Teaching in Collegiate Schools of Nursing

Contributors

Norma J. Briggs   R.N., Ph.D.
Department Chair, Adult Health
   Nursing
School of Nursing
University of Wisconsin—Eau Claire
Eau Claire, Wisconsin

Karen Ehrat   R.N., M.S., Doctoral Candidate
Director, Nursing Administrative Systems
Tucson Medical Center, Tucson, Arizona, and
Lecturer, College of Nursing
University of Arizona, Tucson, Arizona

Alice J. Longman   R.N., Ed.D.
Associate Professor, College of Nursing
University of Arizona, Tucson, Arizona

Teaching in Collegiate Schools of Nursing

Suzanne R. Van Ort R.N., Ph.D.
Associate Professor, College of Nursing
University of Arizona, Tucson, Arizona
  formerly
Dean and Professor, School of Nursing
University of Wisconsin—Eau Claire
Eau Claire, Wisconsin

Arlene M. Putt R.N., Ed.D.
Professor Emerita, College of Nursing
University of Arizona, Tucson, Arizona

Little, Brown and Company
Boston   Toronto

Library of Congress Cataloging in Publication Data

Van Ort, Suzanne R.
    Teaching in collegiate schools of nursing.

    Includes bibliographies and index.
    1. Nursing—Study and teaching.   2. Nursing—Study
and teaching (Graduate)   I. Putt, Arlene M.   II. Title.
[DNLM: 1. Education, Nursing—United States.
2. Teaching.   WY 18 V217t]
RT71.V36   1984   610.73′07′11   84-21804
ISBN 0-316-89715-9

Copyright © 1985 by Suzanne R. Van Ort and Arlene M. Putt

All rights reserved. No part of this book may be reproduced in any form or by
any electronic or mechanical means including information storage and
retrieval systems without permission in writing from the publisher, except by
a reviewer who may quote brief passages in a review.

Library of Congress Catalog Card Number 84-21804

ISBN 0-316-89715-9

9 8 7 6 5 4 3 2 1

ALP

Published simultaneously in Canada
by Little, Brown & Company (Canada) Limited

Printed in the United States of America

Acknowledgments

   Figures 2-2, 2-3, and 2-4: Reprinted by permission of Dr. Patricia Ostmoe,
Dean, School of Nursing, University of Wisconsin—Eau Claire. Figure 2-3 is
also reprinted by permission of Dean Gladys Sorensen, College of Nursing,
University of Arizona, Tucson.
   Figures 3-1 and 3-2: from L.L. Iverson, "The Chemistry of the Brain,"
Scientific American, September, 1979. Copyright © 1979 by Scientific
American, Inc. All rights reserved. Reprinted by permission of W.H.
Freeman and Company.
   Figure 3-3: from N.A. Lassen, D.H. Ingvar, and E. Skinjol, "Brain
Function and Blood Flow," *Scientific American*, October 1978. Reprinted by
permission of Dr. Niels A. Lassen.

Excerpt, p. 70, and Figure 5-1: from Fred F. Harcleroad, C. Theodore Molen, Jr., and Jack R. Rayman, *The Regional State Colleges And Universities Enter The 1970s*, (1973). Reprinted by permission of American College Testing Program, ACT Publications.

Excerpt, pp. 75–76: from "Assumptions Basic to the Scope of Practice" from *Competencies of the Associate Degree Nurse on Entry into Practice*. National League for Nursing Publication No. 23-1731, 1978. Reprinted by permission of Division of Associate Degree Programs, National League for Nursing.

Selected text from Division of Baccalaureate and Higher Degree Nursing Programs, *Characteristics of Baccalaureate Education in Nursing*, National League for Nursing Publication No. 15-1758, 1979. Reprinted by permission of Division of Baccalaureate and Higher Degree Programs, National League for Nursing.

Selected text from Helen Yura, Ph.D., "Who is the Product of the Baccalaureate Nursing Program?" in *Curriculum Process for Developing or Revising a Baccalaureate Nursing Program*, National League for Nursing Publication No. 15-1700, 1978. Reprinted by permission of Division of Baccalaureate and Higher Degree Programs, National League for Nursing.

Figure 6-1: Adapted with the assistance of Joseph H. Markle from "Write a Lesson Plan," Module B-4, Professional Vocational Teacher Education Module, Ohio State University, 1974. This publication was supported by a contract from the National Institute of Education, U.S. Department of Education. Reprinted by permission of The National Center for Research in Vocational Education, Columbus, Ohio.

Chapter 10, "Evaluation of Teaching," is based on Suzanne Van Ort, R.N., Ph.D., "Developing a System for Documenting Teaching Effectiveness" in *Journal of Nursing Education*, Vol. 22, No. 8, October, 1983. Reprinted by permission of *Journal of Nursing Education*.

To my husband, David Paul Van Ort, D.D.S., M.Ed.,
 who shared the peaks with enthusiasm
 and the valleys with equanimity.
 Suzanne R. Van Ort

To all those excellent teachers I have
 encountered over the years,
 and to A.G. Breidenstine in particular,
 for the great impact he made on
 my life many years ago.
 Arlene M. Putt

Preface

Teaching in Collegiate Schools of Nursing is an outgrowth of our academic experiences in which faculty and students have sought information about teaching and the academic world. In response to these colleagues and friends, we have organized the book to provide information on learning, teaching, faculty roles and responsibilities, curriculum development and process, and the issues encountered when teaching nursing in an age of rapidly expanding technology.

The book is designed to serve as a resource for graduate nursing students in courses on clinical teaching, and for new faculty in nursing education. Organized as a four-part handbook, it is also an overview of topics essential to those assuming the faculty role in nursing education.

The chapter on evolution of nursing education provides historical perspective as a foundation for succeeding chapters. The components of the faculty role provide a context within which the content on learning and teaching is meaningful. Part II is focused on the neurophysiology of learning and the psychophysiological theories that lay the groundwork for understanding the learning process. Part III includes content on curriculum development, curriculum process, teaching strategies, and clinical instruction. Evaluation of teaching, evaluation of learning, and program evaluation are also presented in Part III. In the fourth and final part we present an overview of current issues that affect faculty in schools of nursing.

Although we do not claim to have achieved all-inclusive treatment in each of these areas, we offer this work as a resource for faculty and graduate students as they strive for excellence in academic nursing. May the book further serve to explain to others not engaged in teaching why the task of teaching nursing in a collegiate setting is so complex.

Suzanne Van Ort
Arlene M. Putt

Acknowledgments

Throughout our experience as nurse educators, many individuals have contributed to our beliefs about collegiate nursing and thus to this book. Students have tested our thinking and refined our knowledge. Fellow faculty have helped us clarify our concept of nursing as a practice profession and as an academic discipline. Nursing service colleagues have presented us with the realities of patient care in an evolving health care system. All of these individuals are unnamed contributors whom we recognize and appreciate.

Many students and colleagues have systematically or serendipitously contributed to this endeavor. In particular we wish to thank the faculties and students of the University of Arizona College of Nursing and the University of Wisconsin—Eau Claire School of Nursing for helping us to grow as teachers and as human beings.

To our families who displayed strong encouragement and interest throughout our efforts, we express appreciation for their patience and fortitude.

There are several individuals who contributed their unique talents to the book's completion. Mrs. Martha Newsom typed much of the final manuscript; her typing precision and pleasant manner are appreciated. Without the computer expertise and word processing facilities provided by Joseph H. Markle, this creation would have been a much more arduous task. Gratitude is expressed to the entire Markle family, Joe, Edie, Melynda and Krista, for their tolerance of the many disruptions this book brought to their lives. Their steady support and good humor are greatly appreciated. They made writing fun for one author.

Finally, to Ms. Julie Stillman, who in the role of Nursing Editor at Little, Brown and Company has provided encourage-

Acknowledgments

ment and support through the creation process, goes a deep appreciation for her efforts, talent, and friendship. To the staff at Little, Brown and Company, particularly Ann West and Julie Winston, goes recognition for their expert assistance and ready support.

S.V.O., A.M.P.

Contents

Part I: Nursing and the Faculty Role

1   Evolution of Nursing in Higher Education   3
    Study Questions 3
    Evolution of Higher Education in America 3
    Evolution of Nursing Education in America 8
    References 17
    Suggested Readings 17

2   Faculty Role in the Collegiate Setting   19
    Study Questions 19
    Preparation for the Faculty Role 22
    Position Description 23
    Personnel Decisionmaking 28
    Grievance Procedure 35
    Faculty Workload 36
    Alternatives to a Full-time Faculty Position 37
    References 39
    Suggested Readings 39

Part II: Learning

3   What Is Learning?   43
    Study Questions 43
    Neural Connections 43
    Types of Learning 48
    Specialization of Hemispheres 49
    Memory 51
    References 53
    Suggested Readings 54

4 Theories of Learning   56
Study Questions 56
Historical Perspectives 56
Present Century Developments 57
Self-Assessment of Learning Style 62
References 64
Suggested Readings 65

Part III: Strategies for Teaching

5 Curriculum Development and Process   69
Study Questions 69
Curriculum Development 69
Curriculum Patterns for Basic Nursing Education 74
Curriculum Patterns for Graduate Education in Nursing 78
Curriculum Process 80
References 87
Suggested Readings 88

6 Development of a Single Course   90
Study Questions 90
Contribution to the Total Program 90
Course Description 91
Allocation of Credit 93
Prerequisites 93
Course Placement and Learner Level 94
Behavioral Objectives 95
Course Content 96
Teaching Methods 97
Lesson Plan 98
Selection of Learning Experiences 100
Learning Evaluation 100
Grade Assignment 101
Course Evaluation 102
References 105
Suggested Readings 106

7 Teaching and Learning Modes   108
Study Questions 108
Audiovisual Materials 109
Microteaching 115

Contents

    Clinical Student Teaching Under Preceptorship 117
    Classroom Strategies 118
    References 125
    Suggested Readings 126

8 Clinical Instruction: Viewpoints of a Faculty Member and Agency Administrator   128

    Study Questions 128
    Introduction 129

    From a Faculty Viewpoint
    The Value of Clinical Instruction 129
    The Value of Simulated Experiences 130
    Objectives of Clinical Instruction 131
    Factors in Planning Clinical Instruction 131

    From an Agency Point of View
    The Value of Clinical Instruction 143
    The Value of Simulated Experiences 143
    Factors in Planning Clinical Instruction 144

    References 151
    Suggested Readings 152

9 Evaluation of Learning   153

    Study Questions 153
    Learning Domains 153
    Test Development 154
    Reliability 161
    Validity 161
    Scoring and Grading Systems 162
    References 166
    Suggested Readings 167

10 Evaluation of Teaching   168

    Study Questions 168
    Characteristics of Effective Teaching 169
    Evaluation Models 171
    Components of Teaching Effectiveness Evaluation 171
    Measures for Evaluating Teaching 174
    Process for Evaluating Teaching 175
    References 178
    Suggested Readings 179

11 Program Evaluation — 181
Study Questions 181
Types of Evaluation 182
Overall Program Evaluation 185
Internal Program Evaluation 186
External Program Evaluation 191
References 195
Suggested Readings 195

Part IV: Issues in Teaching

12 Education and Practice Issues — 199
Study Questions 199
Entry into Practice 199
Historical Perspective 200
National Efforts in Response to the 1985 Proposal 200
American Nurses' Association Actions 200
National League for Nursing Actions 202
Regional and State Actions 202
Dilemmas 204

Education and Practice Issues
Graduate Education 207

References 209
Suggested Readings 211

13 Continuing Education Issues — 212
Study Questions 212
The Role of Continuing Education in the Nursing Profession 213
Goals of Continuing Education 215
Types of Programs 217
Content Trends of Continuing Education 218
Resources 219
Financing 220
Continuing Education Issues Confronting Faculty 221
References 222
Suggested Readings 223

14 Faculty Role Issues — 225
Study Questions 225
Faculty Clinical Practice 225

Academic Freedom and Tenure 227
Collective Bargaining 228
References 231
Suggested Readings 232

15 Professional Autonomy Issues 233

Study Questions 233
Autonomy of the Profession 233
Economics 236
Credentialing 238
Future Directions 240
References 241
Suggested Readings 242

Index 245

Part I

Nursing and the Faculty Role

Chapter 1

Evolution of Nursing in Higher Education

Suzanne Van Ort, R.N., Ph.D.

Study Questions

1. What events in the 1700s and 1800s contributed to the development of nursing education in America?
2. Where and when was the first baccalaureate nursing program established? How was it different from contemporary baccalaureate nursing programs?
3. How did wars affect the development of nursing and nursing education?
4. What major national studies affected the development of nursing education?
5. What was the effect of the ANA *Position Paper* of 1965 on nursing and nursing education?
6. What has been the role of the federal government in promoting nursing education?

Evolution of Higher Education in America

American higher education evolved from the European patterns of education and became reality in 1636 with the founding of Harvard College. Harvard College, patterned on the British model, adapted the classical curriculum to include divinity, philosophy, classical languages, grammar, logic, mathematics and rhetoric (10). Colonial American colleges developed downward since there were insufficient high schools or preparatory schools to supply students to the colleges. Instead, the colonial colleges copied the British system and curriculum as they offered courses

3

to the small governing elite of the American colonies. Teaching was done by the college president and the one or two other faculty. Teaching focused on transmitting the knowledge of the faculty to students. Furthermore, most colonial colleges had religious roots that gave direction to their curricula and guided the lives of the students (10). Harvard, Yale and Princeton were founded by Calvinists. The College of William and Mary in Virginia and King's College in New York were founded by Anglicans.

As the first American college, Harvard College served as a model for Yale and subsequent colonial colleges (10). These schools were chartered by their respective colonial governments and, initially, focused heavily on religious instruction within the liberal arts curriculum. Since the colleges were privately supported, poverty and a lack of qualified faculty affected the breadth and depth of the curriculum. In 1642, the Harvard curriculum expanded to include geography, history, botany, and Hebrew (10). After 1652, Harvard moved to a four-year curriculum. These developments signaled the beginning of an American curriculum that was an adaptation of the British and continental curricula. Harvard continued to serve as the model for all other colonial colleges (10). With minimal alterations, this model served as a prototype for American higher education until the American Revolution. Following the revolution, American colleges were transformed into primarily secular institutions which added courses in biological and medical sciences, modern languages, law, public administration, and fine arts.

During the nineteenth century, American higher education responded to the nation's egalitarianism by liberalizing the curriculum and accepting students from various walks of life. Industrialization in America necessitated a redefining of curricula to prepare citizens for merchant and manufacturing positions. Colleges diversified and proliferated in the nineteenth century as the West and South developed. Special-purpose institutions, particularly science-oriented technical colleges appeared on the scene. Colleges became universities as electives were offered and institutions organized into departments. The Morrill Act of 1862 provided that each state would use federal funds to support colleges that offered courses in agriculture and mechanical arts (7). This land-grant college movement revolutionized American higher education by challenging each state to define a land-grant institution to meet its own particular state's need.

The evolution of graduate education in America occurred over a period of approximately forty years during the middle 1800s. As colonial colleges matured and public higher education was established, educational leaders recognized the need for universities to provide advanced degrees and professional education. Typically, American educators went to the British or German universities to receive their advanced education. On their return home, they brought to America the European ideas of graduate education. In 1870, the Johns Hopkins University was founded in Baltimore as a university patterned after the great German universities (11). This model included an undergraduate college but focused on scholarship and scientific research as central institutional purposes (11). The German influence on Harvard and Yale led to reforms in their undergraduate programs and ultimately planted the seeds for future graduate education in those institutions (11). Electives were introduced and departments of theology, law, and medicine were established.

At the same time as the colleges were expanding into universities, graduate degrees were offered in various liberal arts and science disciplines. However, recipients of master's degrees were not necessarily graduates of baccalaureate programs. Thus, the quality of the education was often questioned. The Civil War interrupted further progress because enrollment in existing colleges fell as war needs took priority.

Following the Civil War, graduate education began to come into its own. The John Hopkins University became the first American institution initially founded as a university to continue to succeed with graduate education as a primary mission. Thus, the idea of graduate education was finally institutionalized in America.

Throughout the late nineteenth and early twentieth centuries, American higher education strove to define its purposes and ensure itself a meaningful future. Standardization of general education curricula, organization of college preparatory curricula, and the rise of public, state-supported higher education characterized this era (10). In addition, special-purpose institutions for blacks, women, and Roman Catholics began to gain prominence. Professional education expanded, and universities used the elective system to organize the curriculum by clusters of beginning and advanced courses.

In an attempt to upgrade the training of teachers for the public schools, the normal schools which had been instituted in the early 1800s, were changed into teacher's colleges which offered bachelor's degrees (5). In this period of rapid social and technological change, American higher education responded by diversifying the curricula to respond to utilitarian and vocational values.

American higher education in the twentieth century has been characterized by the demise of the classics, the rise of science and technology, the emergence of the professions, and the concept of universal access to higher education (10). The ideas of a departmental major, curricular concentration, specialization, and the increase of electives promoted diversity in higher education. Vocationalism and the growth of career options necessitated the establishment of support services such as counseling and guidance, testing centers, and advising services. Interdisciplinary courses began to appear in college catalogs. In addition, the expansion of fine arts curricula and the introduction of competency-based instruction represented divergent yet popular movements.

Two significant occurrences in the twentieth century affected higher education for the future (10). After World War II, the increased role of the federal government in supporting higher education was evident in the numbers of students attending college on the GI Bill and subsequent federal student loan and scholarship programs. Federal funding enabled many individuals to attend institutions of higher education and, as a result, universal access to higher education was promoted.

The student protest movement of the 1960s was the second significant occurrence (10). Although the student movement failed in its attempt to transform higher education, the movement did result in a reexamination of educational philosophies, purposes, and objectives. At issue was student leadership on campus. One consequence of the protest movement was a renewed commitment to the student as a central focus of the academic setting (10).

As higher education expanded its curricular offerings and responded to societal needs, institutions were restructured and organized to facilitate universal access and opportunity. Normal schools became teachers' colleges and then state colleges; colleges became universities; and a new structure, the community college, came of age (4, 5, 6). The community college movement, an outgrowth of the junior college originally begun in 1906 in Joliet, Illinois, expanded its mission of vocational education to provide a wide variety of vocational, preprofessional, college preparatory, and community service offerings (7).

In 1973, the Carnegie Commission on Higher Education developed *A Classification of Institutions of Higher Education* (1). This classification used eighteen categories to describe 2,827 institutions in the United States. The Carnegie Classification used five main categories:

1. Doctoral-Granting Institutions
2. Comprehensive Universities and Colleges
3. Liberal Arts Colleges
4. Two-year Colleges and Institutions
5. Professional Schools and Other Specialized Institutions (1).

Certain of the main categories were subdivided to reflect institutional differences either in federal financial support or in diversity of academic programs. For example, Doctoral-Granting Institutions were subdivided into Research Universities I, Research Universities II, Doctoral-Granting Universities I, and Doctoral-Granting Universities II. The major differences between Research Universities I and Research Universities II were that the former were among the fifty leading institutions in federal financial support and offered at least fifty doctoral degrees (1, p. 1). The Research Universities II were among the one hundred leading institutions in terms of federal financial support and awarded at least fifty doctoral degrees in 1969–1970 or were among the leading fifty institutions in terms of doctoral degrees awarded from 1960–1961 to 1969–1970 (1, p. 2). A comprehensive university was one which offered a liberal arts program as well as several other professional or occupational programs but did not have a doctoral-granting mission. The Carnegie classification has been widely used in higher education and its terminology adopted for higher education research.

Another feature of post-World War II American higher education has been the development of alternate modes of instruction. Computer-assisted instruction, television teaching, simulation and gaming, modularized instruction, and the expansion of learning resource centers have facilitated the system's ability to meet educational needs of diverse student groups. Educational technology and audiovisual instruction have come of age in the decades since World War II.

As the educational system enters the final decades of the twentieth century, creative retrenchment and increased accountability for educational outcomes are operant. Economic realities such as diminished federal funding for higher education necessitate careful planning for use of scarce resources so that the quality and accessibility of American higher education continue (2). Programs of institutional assessment, educational auditing, program accountability, faculty evaluation, and reexamination of support services are being implemented. Work-study programs, part-time study, and various off-campus programs facilitate student access to higher education while conserving resources. According to the Carnegie Council on Policy Studies in Higher Education:

> ...the following contributions by higher education, it now appears, will be needed by the nation in 2000, and generally also in the years in between:
> 1. Places to accommodate by 2010 approximately the same number of students as were enrolled in 1978.
> 2. Institutions representing at least the degree of diversity we have today.
> 3. Resources to impart higher levels of skill attainment than ever before.
> 4. Capabilities for more advanced scientific research.
> 5. Capabilities to educate a more active, better-informed more humanely oriented citizenry.
> 6. Capabilities to offer greater equality of opportunity and the possibility of a greater equality of earned income.
> 7. Abilities to provide ever more constructive evaluation for national self-renewal.
> 8. Capacities to provide more services to the surrounding community.
> 9. Capabilities to maintain a network of contact and communication (2, pp. 89–95).

These evolutionary trends in American higher education served as the foundation and background for the development of collegiate nursing education in America.

Evolution of Nursing Education in America

In colonial America, nursing care was provided for ill individuals primarily by family members or members of religious orders. Sick individuals were often cared for in their homes. The first hospitals in America were established in the early eighteenth century in New Orleans, Philadelphia, Boston, and New York (3). The first hospital to be organized as such, Pennsylvania Hospital, was built in 1755 in Philadelphia. The early hospitals were staffed by hospital sisters and laywomen who received on-the-job training. American medicine was still in its infancy in the eighteenth century and did not organize the first medical school until the Medical College of Philadelphia, now the University of Pennsylvania, was founded in 1765 (8). The first American medical degree was conferred in 1771 by King's College in New York. Harvard did not start a medical school until 1773.

In 1798, Dr. Valentine Seaman, attending surgeon at New York Hospital, began to provide instruction to nurses (8). His was an early attempt to educate nurses by other than on-the-job training. Several subsequent attempts to reorganize nursing education occurred in the early 1800s. However, modern medicine was just beginning to develop in the United States, and, since nursing was under the aegis of medicine, nursing had to wait for development. Following the model established by Florence Nightingale when she organized the school of nursing at St. Thomas' Hospital in London in 1860, American nursing education began in hospital schools of nursing (3, 8). Two cardinal principles established by Miss Nightingale were that nurses should be trained in hospitals designed to do training and that the nursing education units should be separately administered and not an integral part of hospital administration (3). Since the Nightingale School was privately funded by the Nightingale Endowment Fund, it was feasible to organize it as an autonomous unit. The nurses educated at the Nightingale School at St. Thomas's Hospital received one year of training in hospital nursing which incorporated the concept of home care for patients. Miss Nightingale advocated education for women and proposed nursing as a secular career for educated women.

In 1873 three important schools of nursing which greatly influenced the development of American nursing were established. Although based on the tenets of Florence Nightingale, these schools adapted the Nightingale model to fit the needs of their parent hospital, and, thus, the American diploma school was born. The three pioneering schools were Bellevue Hospital School of Nursing in New York, New England Hospital School of Nursing in Boston, and Connecticut Training School for Nurses in New Haven (3, 8). Although Florence Nightingale had advocated a separating of nursing education and nursing service, for fiscal reasons the U.S. schools chose to merge the two entities under the control of hospital administration. Thus, the autonomy of diploma school education was lost from the beginning.

From the nineteenth century until post-World War II, most nursing education in the United States occurred in hospital schools of nursing on the apprenticeship model (9). Hospital schools of nursing proliferated at the end of the nineteenth century and in the early twentieth century following the tenets of Florence Nightingale. The hospital or diploma school program varied in quality and curricular patterns. However, the typical pattern required one or two years of study and clinical practice. The present three-year curriculum model did not occur until this century (9). Subjects were taught by nurse instructors who frequently were employed as head nurses in the parent hospital. Nursing classes were supplemented by physicians' lectures discussing medical diagnosis and treatment. The curriculum focused on preparing a nurse skilled in nursing procedures and trained to care for ill patients in hospital settings (9).

Although the diploma school model typified American nursing education for many years, periodically there were efforts to suggest that nursing education be placed in the mainstream of American higher education. The first formal challenge to the diploma model came in 1909 with the establishment of a baccalaureate program at the University of Minnesota (3). This three-year curriculum awarded graduates a diploma rather than a degree; but the fact that the program was located in a university setting challenged nurse educators to examine the benefits of university education for nursing.

In 1917 the Standard Curriculum for Schools of Nursing was published in an attempt to unify and upgrade content in nursing schools (8). The advent of World War I delayed the cause of moving nursing education into universities. Although wars may slow progress, the needs for nurses in wartime highlight nursing and ultimately validate the need for nursing education. During World War I, American military nurses served at home and abroad. The Red Cross, Army Nurse Corps, and Navy Nurse Corps recruited American nurses for the war effort. The Army School of Nursing was founded in 1918 in response to the need for nurses. Also, in 1918 the Vassar Training Camp Program was established to train college women for careers in nursing (8). While meeting short-range needs for nurses, the Vassar Training Camp Program also heightened the interest in nursing in colleges and universities.

As a consequence of World War I and progress in medical care, nursing leaders recognized that pre-World War I nursing education needed upgrading in order to meet post-World War I needs. In 1920 a Committee was established to investigate and report on the need for standardization and improvement in nursing education. In 1923, a landmark report entitled *Nursing and Nursing Education in the United States* was published by the Committee (4). This report, sometimes called the Goldmark Report in honor of the contributions of Josephine Goldmark as secretary to the Committee, reported on the investigation, funded by the Rockefeller Foundation, in which all types of nursing education were examined and recommendations offered. Three major points were offered in the Report:

1. Public health was being neglected.
2. Many nursing schools lacked qualified faculty, had inadequate facilities, and failed to relate theory to practice.
3. The chief nurse of the hospital should not be head of the school of nursing.

In 1924 a milestone in nursing education was attained with the establishment of the Yale School of Nursing as the first autonomous collegiate school. The Yale School of Nursing, funded by the Rockefeller Foundation, was the first nursing school in the world to be opened as a separate university department with its own department head (8). Yale offered the Bachelor of Nursing degree following a 28-month course of study.

Subsequent to the success of the Flexner Report which resulted in reforms in medical education, nursing leaders decided to establish a committee to promote upgrading of nursing schools. Thus, in 1925 the Committee on Grading of Nursing Schools was established to grade nursing schools, define the duties and scope of nursing, study the supply and demand of nurses and the problems of public health nursing (8). After seven years of work, the Committee accomplished its charge of studying nursing but failed to carry out the grading of nursing schools. The long-term effects led to upgrading the profession and promoting standardization of requirements. The Committee did recommend that courses in nursing schools should be on a college level, entrance requirements should be similar, and there should be close cooperation between the schools.

Although not all recommendations were completely met, an increasing number of nursing schools was established within universities. According to Deloughery (3), in 1920 there were 180 nursing schools with academic standing; by 1938 there were 45 universities sponsoring complete courses. The Great Depression years saw increased specialization in nursing, improvements in basic nursing education, and documentation of the need for post-graduate education in nursing.

World War II brought new challenges to American nursing and nursing education. Of primary importance in the early 1940s was the recruitment and preparation of sufficient numbers of nurses to meet the needs of both the armed forces and civilian agencies. Consequently, in 1942 the Bolton Act was passed by Congress. This legislation created the U.S. Cadet Corps under the auspices of the Department of Education in the U.S. Public Health Service (8). The U.S. Cadet Nurse corps plan, financed by government appropriations to institutions that prepared nurses, created an essential pool of nurses to meet nursing manpower needs at home and abroad.

Medicine and nursing progressed rapidly during and immediately after World War II (8). Caring for large numbers of wounded in the war stimulated numerous advances in medical science. Psychiatry, neurology, and rehabilitation emerged as medical specialties. Penicillin was first used in battle in 1943. Advances in understanding fluid loss, resuscitation, hepatitis, and prosthetics were made. And, of course, the whole area of atomic research and radiation safety began late in World War II. Public health nursing and psychiatric-mental health nursing expanded as nursing specialties. Finally, in 1946, high school graduation became a universal requirement for professional nurse licensure (8).

A landmark report, entitled *Nursing for the Future*, was published in 1948 (3). Dr. Esther Lucile Brown of the Russell Sage Foundation directed this study which recommended that schools of nursing should have affiliation with universities and should have separate school budgets. The Brown Report recommendations contributed to the development of nursing as a collegiate discipline and to the placement of nurses as integral members of the health team. Dr. Brown was among the first to use the terms professional and technical to differentiate types of nurses.

During the 1950s, baccalaureate nursing education continued to expand, and associate degree nursing education was founded. Baccalaureate nursing education strengthened the generic curriculum and incorporated both public health nursing content and psychiatric-mental health nursing content into the curriculum. Baccalaureate programs began to move from a five-year plan to four years of requirements for the degree. The upper division major in nursing with both foundational and concurrent courses in the liberal arts and sciences became the typical model. This model continued to characterize the baccalaureate nursing program until the advent of the integrated curriculum model in the 1970s.

The associate degree nursing program was initiated to prepare technical nurses through a two-year program located in junior or community colleges. In her doctoral dissertation in 1951, Dr. Mildred Montag proposed a new type of nursing personnel, the nurse technician, who would be trained in a two-year program. In order to test the feasibility of this proposal, a national research project was initiated in 1952. Under the direction of Dr. Montag, the Cooperative Research Project in Junior and Community College Education for Nursing documented the feasibility of associate degree nursing education (3). The first technical nursing program was established at Orange County Community College in Middletown, New York. Associate degree programs proliferated at a fantastic rate for the next thirty years.

Additional forces for educational change in the 1950s included curriculum experimentation, accreditation pressures, growing emphasis on the psychological aspects of nursing care, and the shift in assignments from the traditional hospital shifts to shorter, well-supervised periods of caring for patients. Many diploma schools affiliated with educational institutions and strengthened their educational base.

In addition to progress in basic nursing education, graduate education in nursing was also evolving. The original master's degree programs in nursing were founded in the late 1920s. Continuing as a pioneer, Yale offered the Master of Nursing degree beginning in 1929. However, this master's degree was offered as a generic degree not based upon a baccalaureate degree in nursing. Few nurses pursued graduate education until baccalaureate education became more widespread. Following World War II, master's degree programs in nursing assumed leadership in preparing teachers and administrators (8). During the 1950s nursing research received federal support and began to be recognized as an essential force for the future.

The first doctoral programs in nursing were established at Teacher's College, Columbia University in the early 1920s. However, the doctoral concept did not receive wide acceptance until after World War II. In 1954 the University of Pittsburgh began a

Doctor of Philosophy program in Maternal-Child Nursing, and in 1960 Boston University began a Doctor of Nursing Science program in psychiatric nursing (8). The first comprehensive doctoral programs in nursing were established in 1964 at the University of California.

During the Kennedy administration in the early 1960s, nursing education received additional federal funding as well as federal recognition through the establishment of the Surgeon General's Consultant Group on Nursing. In its report, entitled *Toward Quality in Nursing*, the Consultant Group presented the nation's needs for nursing education and nursing service and set forth goals to meet these needs (8). Among the goals were recruitment of additional students, especially for baccalaureate and graduate programs, upgrading of educational programs, and funding for nurses to obtain advanced degrees. Better utilization of nurses by nursing service was also advocated. Based on the recommendations of the Consultant Group, the Nurse Training Act of 1964 was adopted by Congress. This legislation expanded federal aid for professional nursing education, provided construction grants to schools of nursing, and provided special project grants to improve nursing education. During this era many nurses received doctoral degrees in other fields, particularly education. This extra professional preparation affected the development of nursing theory and nursing research by focusing initially on contributions from the other disciplines, while working diligently to develop nursing as a discipline.

Another significant national action in the 1960s occurred as the American Nurses' Association's *First Position Paper on Education* was published in December 1965 (3). This paper recommended that nursing education should take place in institutions of higher learning, that the minimum preparation for professional practice should be the baccalaureate degree, that the minimum preparation for technical practice should be the associate degree, and that assistants in health service programs should be trained in vocational education institutions. The *Position Paper* generated an outcry among nurses, particularly those graduated from diploma schools, who believed their professional future threatened. Rather than serving only as an impetus for change, the *Position Paper* became a divisive force which pitted nurses against one another. Diploma school advocates united to perpetuate the diploma model and resist both baccalaureate and associate degree expansion. Associate degree advocates grew in numbers and power as new associate degree nursing programs were established. Baccalaureate degree programs became the advocates of the *Position Paper* since the associate degree nurses resented the title of technical nurse. Regardless of the emotional impact of the *Position Paper*, the trend toward collegiate education and away from diploma education continued. Baccalaureate and associate degree programs increased in number and enrollments (3). Table 1-1 shows the ten-year enrollment trend following the *Position Paper*.

The Vietnam War once again reiterated the need for military nurses. Male nurses were appointed to the armed services beginning in 1966. As in previous wars, medical and nursing care advanced during the Vietnam War (8). New techniques and technology were tested in war and adopted in civilian life. Specialties in nursing, such as coronary care nursing, were recognized in the late 1960s, and sophisticated special care units were established in U.S. hospitals. Also in the 1960s, new roles were proposed that focused on independent nursing functions. The nurse practitioner movement, begun at the University of Colorado in 1965 as a program for pediatric nurse practitioners, gained popularity as a way to promote access to and quality of health care. Nurse practitioners were trained as family nurse practitioners, adult nurse practitioners, geriatric nurse practitioners, and pediatric nurse practitioners.

Continuing education programs for nurses were designed to provide short-term courses and workshops to upgrade and maintain the skills of practicing nurses. These programs became increasingly popular as nursing knowledge and health care technology increased dramatically.

Another educational movement in nursing that gained momentum following the ANA *Position Paper* of 1965 was the

Table 1-1 Nursing education programs by type and number, 1965 and 1976

Year	Diploma	Associate degree	Baccalaureate degree	Total
1965	821	174	198	1193
1976	390	642	341	1373

Source: J.C. Vaughn and W.L. Johnson. *NLN Nursing Data Book 1981*. New York: National League for Nursing, 1982.

effort to provide baccalaureate nursing education for registered nurses from diploma or associate degree programs. Recognizing the uniqueness of the "RN Student," many basic baccalaureate programs attempted to provide wide educational experiences for practicing nurses. Also, special career mobility or career ladder programs were established specifically for registered nurse students. These programs enabled qualified graduates of diploma programs to obtain an associate degree or qualified graduates of either diploma or associate degree programs to obtain a baccalaureate degree.

As a direct outgrowth of the Surgeon General's Consultant Group on Nursing, the National Commission for the Study of Nursing Education in the United States was organized in 1967 (8). The National Commission, chaired by Dr. Jerome Lysaught, studied the needs and resources for nursing in the future. Its report, often called the Lysaught Report, entitled *An Abstract for Action*, was published in 1970. The report recommended a renewed focus on nursing practice with increased research in clinical practice and an increase in nurses preparing for expanded nursing roles. In response to this report, numerous nurse practitioners were trained either in certificate programs or master's degree programs. By 1977 there were over 150 nurse practitioner programs and 7000 nurse practitioner graduates.

As nursing education entered the 1980s, economic constraints and public concern for efficient and effective health care necessitated a reexamination of educational outcomes and a renewed accountability for the quality and essentiality of nursing as a positive force for the future in the health care arena.

During the past twenty years, there had been a dramatic shift in the educational preparation of nurses. In 1960, 83 percent of new nurse graduates were trained in diploma programs; by 1980, 80 percent of new graduates had been educated in colleges and universities (13, p. 39). In addition to basic nursing education, increasing numbers of registered nurses received college degrees (12, p. 464). In 1970–1971, 2214 registered nurses graduated from 234 programs (13, p. 56); by 1981–1982 this number had increased to 9344 graduates from 424 programs (12, pp. 463–464).

Graduate education in nursing also expanded. In 1960, 1009 nurses graduated from 43 master's degree programs in nursing (13, p. 90). In the academic year 1981–1982, there were 5193 graduates from 154 master's degree programs in nursing (12, p. 464). There were only 11 graduates from the four existing doctoral programs in nursing in 1960–1961 (13, p. 79). In

1981–1982, 137 nurses graduated from the 25 doctoral programs in nursing (12, p. 464).

These educational shifts foretell a more active place for nursing in the health care arena of the future. Educationally prepared nurses will assume leadership in identifying health needs and proposing nursing's response to the health needs of the American people.

References

1. Carnegie Commission on Higher Education. *A Classification of Institutions of Higher Education.* Berkeley: Carnegie Commission on Higher Education, 1974.
2. Carnegie Council on Policy Studies in Higher Education. *Three Thousand Futures.* San Francisco: Jossey-Bass, 1980.
3. Deloughery, G.L. *History and Trends of Professional Nursing.* (8th ed). St. Louis: Mosby, 1977.
4. Harcleroad, F.F., Molen, C.T., Jr., and Rayman, J.R. *The Regional State Colleges and Universities Enter the 1970s.* Iowa City: American College Testing Program, 1973.
5. Harcleroad, F.F. Molen, C.T., Jr., Van Ort, S. *The Regional State Colleges and Universities in the Middle 1970s.* Tucson: University of Arizona, 1976.
6. Harcleroad, F.F., Sagen, H. and Molen, C.T., Jr. *The Developing State Colleges and Universities.* Iowa City: American College Testing Program, 1969.
7. Henderson, A.D. and Henderson, J.G. *Higher Education in America.* San Francisco: Jossey-Bass, 1975.
8. Kalisch, P.A. and Kalisch, B.J. *The Advance of American Nursing.* Boston: Little, Brown, 1978.
9. Putt, A.M. *Nursing Gains a Place in Higher Education.* Tucson: University of Arizona, (unpublished paper), 1967.
10. Rudolph, F. *Curriculum.* San Francisco: Jossey-Bass, 1977.
11. Storr, R.J. *The Beginnings of Graduate Education in America.* Chicago: University of Chicago Press, 1953.
12. Vaughn, J.C. Educational Preparation for Nursing—1982. *Nurs. and Health Care* 4(8):460, 1983.
13. Vaughn, J.C. and Johnson, W.L. *NLN Nursing Data Book, 1981.* New York: National League for Nursing, 1982.

Suggested Readings

Aiken, L.H., (ed.). *Nursing in the 1980s.* Philadelphia: Lippincott, 1982.
Barzun, J. *The American University.* New York: Harper & Row, 1968.
Bridgeman, M. *Collegiate Education in Nursing.* New York: Russell Sage, 1953.

Carnegie Commission on Higher Education. *A Classification of Institutions of Higher Education.* Berkeley: Carnegie Commission on Higher Education, 1974.

Carnegie Council on Policy Studies in Higher Education. *Three Thousand Futures.* San Francisco: Jossey-Bass, 1980.

Chaska, N.L. *The Nursing Profession: A Time to Speak.* New York: McGraw-Hill, 1983.

Chaska, N.L. *The Nursing Profession: Views Through the Mist.* New York: McGraw-Hill, 1978.

Deloughery, G.L. *History and Trends of Professional Nursing* (8th ed). St. Louis: Mosby, 1977.

Dolan, J.A., Fitzpatrick, M.L., and Herrmann, E.K. *Nursing in Society: A Historical Perspective.* Philadelphia: Saunders, 1983.

Flanagan, L. *One Strong Voice.* Kansas City: American Nurses Association, 1976.

Harcleroad, F.F., Molen, C.T., Jr., and Rayman, J.R. *The Regional State Colleges and Universities Enter the 1970s.* Iowa City: American College Testing Program, 1973.

Harcleroad, F.F., Molen, C.T., Jr., Van Ort, S.R. *The Regional State Colleges and Universities in the Middle 1970s.* Tucson: University of Arizona, 1976.

Harcleroad, F.F., Sagen, H.B., and Molen, C.T., Jr., *The Developing State Colleges and Universities.* Iowa City: American College Testing Program, 1969.

Henderson, A.D. and Henderson, J.G. *Higher Education in America.* San Francisco: Jossey-Bass, 1975.

Kalisch, P.A. and Kalisch, B.J. *The Advance of American Nursing.* Boston: Little, Brown, 1978.

Palmer, I.S. Nightingale Revisited. *Nurs. Outlook* 31:229, 1983.

Palmer, I.S. From Whence We Came. In N.L. Chaska, *The Nursing Profession: A Time to Speak.* New York: McGraw-Hill, 1983.

Rudolph, F. *Curriculum.* San Francisco: Jossey-Bass, 1977.

Safier, G. *Contemporary American Leaders in Nursing.* New York: McGraw-Hill, 1977.

Vaughn, J.C. and Johnson, W.L. *NLN Nursing Data Book, 1981.* New York: National League for Nursing, 1982.

Chapter 2

Faculty Role in the Collegiate Setting

Suzanne Van Ort, R.N., Ph.D.

Study Questions

1. What impact does the structure of the collegiate setting have on the role of faculty in an institution?
2. What effect does the place of nursing in the institution have on faculty roles in the institution and nursing program?
3. What are the three primary roles of faculty in academic settings? What preparation is offered for these roles?
4. What are the components typically included in a description of a faculty position?
5. What are the components of personnel decisionmaking in an academic setting? What are the typical mechanisms for appointment and retention of faculty?
6. What are the decisionmaking patterns and requirements for promotion and tenure in an academic setting? How do these vary in institutions?
7. What are the components of the faculty workload? How are these being quantified at present? What are some alternatives for the future?
8. What are some patterns for working part-time in a collegiate nursing program?

The role of faculty in a collegiate setting involves a complex set of expectations that varies considerably depending upon the institutional mission, program missions, and governance structures of the institution and program. The primary missions of higher education institutions are teaching, research, and community service. In considering these overall missions, individual institutions may emphasize one more than another. For example, research degree-granting institutions may emphasize research whereas comprehensive universities may place greater emphasis on their teaching mission. None of the institutions specifically excludes teaching, research, or community service. However, the institutional emphasis is important as it affects the mission of individual programs and the expectations of faculty within the institution.

The organizational structure of institutions also reflects the institutional mission. A basic organizational structure for a four-year university is illustrated in Figure 2-1.

The organization table shown in Figure 2-1 indicates that in a typical collegiate setting, faculty in the school of nursing are directly responsible to a department chairman who reports to the dean of the school of nursing. The dean usually reports to a vice-president in charge of academic programs who, in turn, reports to the president of the institution. Other vice-presidents in areas such as business services, student services, or research interface with the academic vice-president's office to provide support services. Deans of other academic programs or schools in the institution also report to the academic vice-president and are on a parallel line relationship with the dean of the school of nursing. Thus, the governance structure of the institution is organized as a line organization with hierarchical relationships.

Typically, there is an institutional faculty senate, elected by faculty and representative of various faculty constituencies in the

Figure 2-1 Organizational structure of four-year university with school of nursing

President			
Vice President, Business Services	Vice President, Student Services	Vice President, Academic Affairs	Vice President, Research
Dean, Liberal Arts and Sciences	Dean, Education	Dean, Nursing	Dean, Business
Department Chairmen	Department Chairmen	Department Chairmen	Department Chairmen
Faculty	Faculty	Faculty	Faculty

institution, which provides for faculty input into institutional governance. The specific role of the faculty senate is determined by each institution. If the institution has collective bargaining, the role of the faculty senate may be to act as a bargaining agent or unit. In non-collective bargaining institutions, the faculty senate is theoretically viewed as a partner with administration in the concept of shared governance.

The place of nursing within the institution is an important factor in determining nursing faculty's role and autonomy. In academic health science centers, nursing is often located within the health science center structure. By contrast, in many four-year comprehensive colleges and universities, nursing may be the only health profession program on the campus. Each of these models has its challenges and opportunities. For example, the academic health science center offers opportunities for interprofessional collaboration among faculty in medicine, nursing, pharmacy, and allied health disciplines. However, the influence of the medical model may impinge on nursing's autonomy. Conversely, if nursing is the only health profession program on a campus, the program's autonomy may be greater, but the absence of support colleagues in other health disciplines may be a deleterious factor. Competition for funding in a health science center is very different from competition for funding in a comprehensive university. The important consideration for nursing faculty is to understand the institutional mission and structure and their impact upon the nursing program and faculty.

As mentioned previously, the primary missions of a collegiate setting are teaching, research, and community service. Faculty roles flow from and correspond to these missions. Thus, faculty have role responsibilities in teaching, research, and community service.

The teaching role of faculty encompasses classroom and clinical teaching, advising and counseling students, course development and evaluation, and professional growth activities related to improvement of instruction. According to a study at the University of Iowa, faculty members in nursing spend at least 65 percent of their work-related time in teaching activities (13).

The research role of faculty includes the conduct of and participation in formal research studies, provision of research consultation to faculty or agency colleagues, preparation and presentation of scholarly papers, and professional growth related to scholarliness.

Community service faculty role responsibilities include participation in activities of various community agencies that relate to health. For example, serving on the board of directors of a Health Systems Agency, the local unit of the American Heart Association, or the American Cancer Society, volunteering to assist with health teaching activities in the community, or serving as a consultant to health care practitioners in the community may be included under the category of community service.

Preparation for the Faculty Role

Several mechanisms exist to prepare faculty for their multifaceted role. First, formal academic preparation is offered in master's degree and doctoral programs that provide content in teaching as a functional area or higher education as an area of concentration. At the master's degree level, students who select the functional area of teaching usually have formal classes on curriculum development and curriculum process, teaching methods, use of audiovisual materials, and evaluation methods. Also, supervised teaching with faculty preceptors is often included in the master's degree program in nursing.

Another mechanism for preparing faculty members to assume their role is the use of a mentoring system for neophyte faculty members. Senior faculty members may serve as role models and advisors to new faculty as they learn the academic role. Usually this is an informal rather than a formal mechanism. Mentorship in academic nursing, although a relatively new phenomenon as a formal endeavor, promises to have an important place in nursing's future (8).

In addition, faculty development opportunities on an individual or group basis are available to facilitate professional growth of faculty. These faculty development activities may include organized group programs or seminars, independent participation in workshops or conferences, formal degree-oriented programs of study, informal discussions among faculty, or individual efforts to develop an area of expertise (6). The Southern Regional Education Board sponsored a project in which faculty in associate degree, and baccalaureate and higher degree nursing programs in the South responded to questionnaires regarding faculty development activities (6). Faculty reported little relationship between faculty development activities and institutional rewards.

However, as individuals faculty believed faculty development activities to be valuable in terms of professional growth.

A serendipitous mechanism for preparing faculty is interaction with students in the academic setting. Students, as the consumers of a faculty member's teaching, are interested in the development of teaching excellence. Often, students are willing and able to provide feedback to faculty on the success (or failure) of a teaching experience. Faculty who learn to listen to students' comments will ultimately be the better for it. Students' respect for one's teaching is a worthwhile goal and the ultimate ambition that accompanies good learning and good teaching in the academic setting.

Within specific schools of nursing, new faculty also receive preparation on a day-to-day basis through working within the governance structure of the school, serving with other faculty on various committees, and participating with the teaching team. This informal education is usually very beneficial, although it is difficult to specifically describe since it is a high individual process for each new faculty member.

Position Description

The description of a faculty position in nursing typically includes, but is not necessarily limited to, the following six areas of expected faculty participation.

1. teaching responsibilities
2. advising students
3. committee work
4. research and scholarly endeavors
5. community service
6. professional involvement

Each of these areas will be briefly discussed as a separate entity, although their composite, the faculty role, is often greater than the sum of these parts.

Teaching Responsibilities

The primary responsibility of faculty in a collegiate nursing program is teaching. Teaching responsibilities may include formal classroom teaching, supervision of seminars or discussion groups, and teaching of students in the clinical setting. Faculty are responsible for development of instructional materials, preparation for classroom and clinical teaching, and evaluation of students in both classroom and clinical settings. In order to effectively carry out teaching responsibilities, faculty need to be aware of current nursing practices and the current literature in nursing and health care.

Since teaching methods, clinical instruction, and evaluation of learning and teaching are discussed in succeeding chapters, the reader is referred to these chapters for additional information relevant to the teaching role.

Advising Students

The role of academic advisor to students is an essential but often undervalued component of the faculty role. Students need academic advising to develop a program of study, select appropriate learning experiences, and monitor their progress through the program of study. The academic advisor must be cognizant of university requirements, nursing program requirements, and the goals and special needs of the individual student. In attempting to achieve a good fit between the student's learning needs and program offerings, the academic advisor serves a pivotal role. Also, the academic advisor is important as a source of information for students and a consultant in terms of nursing and professional issues.

One difficulty often encountered in the advising role is the necessity of separating the academic advising role from the personal counseling role. Frequently, faculty in schools of nursing are in close contact with students because of assigned clinical supervision and interpersonal contacts. Faculty and students come to know each other well, and, therefore, it often seems natural for the faculty member to assume a personal counselor or confidante role. While occasionally this may serve a useful purpose, as an ongoing practice the faculty member should strive to limit faculty advising to academic matters. Faculty in a personal counselor role may jeopardize the objectivity necessary for fair evaluation of student performance and assigning objective grades. Also, faculty are not always prepared by education or experience to deal with the complexity of student counseling concerns. Most colleges have a counseling service to which students may be referred for personal counseling or assistance in other than academic areas.

Committee Work

School of nursing faculty participate in three complex organizational structures: university governance, the school of nursing organization, and the organization in those clinical agencies in which they supervise students. There are obvious interfaces between the university governance structure and the school of nursing since the latter functions within the overall university governance structure.

The relationship between the university and clinical agencies is specified in negotiated agreements that describe the expectations and responsibilities of the university, school of nursing, and clinical agency in providing for student learning experiences. School of nursing faculty may be invited to participate in the clinical agency on committees that consider nursing practice, nursing education, or nursing research issues. Concomitantly, representatives from clinical agencies may participate in school of nursing committee work. These interchanges facilitate the articulation of nursing education and nursing service.

Within the university governance structure, faculty may be appointed or elected to various Faculty Senate committees, campus-wide program committees, or ad hoc committees for specific projects. Schools of nursing usually have a set of bylaws in which the school committee structure is codified and described. Standing committees of the faculty often include a curriculum committee, admissions committee, faculty development committee, scholarship committee, student progress committee, promotion and tenure committee, and a long-range planning committee. In addition, ad hoc committees of the faculty may be appointed to complete specific tasks.

Research and Scholarly Endeavors

As part of the faculty role, each faculty member in a collegiate school of nursing has an obligation to participate in research and scholarly endeavors. Depending upon the institution, research may be a requirement for promotion and tenure. Regardless of the requirement, faculty in an academic setting need to develop the scholarly aspects of the profession in order to contribute to both the present and future knowledge base in nursing. Nursing faculty may conduct research in clinical nursing practice, nursing theory development, nursing education issues such as computer applications in nursing, or basic research in their area of expertise. Research support in the form of intramural and extramural funding, computer support, statistical consultation, laboratory facilities, and library resources are essential to assist faculty researchers.

Both individual research and collaborative projects need to be encouraged. Interprofessional and intraprofessional studies are needed to specify and validate the domains of nursing.

Publication of research and scholarly endeavors is an obligation concomitant with the research role. Assistance to faculty in terms of typing, word processing, and duplicating services is important in school budget planning. Also, faculty need support to prepare and present scholarly papers, poster sessions, research papers, or symposia as a mechanism for disseminating and discussing the results of research and scholarly endeavors.

Scholarly endeavors for faculty may include development of a theoretical model for nursing phenomena, consideration of a sociopolitical strategy involving nursing, or development of instructional materials of a unique, marketable nature. Each school usually specifies scholarly activity and attempts to delineate this category of faculty activity.

Community Service

The community service role of faculty provides a vehicle for nursing to be represented in community agency activities and for faculty to contribute in an area of interest or expertise. Community service activities of faculty may include serving on boards or committees of voluntary or governmental agencies, providing consultation to community agencies, participating in charitable organization functions, or becoming involved in the health care political arena. When participating in community service activities, faculty members must be careful to define whether they represent themselves, the school of nursing, or both. Particularly in the political arena, the faculty member should define representation as an individual rather than an academic activity.

Community service activities of faculty benefit not only the individual, the school, and the agency involved. The increased visibility of nurses as concerned, contributing citizens promotes a positive public image of the nursing profession.

Position Description

Professional Involvement

As members of the profession, nurses who are faculty members in schools of nursing have an obligation to participate in professional activities. These professional activities may include active participation in the professional organization, the American Nurses' Association or its structural units, involvement in the National League for Nursing or its constituent units, any of the various nursing specialty organizations, or other scientific and disciplinary organizations.

Professional involvement in nursing organization activities provides an opportunity to give nursing input into nursing's present and future. Critical decisions regarding nursing practice, nursing education, and nursing research require the input of many nurses in order for representative outcomes to be achieved.

Also, faculty members may be called upon to represent the professional organization in the legislative arena at local, state, or federal levels. In these critical economic times, testimony of experts in nursing is essential if nursing is to garner its share of resources in order to provide quality nursing care.

In most higher education institutions, faculty are categorized into four academic ranks. The four most common ranks in ascending order are Instructor, Assistant Professor, Associate Professor, and Professor. Faculty in each rank have role responsibilities related to the institutional missions of teaching, research, and community service. The type and extent of these faculty responsibilities increase as a faculty member progresses through the ranks. Faculty workloads and teaching assignments usually reflect the expectations of each rank. For example, in a typical university a neophyte Instructor is expected to focus upon teaching responsibilities and development of skill in the teaching role. Less of the Instructor's attention is placed upon research or community service. As the Instructor matures in that rank and prepares for promotion to Assistant Professor, the faculty responsibilities expand to include leadership of a course group, participation with other faculty in research, and participation in community service.

Once the Assistant Professor rank is attained, increasing role responsibilities for leadership in courses, expending expertise in teaching, participating in university governance and school committee work, increasing scholarly activity and publications, participating in professional meetings and as consultant in community service activities, and developing a defined research interest are expected. The expanded responsibilities are prerequisite to promotion to Associate Professor.

At the Associate Professor level, the faculty member is expected to be a master teacher, serve the school and university in a leadership capacity, conduct research and disseminate findings, serve as a mentor for other faculty, be a leader in professional and community activities, and participate in state, regional, and national professional activities. The Associate Professor is usually expected to participate in long-range planning activities and serve as a consultant in the areas of his/her particular research interest.

Attainment of the rank of full Professor assumes that the faculty member fulfills the role responsibilities of preceding ranks, is recognized as a national leader in teaching and research, and is recognized as a state or regional leader in community service. In addition, the Professor assumes leadership responsibilities in school and university governance. The Professor rank exemplifies the epitome of the scholar who is a recognized leader in the profession as well as a leader in the academic world.

Thus, six components of the faculty role, collectively and as individual entities, describe a full-time faculty commitment in various academic ranks in a collegiate school of nursing. Since faculty members still need to be individuals and unique persons in their own right, they need to be aware of the expectations of a faculty role and the responsibilities of each position for which they apply. It is a joint responsibility of the dean of the school of nursing and the faculty applicant to ensure a good fit between the school's needs and resources and the unique qualifications of the applicant. When this good fit is achieved and nurtured on an ongoing basis, faculty role satisfaction is attained.

Personnel Decisionmaking

One of the most important components of institutional governance is personnel decisionmaking. Whether the institution is public or private, large or small, some mechanism exists to make personnel decisions regarding appointment, reappointment, promotion, and tenure of personnel. As the institution becomes larger and more complex, the personnel decisionmaking process tends to increase in complexity and become more codified. The succeeding paragraphs will describe personnel (faculty) decisionmaking procedures. Each institution has the prerogative of specifying its particular process.

Appointment

The appointment of a faculty member is the culmination of a series of interactions between a prospective faculty member and the dean or program administrator. Initially, the prospective faculty member or applicant may have responded to an advertisement placed by the school in a journal or may have been contacted personally by a colleague or the program administrator. Most schools request a letter of application, curriculum vita, and names of references before an applicant can be considered. Some schools require that copies of transcripts of undergraduate and graduate work be submitted. Also, schools may request a statement of the applicant's philosophy of nursing and/or professional goals. The latter enables the program faculty to predict whether the applicant's philosophy is complementary to the philosophy of that program.

Once the applicant's credentials are received, if both the applicant and program faculty are interested in pursuing the appointment, the applicant is usually invited for one to two days of interviews. The interviews provide a mutual opportunity to respond to questions, provide information, and assess compatibility between the applicant and the program (9, 12). Opportunities are provided for the applicant to meet with university administrators, nursing program administrators, and faculty. Often arrangements are made for the applicant to visit representative clinical facilities and get a sense of the community as a whole. Sometimes nursing students also participate in the interview process. The final session in the interview process may be used by the program administrator to discuss administrative procedures for effecting (or not effecting) a faculty appointment. Possible salary, rank, tenure, and role expectations are also discussed.

Following the interview process, the program administrator, with faculty input, decides whether a faculty appointment will be offered to the applicant. If an appointment is not to be offered, the applicant should be promptly notified of the decision. If an appointment is offered, the applicant is usually contacted by the program administrator. An official contract usually is issued by the institution's chief executive officer.

Reappointment

Depending upon the institutional procedures, faculty members may receive one year or multiple year contracts. Reappointment beyond the contract period typically involves a review of the faculty member's performance. Similar procedures and criteria may be used for peer evaluation of nontenured continuing faculty. Criteria for the performance review are developed by program faculty. These criteria reflect the institutional and program missions in the areas of teaching, research, and community service.

Figure 2-2 presents examples of performance criteria that may be utilized for reappointment. Note that reappointment criteria reflect the areas of teaching, research, and community service.

Promotion in Rank

As stated previously, collegiate institutions have adopted four academic ranks to which faculty are appointed. In ascending order these ranks are: Instructor, Assistant Professor, Associate Professor, and Professor. Institutional procedures specify the qualifications for each rank including time periods of service in one rank before promotion to the next rank.

Promotion decisions are based upon criteria that reflect the teaching, research, and community service missions of the institution. Promotion criteria are developed by program faculty in cooperation with institutional faculty and administration.

Promotion decisions usually involve recommendation by a faculty committee to the dean or program administrator, then through institutional channels to the chief executive officer. In some instances, promotion to the highest ranks may require action by the institution's governing board.

Figure 2-3 presents examples of promotion criteria for the areas of teaching, research, and community service at the Associate Professor rank. Promotion to a higher rank assumes that criteria for the lower ranks are met as well as specific criteria for the higher rank. Note the similarities and differences between the two institutions. The first example is a Research I institution and thus emphasizes its research mission. The second institution

Figure 2-2 Examples of reappointment criteria

Area Evaluated and Suggested Behaviors

I. General Education Service: Responsibility and Leadership
   A. On teaching team
   B. As school of nursing faculty
   C. As university faculty member

II. Teaching
   A. Classes
      1. Prepares adequately for classes
      2. Utilizes effectively the teaching methods employed
      3. Evaluates student achievement at regular intervals
   B. Clinical
      1. Prepares adequately for laboratory experiences
      2. Guides students effectively in clinical setting
      3. Evaluates students' achievement periodically throughout the semester

III. Advising
   A. Available for consultation
   B. Perceptive to student needs
   C. Treats information with confidence

IV. Professional
   A. Wide knowledge in specialized field
   B. Membership in professional organizations
   C. Attends professional meetings
   D. Keeps current with advancements in field
   E. Continues own education
   F. Acts with professional integrity

V. Community
   A. Contributes to the extension of knowledge into the community
   B. Engages in activities outside of field of nursing

Source: Adapted from Reappointment Criteria, School of Nursing, University of Wisconsin—Eau Claire. Used with permission.

Figure 2-3 Examples of criteria for promotion from assistant professor to associate professor

Criteria	Research university	Comprehensive university
Education	Effective teaching record	Minimum 7 years full-time teaching including no less than 3 years full-time college teaching Effective teacher Competent in evaluation methods
Research	Funded research	Writes and directs research projects
Publications	At least 6–8 scholarly publications with emphasis on refereed publications and primary or major authorship	Recent (within 5 years) publication or other creative production
Leadership	Leadership in professional service, academic and community service activities, local and regional Positive external reviews	Recognized as expert in one or more areas Successful coordination of one or more courses Promotes constructive community action Membership and visibility in specialty areas Presents professional papers at workshops Participates in graduate education Successfully manages the responsibility of administratively-defined positions

Source: Adapted from Reappointment Criteria, College of Nursing, University of Arizona and School of Nursing, University of Wisconsin—Eau Claire. Used with permission.

is a comprehensive university with teaching as its primary mission.

Tenure

The concept of tenure in academic institutions came into existence as a mechanism to protect the academic freedom of faculty. Tenure guaranteed the faculty member freedom to express his/her opinions and teach openly in the classroom without fear of reprisal. In recent years tenure has been incorrectly associated with job security. While by definition tenure implies that a faculty member will receive a continuing contract until retirement, the intent is preservation of academic freedom, not job security.

Tenure is defined as a commitment on the part of the institution to offer the faculty member a continuing appointment until the faculty member retires, elects to resign, or is dismissed for cause. The only other reasons for abrogating a tenure appointment would be discontinuance of the program to which the faculty member is assigned or financial exigency of the institution. Thus, a tenure appointment involves a long-term fiscal and programmatic commitment on the part of the institution. It is, therefore, a most serious personnel decision, and a tenure review is conducted rigorously.

In most academic institutions, a faculty member may be considered for tenure at any time after the initial appointment. Usually faculty must achieve tenure by the sixth year of appointment. If a positive tenure recommendation is not made during the sixth year, the faculty member is usually granted a seventh and terminal year. Recommendations for tenure begin at the faculty committee level, are forwarded to the dean or program administrator, the academic vice-president, chief executive officer, and governing board. Because of the fiscal and programmatic implications, tenure recommendations receive close scrutiny at every level.

Figure 2-4 presents examples of criteria for tenure in the areas of teaching, research, and community service. Although in some institutions tenure may be awarded at the Instructor rank, usually tenure is associated with Assistant or Associate Professor rank. Since tenure decisions are often associated with appointment to Associate Professor, the criteria for promotion and tenure are parallel in that instance.

Requirements for tenure in an institution reflect the teaching,

Figure 2-4   Examples of criteria for tenure

Candidates for tenure will be requested to submit data which addresses the following categories to be evaluated for tenure. Data will include a current curriculum vita and other supportive documents as designated by the Personnel Committee.

1. Educational Preparation
   A. Earned doctorate
   B. The Masters degree in nursing
   C. The Baccalaureate degree in nursing

2. Professional Activities
   A. Membership in professional and profession-related organizations
   B. Presentation at professional meetings
   C. Community service activities
   D. Representation of nursing in the health care arena

3. Professional Practice
   A. Recognition as expert clinician
   B. Professional consultation

4. Teaching Experience and Expertise
   A. Courses taught
   B. Courses coordinated
   C. Courses initiated or developed
   D. Teaching effectiveness

5. Leadership
   A. Responsibility for planning and implementation of programs
   B. School and university committees
   C. Activities facilitating achievements of course, program, and school goals

6. Scholarly Endeavors
   A. Research, publications, and media
   B. Honors and awards

Source: Adapted from Reappointment Criteria, School of Nursing, University of Wisconsin—Eau Claire. Used with permission.

research, and community service missions. Interestingly, a study by Sorensen and Van Ort found that 63 percent of a sample of nursing programs in Research I and II universities required the doctoral degree for promotion to Associate Professor, while only 45 percent required the doctorate for tenure (14). Research I universities had, as expected, more stringent expectations for doctoral preparation that did Research II institutions in the same study. Emphasis upon research is, of course, greater in research degree-granting institutions. However, most academic institutions require some evidence of ongoing scholarly activity as well as excellent teaching and participation in community service. Grantsmanship and research are becoming increasingly important in collegiate nursing education and are included among the tenure criteria in most baccalaureate and high degree nursing programs. The reader is referred to Chapter 14 for a discussion of tenure as an issue.

Grievance Procedure

Institutions of higher education are obliged to provide an academic grievance procedure in order to ensure that due process is available for faculty who are dissatisfied with a personnel decision. The primary requirement of academic due process includes the right to have a hearing at which all facts from both sides of the question are presented, with full disclosure assured.

Faculty members who believe they have a grievance are usually first advised to institute an appeal to the Personnel Committee for reconsideration of the committee's decision. If the appeal to the Personnel Committee is unsuccessful, the grievance procedure usually moves to the department level and then to the dean. If the intraschool appeals are unsuccessful, the faculty member has recourse to appeal through other institutional committees and administrative structures. The final institutional decision usually rests with the chief administrative officer of the institution. If the grievance is not settled within the institution, the faculty may seek redress through the civil courts.

This section has presented information regarding personnel decisionmaking mechanisms in collegiate education. Recognizing that institutional nuances exist, typical procedures for appointment, reappointment, promotion in rank, and tenure are discussed, and sample criteria presented. Prospective faculty need to be aware of the personnel decisionmaking patterns and expectations of an institution before a commitment to a faculty position is made. This prevents misperceptions from occurring later when a personnel decision is made.

Faculty Workload

Closely related to personnel decisionmaking is the determination of faculty workload. Although each institution has its own policies and procedures for determining faculty workload, examples are presented in succeeding paragraphs to illustrate possible methodologies.

Typical methods for determining faculty workload involve quantification of faculty responsibilities in the areas of teaching, research, and community service. Institutions may use the credit hour of instruction, the student contact hour, or a specific formula devised to quantify workload. The credit hour approach, as utilized in nursing and most other academic disciplines, equates a classroom teaching hour with a credit hour (3, p. 40). In a national study of associate degree and baccalaureate faculty workloads, Coudret found that the credit hour approach was least preferred by faculty (3). Difficulties arose in quantifying clinical instruction time by credit hours and team teaching was difficult to quantify by credit hours (3, p. 39).

Use of student contact hours as a method for quantifying faculty workload is commonly found in associate degree nursing programs and unionized baccalaureate programs. In this approach, faculty workload is measured by actual time spent with students, thus reflecting clinical instruction time accurately.

Formulas designed specifically for faculty workload quantification were preferred by faculty but used less frequently, according to the Coudret study (3). Formulas were seen as more flexible in terms of incorporating activities other than teaching. Particularly in baccalaureate programs, formulas recognized research, committee work, community service, and other expectations of faculty in colleges and universities.

Crawford and her colleagues described a formula for faculty workload that incorporates equitable weighting for classroom and clinical teaching (4). In addition, the formula provides for inclusion of research, faculty practice, committee work, administrative responsibilities, and community service activities (4, p. 286).

At the University of Texas at Austin, an administrative costing methodology provides for allocation of program resources as well as costing out of faculty workload (2). Faculty salary allocations reflect contributions to instruction, writing, research, committee work, and community service (2, p. 586). Faculty workload activities are weighted and formulas utilized to allocate instructional costs and derive faculty salaries (2, p. 589).

Formulas for faculty workload recognize the uniqueness of the nurse faculty role as well as the role expectations of nursing as an academic discipline. Faculty in nursing programs in the coming years will be expected to establish a workload policy congruent with the parent institution yet cognizant of nursing's professional uniquenesses.

Alternatives to a Full-time Faculty Position

In recent years, alternatives have been developed to facilitate the employment of faculty who elect not to accept a full-time faculty position for a variety of reasons. Part-time faculty appointments, joint appointments, or shared appointments may be used as alternatives to a full-time position in one institution. Also, flexible scheduling may be used to accommodate the needs of the institution as well as the individual.

Part-time faculty appointments are utilized in collegiate nursing programs to varying degrees and in diverse ways. Bower and her colleagues surveyed a national random sample of 91 accredited baccalaureate nursing programs regarding their use of part-time faculty (1, p. 44). The Bower study found that part-time faculty were employed primarily for classroom and clinical teaching (1, p. 45). The majority of respondent schools did not include part-time faculty on the tenure track, nor did part-time faculty accrue time toward promotion (1, p. 45). However, if part-time faculty served on school or university committees, full voting privileges were accorded (1, p. 45). Salary and benefit allocations varied among institutions, with many institutions offering limited fringe benefits to part-time faculty (1, p. 45).

According to MacQueen, part-time faculty positions provide mutual benefits for nursing programs and faculty who, primarily because of family responsibilities, cannot work full-time (7). MacQueen advocates a flexible approach to the appointment of part-time faculty in which the status, benefits, and job security of part-time faculty are improved (7, p. 103).

Other alternatives to a full-time faculty appointment include the use of *flex-time, job sharing,* or *joint appointments.* Flex-time involves the mutual arrangement by the employer for a work schedule that differs from the usual schedule, yet facilitates work completion while accommodating the individual faculty member's needs (7, p. 103).

Job sharing involves an arrangement whereby two nurse faculty members share one full-time faculty position (10, p. 411). O'Kane and Meyer describe their experiences in sharing a faculty position in a baccalaureate nursing program (10, p. 411). All components of the faculty position (teaching, research, community service) are included in the job-sharing arrangement. The difficulties perceived by O'Kane and Meyer involved specific allocation of time for each participant and interpretation of the job-sharing arrangement to colleagues and administrators.

Another potential alternative to a full-time faculty position is the joint appointment. Joint appointments are particularly attractive to nurse faculty who prefer ongoing appointments in nursing practice while serving on a faculty. Kuhn (5) describes a joint appointment in which she contributed 20 percent of her time to nursing service in exchange for 20 percent of staff nurses' time spent serving as clinical preceptors for nursing students (5, p. 1570). Joint appointments may be arranged for nurse faculty to work in direct patient care, clinical research, staff development, or consultant roles. One caution for those anticipating a joint appointment is that time must be allocated carefully to prevent the individual from working essentially two full-time positions. A carefully written job description with specific delineation of expectations in each portion of the joint appointment is essential.

This chapter described various components of the faculty role and the expectations for achieving success in that role. O'Shea suggests that orientation to the faculty role and the development of peer support systems for nurse faculty would be useful for new faculty in adjusting to the multifaceted faculty role (11, p. 310). In the future, flexible alternatives and faculty support systems will be devised to capitalize on nurse faculty member capabilities while recognizing the uniqueness of the role of nurse faculty member in an academic setting.

References

1. Bower, D., Fairchild, N., Hawkins, J., and Koundahjian, E. Part-time Faculty: Responsibilities, Opportunities, Employment Terms. *Nurs. Outlook* 28:43, 1980.
2. Brown, B.J., Lasher, W.F., and Embrey, C.L. A Costing Methodology for Schools of Nursing. *Nurs. Outlook* 27:584, 1979.
3. Coudret, N.A. Determining Faculty Workload. *Nurse Educator* 6(2):38, 1981.
4. Crawford, M.E., Laing, G., Linwood, M., Kyle, M.. and DeBlock, A. A formula for Calculating Faculty Workload *JNE* 22:285, 1983.
5. Kuhn, T.K. An Experience with a Joint Appointment. *Am. J. Nurs.* 82:1570. 1982.
6. Lane, E.B., Lagodna, G.E., Brooks, B.R., Long, N.J., Parsons, M.A., Fox, M.R., and Strickland, O.L. Faculty Development Activities. *Nurs. Outlook* 29:112, 1981.
7. MacQueen, J. In Support of Part-Time Faculty. *Nurs. Outlook* 29:102, 1981.
8. May, K.M., Meleis, A.I., and Winstead-Fry, P. Mentorship for Scholarliness: Opportunities and Dilemmas. *Nurs. Outlook* 30:22, 1982.
9. Mooneyhan, E.L. Evaluating a Potential Employer in Academia. *Nurs. Outlook* 26:697, 1978.
10. O'Kane, P.K., and Meyer, M. Sharing a Faculty Position. *Nurs. Outlook* 30:411, 1982.
11. O'Shea, H.S. Role Orientation and Role Strain of Clinical Nurse Faculty. *Nurs. Res.* 31:306, 1982.
12. Schlotfeldt, R.M. Recruiting, Appointing, and Renewing Faculty: A Shared Responsibility. *Nurs. Outlook* 24:154, 1976.
13. Solomon, H., Jordison, N., and Powell, S. How Faculty Members Spend Their Time. *Nurs. Outlook* 28:160, 1980.
14. Sorensen, G.E. and Van Ort, S.R. *Faculty Mobility in Selected Baccalaureate and Higher Degree Nursing Programs.* Paper presented at Second Annual Research in Nursing Education Conference, San Francisco, CA, January 20, 1984.

Suggested Readings

Andreoli, K.G. Faculty Productivity. *J. Nurs. Admin.* 9(11):47, 1979.

Barley, Z.A. and Redman, B.K. Faculty Role Development in University Schools of Nursing. *J. Nurs. Admin.* 9(5):43, 1979.

Barzun, J. *Teacher in America.* Garden City: Doubleday, 1954.

Beyer, J.E. and Marshall, J. The Interpersonal Dimension of Collegiality. *Nurs. Outlook* 29:662, 1981.

Bower, D., Fairchild, N. Hawkins, J., and Koundahjian, E. Part-time Faculty: Responsibilities, Opportunities, Employment Terms. *Nurs. Outlook* 28:43, 1980.

Bueche, M.N. Academic Tenure: A Reexamination for the Eighties. *Nurse Educator* 8(1):3, 1983.

Chaska, N.L. *The Nursing Profession: A Time to Speak.* New York: McGraw-Hill, 1983.

Conway, M.E. and Andruskiuw, O. *Administrative Theory and Practice.* Norwalk, CT: Appleton-Century-Crofts, 1982.

Conway, M.E. and Hardy, M.E. *Role Theory: Perspectives for Health Professionals.* New York: Appleton-Century-Crofts, 1978.

Coudret, N.A. Determining Faculty Workload. *Nurse Educator* 6(2):38, 1981.

Crawford, M.E., Laing, G., Linwood, M., Kyle, M., and DeBlock, A. A Formula for Calculating Faculty Workload. *JNE* 22:285, 1983.

Disbrow, M.A. Conducting Interdisciplinary Research: Gratifications and Frustrations. In N.C. Chaska, *The Nursing Profession: A Time to Speak.* New York: McGraw-Hill, 1983.

Fagan, M.M. and Fagan, P.D. Mentoring Among Nurses. *Nurs. and Health Care* 4:77, 1983.

Fleming, J.W. Tenure Today. *Am. J. Nurs.* 83:279, 1983.

Garrity, M., Miller, V., Osborn, M., and Vanderlinden, M. Developing Criteria for Promotion and Tenure. *Nurs. Outlook* 28:187, 1980.

Henry, J.K. Nursing and Tenure. *Nurs. Outlook* 29:240, 1981.

Highet, G. *The Art of Teaching.* New York: Vintage Books, 1950.

Kuhn, T.K. An Experience with a Joint Appointment. *Am. J. Nurs.* 82:1570, 1982.

MacQueen, J. In Support of Part-Time Faculty. *Nurs. Outlook* 29:102, 1981.

O'Kane, P.K. and Meyer, M. Sharing a Faculty Position. *Nurs. Outlook* 30:411, 1982.

O'Shea, H.S. Role Orientation and Role Strain of Clinical Nurse Faculty. *Nurs. Res.* 31:306, 1982.

Peterson, C.W. Overview of Issues in Nursing Education. In N.L. Chaska, *The Nursing Profession: A Time to Speak.* New York: McGraw-Hill, 1983.

Werley, H.H. and Newcomb, B.T. The Research Mentor: A Missing Element in Nursing? In N.L. Chaska, *The Nursing Profession: A Time to Speak.* New York: McGraw-Hill, 1983.

Part II

Learning

Chapter 3

What Is Learning?

Arlene M. Putt, R.N., Ed. D.

Study Questions

1. What is your definition of learning? Write your definition before and after reading the chapter.
2. What happens to neurotransmitters after they are released into the synapse?
3. How can a neuron be inhibited from firing?
4. How does one enhance attention?
5. What happens in habituation?
6. What is the dominant hemisphere pattern of persons who write in the lateral position compared to the pattern of persons who write in the hooked-hand position?
7. How are memories stored? Describe two theories.
8. What techniques help you to remember material?
9. Why is an understanding of the processes of learning important to the teaching of nursing?

Since learning is the primary issue in teaching, one must consider what takes place in learning before attempting to describe ways to achieve teaching that will foster learning. While space in this volume is inadequate to review all of the present knowledge of learning, some basic facts must be presented.

Neural Connections

Unraveling the complex process of learning is one of the present day challenges of neuroscience. Miller (18, p. 51) states that "studying how the brain functions greatly increases our respect for what is involved in different kinds of behavior...." Milgram (14, p. 50) concludes there is "...essential unity within psychology—the understanding that all psychological events rest on a biological substrate...." As a primary function of the nervous system of the body, learning is, in essence, a matter of making neural connections via the action of nerve complexes, neurotransmitters, and neuromodulators. Learning, then, is the establishment of neural connections through the refinement of neural pathways. Learning is also more than a change in behavior resulting from experiences for it is possible for learning to have occurred without observable changes in behavior.

The nervous system, the controlling system of the body, has been estimated to contain approximately 10 billion nerve cells (7). These nerve cells, called *neurons*, are the functioning units of the nervous system and consist of a cell body, or *soma*, with multiple short branches, termed *dendrites*, and a single long projection called an *axon*. A gap between neurons is called a *synapse* (9). Figures 3-1 and 3-2 contain diagrams of neurons with the various parts labeled.

Neurons react to either electrical or chemical stimulation by releasing tiny packets of neuron-manufactured neurotransmitter substance from the terminal area of the axon into the synaptic gap where the transmitter can interact with the receptor of the next neuron. The unused neurotransmitter is then either recycled or, as in the case of acetylcholine, destroyed by a specific enzyme, acetylcholinesterase (9). At one time excitation was thought to be unidirectional, proceeding from the reception of the nervous impulse by the dendrites, conducting toward the soma, and then out the axon to the synapse. Now it is known that neurons can interact in a variety of ways: soma to soma, soma to dendrites, soma to axon, axon to soma, axon to dendrites, axon to axon, dendrites to soma, dendrites to dendrites, and dendrites to axon. Given these possibilities with 10 billion cells, the permutations are beyond comprehension. One estimate of the capacity of the nervous system to handle information is 100 trillion bits of information (8). All of these bits of information must be communicated from one neuron to the next by neurotransmitter substances. When a neuron is excited by a stimulus, it fires or discharges; that is, the cell membrane changes its ionic concentration at one spot, creating a wave of depolarization that travels by self-propagation down the nerve to the synapse. Then, the neurotransmitter is released into the synaptic gap where it binds to the

Figure 3-1 Neuron with component parts and types of synapses

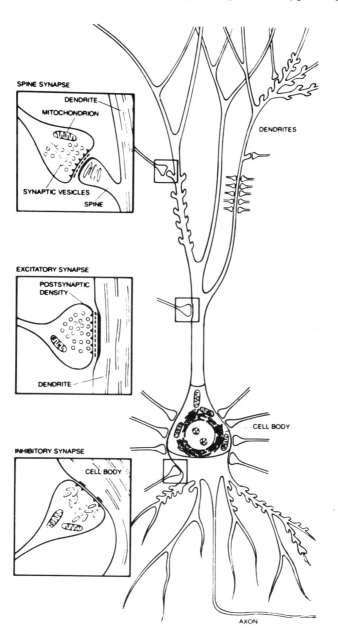

Source: Iverson, L. The Chemistry of the Brain. *Sci Am.* 241 (3):134, 1979.

What is Learning?

Figure 3-2   Physiologic flow patterns within neurons

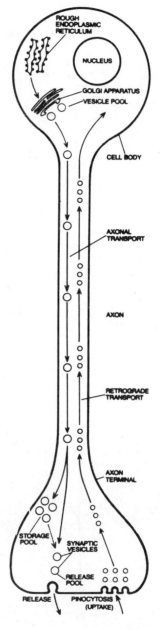

Source: Iverson, L. The Chemistry of the Brain. *Sci. Am.* 241 (3):134, 1979.

receptors of the next neuron, thus stimulating that neuron. In addition to excitation of the neuron, prevention of firing, inhibition, can occur. If inhibition occurs, the neural membrane becomes hyperpolarized and then cannot fire. In addition to excitation and inhibition, the possibility exists for the response to be modulated. One way in which modulation can occur is in the number of units which become involved and activated. Strong stimuli arouse more units, and weak stimuli arouse less units. Modulation can be learned. Evidence exists to show that man can learn to fire a single neuron out of the 10 billion neurons he possesses (8). Such precise control can only be obtained by extensive learning, coaching, and practice. However, this serves to illustrate that the power and versatility of learning can assume awesome proportions.

Well known is the fact that man can achieve very fine control over his skeletal muscles via coaching and practice. A less well-known fact is that man can control his autonomic nervous system. The autonomic nervous system consists of the largely automatic sympathetic division of this nervous heritage which takes over body control in situations of flight or fright, plus the opposing parasympathetic division which controls such resting functions as digestion and relaxation. The reader is referred to any physiology text for fuller descriptions of autonomic functioning. The fact that autonomic responses are subject to learning and voluntary control has been classically demonstrated in the work of Miller (17) and DiCara (5). Through a series of rewards for responses in the desired direction, animals can learn to reshape their autonomic responses in one direction or another. The same is true of man.

Originally, a neuron was thought to produce only one transmitter substance, but evidence exists that two or even three transmitters may be produced in some neurons (15). The role of the second transmitter is unclear but may be that of a modulator at the synapse. The third neurotransmitter is inhibitory in nature. To understand the roles of the additional transmitters, additional research is necessary.

No one knows how many transmitter substances there are. Over 30 have been identified with new information accumulating rapidly (9, 11). In Table 3-1 are listed most of the presently recognized transmitters. Many of these substances occur at multiple locations in the body. Some transmitters serve dual roles, being excitatory at one location and inhibitory elsewhere (9, 11).

What is Learning?

Table 3-1 Known and suspected synaptic transmitter agents and neural hormones

Acetylcholine	Glutamic acid (glutamate)	Norepinephrine
Adrenocorticotropic hormone (ACTH)	Glycine	Oxytocin
Angiotensin II	Gonadotrophin-releasing hormone	Prolactin-inhibiting hormone (PIH)
Beta endorphin	Growth hormone inhibiting hormone (GIH,GHIH, somatostatin)	Prolactin-releasing hormone (PRH)
Bombesin	Growth-releasing hormone (GRH)	Serotonin
Carnosine	Histamine	Substance P
Cholecystokinin-pancreozymin (CCK-PZ)	Luteinizing releasing hormone (LRH)	Taurine
Corticotropic-releasing hormone (CRH)	a-Melanocyte-stimulating hormone	Thyroid-releasing hormone (TRH)
Dopamine	Met and leu enkephalin	Thyrotropin
Epinephrine	Neurophysin	Vasoactive intestinal peptide
Gamma-aminobutyric acid (GABA)	Neurotensin	Vasopressin

Types of Learning

In looking at the nature of learning, two basic types of learning beyond classical conditioning have been identified: *sensitization* and *habituation* (10). Sensitization refers to an awareness of the newness or difference from past experience, causing a response of increased alertness and greater attention in the individual. In contrast, habituation is the result of repetition of the sameness of the stimuli with the consequence of lower levels of awareness and more attenuation of response until the conscious mind opts to ignore the stimulus entirely. The mind monitors the incoming stimuli for novelty and then decides whether or not to attend. Classical conditioning might be considered a form of habituation.

Bloom (3, 21) has categorized learning into three domains: *cognitive, affective,* and *psychomotor.* In his cognitive domain, which reflects knowledge, he has further classified levels of knowing from low to high order. In his affective domain, Bloom describes learnings in the emotional modes. Bloom's psychomotor domain applies attitudes and knowledge to motor behavior in life situations (21). Thus, Bloom has taken the two types of learning and organized them into levels of knowing and responding. These levels of knowing and responding will be discussed in more detail in Chapter 4.

Specialization of Hemispheres

Specialization of the functions of each of the hemispheres of the brain is another topic under extensive current research. For the majority of people, the *left hemisphere* is the dominant side of the brain, controlling reasoning, analytical and scientific thinking, written and spoken language as well as the motor function of the right side of the body. In contrast, the *right hemisphere* of the brain is involved with music, art, spatial relationships, insight, creativity, three-dimensional forms, and the control of the left side of the body (2). One discovery is the relationship of the writing hand position to the pattern of cerebral dominance. Those individuals who write in the lateral position have contralateral cerebral dominance. That is, the right-handed person who writes in a lateral orientation has left cerebral dominance, and the left-handed person writing in the lateral orientation has right hemisphere dominance. Those individuals who write in a hooked-hand position have ipsilateral cerebral dominance (13). The left-handed hook-hand writer has a left hemisphere dominance, and the right-handed person who writes with a hooked-hand position has a dominant right hemisphere. Which hemisphere dominates depends upon heredity and environmental factors in which compelling needs open new pathways. Within each hemisphere, there are areas of specialized function such as sensory perception, motor, visual and auditory reception, and association.

With the aid of computerized axial tomography (CAT) scan procedures, or evolved electrical potentials, patterns and magni-

What is Learning?

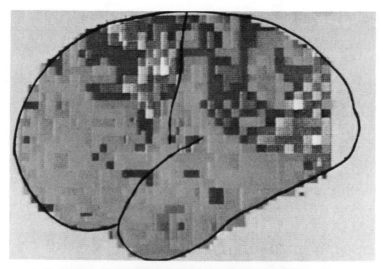

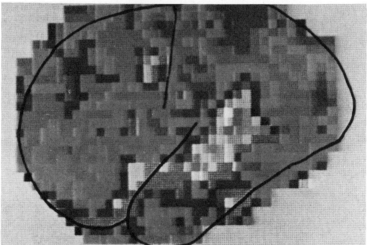

Figure 3-3 Altered brain blood flow during attention

Top: Changes from resting baseline during visual attending. Active areas while tracking a moving object with eyes are frontal eye field, upper frontal lobe supplemental motor area and occipital visual association area.

Bottom: Changes from resting baseline during auditory attending. Active area while listening to spoken words are the temporal lobe auditory cortex and Wernick's area which is adjacent. Wernick's area mediates the understanding of speech.

Source: Lassen, N.A., Ingvar, D.H., and Skinjol, E. Brain Function and Blood Flow. *Sci. Am.* 239(4):63, 1978.

tude of metabolic activity in the brain can be mapped while the subject is attending to a wide array of intellectual tasks. In this manner, areas of the brain involved in learning and memory can be identified as illustrated in Figure 3-3 (12).

A basic principle of body functioning is that of the *use-disuse phenomenon*. If a part of the body is utilized, that part of the body develops and its function is facilitated and refined. If a part of the body is not utilized, that body part tends to wither and atrophy and its function decreases. This principle is true of learning also. One must learn to learn: one must practice learning skills; one must solve problems to become competent; one must use language to become skillful; and one must practice analysis and synthesis to develop these skills. *Memory* facilitates the learning process by supplying facts, figures, and impressions to be integrated into the total life experience. The learning process is and always remains an active process requiring the exchange of energies. Information is a form of energy that can be transferred from one setting to another and manipulated in a variety of ways. All of this requires the expenditure of some form of energy by the body. While some forms of learning are more passive than others, resulting in minimum response from the body, the fact remains that the response is there, and the stimuli received must be integrated into the total body experience which is a unique constellation of experiences for each individual.

Memory

If such is the nature of learning, what then is memory? Memory is the primary way in which an individual records experiences, *sans* writing, *sans* photography, *sans* art, *sans* audio records. Memory is the collection of individual perceptions, stored in the brain, which are available for repeated comparisons with incoming impressions. Memory has been described as a magic slate, but that description is not accurate as memory exists in at least three forms: iconic, short-, and long-term memory (19).

Iconic memory is photographic memory, a skill often found in children, in which, for a very few seconds, the individual can reproduce the entire page mentally and read the information desired. This skill tends to disappear in adulthood.

Short-term memory is that brief memory that exists for the moment. Short-term memory is what the individual is focusing

51

upon at any point in time. An example is the phone number that is checked just prior to dialing. If an interruption occurs, the content of short-term memory is erased and cannot be recalled. Evidence exists to show that the neurotransmitter, acetylcholine, must be present or short-term memory does not exist (18). Short-term memory must be converted to *long-term memory* to be saved.

Less likely to be verbatim, long-term memory is apt to be paraphrased experience, synthesis of meaning, and relationship of concepts.

The location and mechanisms of memory remain enigmas. Does the brain store everything or is it selective? Where is memory stored? How is memory stored? Answers to these questions continue to be sought. Halstead and Rucker (6) support Hebb's model of short-term memory as a reverberating circuit and long-term memory as some changes in the synaptic membrane.

Agranoff (1) demonstrated that short-term memory in goldfish was disrupted by the injection of an antibiotic into the fish brains. After the injection of the antibiotic, the fish could no longer recall the pattern of the maze they had just learned to swim. If the antibiotic was injected after an interval of thirty minutes from the time of the learning, no deficit appeared in the fish's memory, and they could swim the maze they learned. Antibiotics are known to interfere with the synthesis of protein, and this gives substance to the idea that memory, in one form or another, may be encoded in protein. Herbert (7) describes work that leads to the conclusion there are two pathways for memories: spatial memories via the hippocampus and thalamus, and emotional memories via the amygdala and thalamus. Vasopressin is reported to improve memory (10). Also, as memory gets older, it is more difficult to dislodge (4).

However, Pribram (20, p. 46) in another hypothesis, considers memory to be a hologram where recall of a small fragment of the scene will generate the total picture again. The uniqueness of the hologram is "...every element in the original image is distributed over the entire photographic plate" (20, p. 46) With this concept, Pribram believes memories are the result of chemical patterns of changes which have passed through millions of synapses. As early as 1893, Tanzi postulated that the passage of neural impulses caused changes in the synapses (4). In this view, memory is lodged in the trace of changes at the synapses with each synapse having billions of memories. For a full recall of the situation, clues serve to revive additional aspects of memory. Sometimes the memory process depends upon the removal of current happenings by removing the inhibitory control of specific neurons so that happenings of more distant past can be retrieved (16). By whatever mechanisms it occurs, memory provides the continuity to life and permits the individual to learn from past experiences through the process of memorizing—a quick, effortful way to store information for future use (7). The memory process, according to Miskin (7), develops in early childhood.

The processes of learning—receiving, transmitting, ordering, and storing information—are basic to using that information to direct behavior toward established goals. While much information remains to be discovered, one must try to understand the processes involved in learning if one desires to aid the acquisition of knowledge and skills by another person. In other words, one must know both learning and nursing in order to teach nursing.

References

1. Agranoff, B.W. Protein Synthesis and Memory Formation. In A. Lajtha (ed.), *Protein Metabolism of the Nervous System.* New York: Plenum, 1970.
2. Attention is a Right-Sided Function. *Science News* 113:122, 1978.
3. Bloom B. (ed.). *Taxonomy of Educational Objectives: The Classification of Educational Goals.* Handbook I. Cognitive Domain. New York: David McKay, 1956. Handbook II. Affective Domain. New York: David McKay, 1964.
4. Deutsch, J.A. The Neural Basis of Memory. *Readings in Psychology Today.* Del Mar: Communications/Research/Machines, Inc., 1968. P. 105.
5. DiCara, L.V. Learning in the Autonomic Nervous System, *Sci. Am.* 220(1):30, 1970.
6. Halstead, W.C. and Rucker, W.B. Memory: A Molecular Maze. *Readings in Psychology Today.* Del Mar: Communications/Research/Machines, Inc., 1968. P. 102.
7. Herbert, W. Remembrance of Things Partly. *Science News* 124:378, 1983.
8. Hunt, M. *The Universe Within: A New Science Explores the Human Mind.* New York: Simon & Schuster, 1982.
9. Iverson, L. The Chemistry of the Brain. *Sci. Am.* 241(3):134, 1979.
10. Kandel, E.R. and Schwartz, J.H. Molecular Biology of Learning: Modulation of Transmitter Release. *Science* 218:433, 1982.
11. Kreiger, D.T. Brain Peptides: What, When, and Why? *Science* 222:975, 1983.

12. Lassen, N.A., Ingvar, D.H., and Skinjol, E. Brain Function and Blood Flow. *Sci. Am.* 239(4):63, 1978.
13. Levy, J. and Reid, M. Variation in Writing Posture and Cerebral Organization. *Science* 294:337, 1976.
14. Milgram, S. Understanding Psychological Man: Contribution. *Psychol. Today* 16(5):49, 1982.
15. Miller, J. Cells of Babel. *Science News* 122(25&26):394, 1982.
16. Miller, J. One Archive of Memory. *Science News* 124:380, 1983.
17. Miller, N. *Selected Papers.* Chicago: Aldine-Atherton, 1971.
18. Miller, N. Understanding Psychological Man: Contribution. *Psychol. Today* 16(5):51, 1982.
19. Patrusky, B. How Do We Remember? *Science 81* 2(1):96, 1981.
20. *The Human Body: The Brain: Mystery of Matter and Mind.* Washington D.C.: U.S. News Books, 1981.
21. Tuckman, B.W. A Four-Domain Taxonomy for Classifying Educational Tasks and Objectives. *Educ. Technol.* 12(12):36, 1972.

Suggested Readings

Axelrod, J. Neurotransmitters. *Sci. Am.* 230(6):58, 1974.

Bruner, J. Understanding Psychological Man: Contribution. *Psychol. Today.* 16(5):42, 1982.

deTornyay, R. and Thompson, M.A. *Strategies for Teaching Nursing* (2nd ed.). New York: Wiley, 1982.

Galaburda, A.M., LeMay, M., Kemper, T.L., and Geschwind, N. Right-Left Asymmetries in the Brain. *Science* 199:852, 1978.

Geschwind, N. Specialization in the Human Brain. *Sci. Am.* 241(3):180, 1979.

Guinee, K. *Teaching and Learning Nursing.* New York: Macmillan, 1978.

Hubel, D.H., The Brain. *Sci. Am.* 241(3):44, 1979.

Jacobson, M. and Hunt, R.K. The Origins of Nerve-Cell Specificity. *Sci. Am.*, 228(2):35, 1973.

Kreiger, D.T. Brain Peptides: What, Where, and Why? *Science* 222:975, 1983.

Maslow, A.H. *The Farther Reaches of Human Nature.* New York: The Viking Press, 1971.

Miller, J.A. A Shared Chemistry for Brain and Body. *Science News* 123:180, 1983.

Ojemann, G. and Mateer, C. Human Language Center: Localization of Memory Syntor and Sequential Motor-Phonemi Identification Systems. *Science* 205:1401, 1979.

Phillips, J. *The Origins of Intellect: Piaget's Theory.* San Francisco: W.H. Freeman, 1969.

Schmitt, F.O., Dev, P. and Smith, B.H. Electrical Processing of Information by the Brain Cells. *Science* 193:114, 1976.

Skinner, B.F. *Beyond Freedom & Dignity.* New York: Bantam, 1971.

Suggested Readings

Sinclair, J.D. How the Mind Recharges Batteries. *Psychol. Today* 16(11):96, 1982.

Stevens, C.F. The Neuron. *Sci. Am.* 241(3):55, 1979.

Wonder, J. and Donovan, P. *Whole-Brain Thinking—Working from Both Sides of the Brain to Achieve Peak Job Performance.* New York: Morrow, 1984.

Woody, C.D. *Memory, Learning and Higher Function: A Cellular View.* New York: Springer, 1982.

Chapter 4

Theories of Learning

Arlene M. Putt, R.N., Ed.D.

Study Questions

1. What ideas of learning are associated with:
Pavlov	Skinner	Rogers
Dewey	Bruner	Cognitive psychologists?
Gestalt	Bloom	
Piaget	Maslow	
2. How does one form concepts?
3. What are the dimensions and categories into which Bloom organizes learning?
4. Critics of behaviorists note shortcomings in the behavioristic approach to learning. What are these shortcomings?
5. What is cognitive psychology?
6. What is your own primary mode of learning? Compare it with that of your peers.
7. What principles of learning and teaching do you consider important enough to include in your own learning?

Historical Perspectives

How the mind works has been a matter of constant speculation over the centuries. Some knowledge of past thinking is important to understand the present level of theory. Without a knowledge of past thought, one could assume that all of the present thinking is new thought, a common fallacy.

With the ancient peoples the properties of the mind were the concern of the philosophers such as Aristotle and Plato, who utilized their beliefs regarding learning in the teaching of their disciples. The Greek philosophers and the religious leaders became the models for teachers for many generations. Over the years divergent views developed, mainly the metaphysical reasoning of Descartes in the seventeenth century and Kant in the eighteenth century as contrasted with the observational approach to the workings of the mind ascribed to by Hume and Locke (17). Hume, in the eighteenth century, thought the mind associated events it perceived, while Locke, in the nineteenth century, compared the infant's capacity to learn to a *tabula rasa*, or clean slate, where events were recorded.

While historical perspectives of the theories and trends espoused by these and other men of thought are of interest, the scope of this chapter will be limited to discussion of the developments within the present century.

Present Century Developments

The dawn of the twentieth century saw the shifting of emphasis from philosophers' speculation to the experimental approach for extracting truth regarding the nature of learning. Early in the century, Pavlov demonstrated that learning could be conditioned so that an artificial stimulus could be substituted for one that evoked a response. Thus began the field of classical conditioning and *Stimulus-Response* (S-R) *theory* through the work of Watson, Hull, Skinner, and Guthrie. Stimulus-Response theory focuses attention upon observable events and what stimuli can be used to elicit desired responses (7, 11).

Thorndike's laws of learning, derived from his experimental work, spelled out principles to govern education, namely:

1. Put together that which should go together.
2. Reward desirable connections and do not reward undesirable connections (11, 9).

Another person who took a slightly different view of learning at this time was Dewey (11). Dewey's belief was that the stimulus and the response are not sharply distinguished but are related in the organism (11, p. 11). Dewey also tied in interest by the learner to aims and intelligent action. This interrelatedness of aims, interest, and intelligent action is his contribution to the understanding of learning. According to Dewey, learning is problem-solving, or intelligent action, based upon constant evaluation of experiences and their consequences.

Some of the principles arising from the early thinking of Thorndike and Dewey are visible in the following dictums from present day psychology (8, 17):

1. Rewards produce learning, but learning can occur without rewards.
2. Latent learning does take place.
3. Learning is aided by reinforcement.
4. Partial reinforcement is less effective than full reinforcement.
5. Discrimination is associating cue with reward.
6. Learning can be removed by practicing extinction and desensitization.
7. In operant conditioning, spontaneous behavior is linked to rewards and to shaping behaviors.
8. In operant escape, the learner learns avoidance.

From S-R theory arose the school of behaviorism which said human behavior can be explained by conditioning and shaping the behaviors. To the behaviorists, learning is simply a matter of forming connections. The mind was not considered important in understanding behavior so the behaviorists began to hunt for principles of conditioning that would hold true for all animals (17). Chief proponent of behaviorism over the last half century has been Skinner (7). The work of Skinner, while popular in some circles, has evoked criticism in other groups because of its shortcomings. The greatest of these shortcomings is that people do think and find reason to change their behaviors in spite of external pressures, rewards, and punishments. The laws of learning as set forth by the behaviorists are found to be too general. In practice, the theory of association did not work as well in the classroom as in the laboratory. Thinking can speed learning while overt responses delay it (8). Rules of learning are not just applied, but rather the material is learned and understood. For example, verb tense can be shifted and the material restructured without losing the content and the essence of the meaning. By selective attention, the individual can focus upon clues in selected ways. Thus, thinking does affect learning. Bruner (3), Lazarus (9), and Miller (12) are a few of the psychologists who presently hold this view. As he has for half a century, Skinner still claims that behavior will be understood by technical analysis of behavior patterns which he believes are completely shaped by reinforcing consequences from the past. The consequences then become the stimulus for further behavior. Skinner claims the further use of technical analysis techniques will be adequate to decipher increasingly complex behaviors (16).

Important to learning is the concept formation process studied extensively by Piaget (17). His work was the basis for the field of cognitive development. Best known of Piaget's work is his stage theory which identifies stages of learning through which children go. In Piaget's theory, a child goes through a sensorimotor stage from birth to 18–24 months. By one and a half years, the child is at the stage of object concepts. From two to seven years, the child acquires images and concepts to use in preoperational thought. By seven years, the child can deal with concrete operations and can manipulate symbols. Around 11–15 years, the teenager can deal with abstract relationships and formal operations (17).

The problems with Piaget's scheme are these. Piaget conceived adult thinking as a process of formal logic. The logic model of adult thinking is not correct; much of thinking is illogical as the mind does not naturally operate in a formal logical mode. This is a carry-over from childhood. Formal logic demands a constraint to rules that normally do not exist in free thinking (8). Also, abilities may appear at different times than at the time specified by Piaget. Some abilities fail to appear and others appear early. Therefore, it is much easier to speak of cognitive abilities as they develop and to disregard age ranges set by Piaget.

Piaget rejected all ideas of preprogramming. Evidence has been found that the brain comes with tendencies to interpret and assimilate experiences in ways that structure concepts of time, space, number, and causality very early in life. All humans respond to gravity, three dimensions (time, quantity, and causality), and learn to refine these concepts (8). Many experiences cannot be perceived or interpreted until neural pathways mature, and the insulating myelin sheath is complete. Bowel and bladder control are examples. Piaget focused upon the right questions, but observation alone does not give adequate answers to questions of how behaviors develop.

All of this knowledge affects the way individuals learn. Education, as described by Bruner (2), is a process of structuring one's learnings. The human being creates order out of nonorder by the process of recognizing patterns (8). One person who has created order out of varying aspects of learning is Bloom.

Bloom (1) has categorized learning into three domains: *cognitive, affective,* and *psychomotor*. In his cognitive domain which reflects knowledge, he has further classified levels of knowing from low to high order; namely, from *knowledge, comprehension, application, analysis, synthesis,* and finally, *evaluation*. In his first order of knowing, knowledge is equated with fact recall or remembering. In the second order, comprehension, the learner knows what is being communicated and can use the information without understanding the full implications. In the third order, application, rules and abstract ideas are attached to the information which is then utilized in particular concrete situations. In the fourth order, analysis, the information is broken down into its specific parts to clarify and to explain the relationships contained therein. In the fifth order, synthesis, the opposite process is used, that of combining and arranging the component parts to produce a unified whole. In the sixth or highest order, Bloom uses evaluation or judgment based upon determined criteria as a basis for comparison of information.

In his affective domain, Bloom describes learning in the *emotional modes*, those of *receiving, responding, valuing, organizing,* and *characterizing* values. Receiving, as used by Bloom, means attending or becoming sensitive to certain stimuli. By responding, the individual shows interest or reaction to the situation, accepting or rejecting the value presented. In organizing, the individual determines interrelatedness of several values, identifies dominant and passive values, and places the values into a hierarchy and into a system. In characterizing, the total package of values is made consistant with a total philosophy or a global view.

Bloom's psychomotor domain applies attitudes and knowledge to motor behavior in life situations (18). The steps that Bloom identifies in this domain are those of *perception, set, guided response, mechanism* or patterning, and *performance*. In perception, the learner becomes aware of objects in situations utilizing human senses. Using combined awareness, the individual creates a set of readiness for response. For initial responses of complex acts, the format of guided response with the aid of an instructor is utilized. Under patterning, the response is refined and the pattern perfected. Finally, the complex act is performed as needed. Thus, Bloom has taken two types of learning, sensitization and habituation, and organized them into levels of knowing and responding. Bloom's organization is useful in both learning and teaching as evidenced by the applications made by deTornyay and Thompson who use Bloom's taxonomy to structure classroom learning situations (4). Bloom's taxonomy is summarized in Table 4-1.

On strains of thought differing from the behaviorist viewpoint, the German movement of *Gestalt* gained prominence in the early decade of the century. In Gestalt (6), recognition was made of the whole situation and its need to remain a whole for the sake of interpretation. In time Gestalt merged with field theory espoused by Lewin who emphasized that learning takes place in a social milieu where social change is occurring (6, 11). While Lewin put emphasis on the social impact of learning, Maslow (10) and Rogers (15) began putting emphasis upon the individuality of man. Maslow (10) described a process of growth of self through several stages of maturation to an end product of self-actualization of the inner self and full development of individual capabilities. Rogers (15) in turn, asked such questions as: What is my purpose? What do I want to be? Answers to these questions profoundly influence learning. To achieve an optimum self, Rogers advocated being open to experiences with the goal of becoming an even better, more complete human being—the ultimate goal of all learning.

From these beginnings evolved the present day *cognitive psychologists* who see individuals as information-seekers who try to understand how information is acquired, processed, understood, and utilized (13). Cognitive psychologists tend to agree that individuals choose most of what they know. The choices are made through selective attention and cognitive skills and strategies put to use as the individuals continue to explore the surrounding environment (13).

Table 4-1 Summary of Bloom's taxonomy

	Domains		
	Cognitive	Affective	Psychomotor
Levels	Knowledge	Receiving	Perception
	Comprehension	Responding	Set
	Application	Valuing	Guided
	Analysis	Organizing	responses
	Synthesis	Characterizing	Patterning
	Evaluation	values	Performance

Fox (5) summarizes the state of the thinking at the present time. He raises the question of whether the neuroscientists can provide an adequate theoretical base for understanding learning. Fox describes Kandel's work as localized learning in which changes at synapses are modulated. In the neuroselection theory of Changeux, as described by Fox, learning is a process of choosing the neural pathways that will be enhanced. This thinking is in agreement with the principle of use-disuse in which the utilization of a function enhances its anatomical and physiological basis and nonuse leading to atrophy. There is a process in the nervous system by which, at an early age, neural connections are refined and reduced in number. Changeux has termed this selection and stabilizing process to be "resonance" (5). Fox goes on to quote Singer who describes "learning as the prolongation of a self-organizing process" (5, p. 1220). In early life, this adaptive self-organizing process resembles associative learning or Pavlovian conditioning. Again, bowel and bladder training are examples.

Only language sets humans apart from other animals. Cognitive scientists say that language is a solution to sets of communication problems while Chomsky sees language metaphorically as an organ with a described function (5).

While all of the mechanisms involved in learning are still not fully understood, the process of learning and its component parts is evolving steadily. Learning is a life-long process from which no individual can escape. To understand as much as possible about this process is to be able to use it more effectively to achieve one's goals and to provide effective teaching for others.

Self-Assessment of Learning Style

As time goes by, individuals tend to develop patterns of preferred modes of learning. Some persons learn primarily by sight, while other persons depend upon sound. Some individuals require both sight and sound, while still others may add tactile and olfactory perceptions to solidify their learnings. In reality, each person develops a rather solitary pattern to his learning style. A writer-developed tool to identify aspects of the individual's pattern of learning is found in Figure 4-1.

On the Likert-type scale in Figure 4-1, the learner can identify some of the preferred modes of learning. This information is then

Self-Assessment of Learning Style

Figure 4-1 Self-assessment of learning patterns

I learn best when (Check the dot nearest to your perception of yourself).

Instruction is slow paced	. . . . . .	Instruction is fast paced
Instruction is structured	. . . . . .	Instruction is not structured
I take notes	. . . . . .	I listen without taking notes
My anxiety is high	. . . . . .	My anxiety is low
I have internal control	. . . . . .	I have external control
I am given norms	. . . . . .	I set my own norms
I use short-term memory	. . . . . .	I use long-term memory
I see immediate value	. . . . . .	I see later value
I organize my own ideas	. . . . . .	The instructor organizes ideas
Objectives are given	. . . . . .	I make my objectives
Evaluation is upon mastery	. . . . . .	Evaluation is upon contract
I am in a lecture	. . . . . .	I am in a discussion
I participate in class	. . . . . .	I am silent in class
I am hungry	. . . . . .	I am well fed
I am rested	. . . . . .	I am tired
Audiovisuals are used	. . . . . .	Presentation is live
I have to discover answers	. . . . . .	The answers are given
Examples precede rules	. . . . . .	Rules precede examples
I ask numerous questions	. . . . . .	I let others ask questions

Source: Arlene M. Putt, Ed.D.

of use to the learner who can capitalize upon individual preferences and also of use to the instructor who can consider individual preferences in devising teaching strategies that will be of maximum benefit to the learner by helping structure learnings in meaningful ways.

References

1. Bloom, B. (ed.). *Taxonomy of Educational Objectives: The Classification of Educational Goals.* Handbook I. Cognitive Domain. New York: David McKay, 1956. Handbook II. Affective Domain. New York: David McKay, 1964.
2. Bruner, J. *Toward a Theory of Instruction.* Cambridge: Harvard University Press, 1966.
3. Bruner, J. Understanding Psychological Man: Contribution. *Psychol. Today.* 16(5):42, 1982.
4. deTornyay, R. and Thompson, M.A. *Strategies for Teaching Nursing* (2nd ed.). New York: Wiley, 1982.
5. Fox, J. Debate in Learning Theory is Shifting. *Science* 222:1219, 1983.
6. Hilgard, E. The Place of Gestalt Psychology and Field Theories in Contemporary Learning Theory in National Society for the Study of Education. *Theories of Learning and Instruction.* Chicago: University of Chicago Press, 1964.
7. Hill, W. Contemporary Developments within Stimulus-Response Learning Theory in National Society for the Study of Education. *Theories of Learning and Instruction.* Chicago: University of Chicago Press, 1964.
8. Hunt, M. *The Universe Within: A New Science Explores the Human Mind.* New York: Simon & Schuster, 1982.
9. Lazarus, R. Understanding Psychological Man: Contribution. *Psychol. Today* 16(5):43, 1982.
10. Maslow, A. *The Farther Reaches of Human Nature.* New York: Viking Press, 1971.
11. McDonald, F. The Influence of Learning Theories on Education (1900–1950) in National Society for the Study of Education. *Theories of Learning and Instruction.* Chicago: University of Chicago Press, 1964.
12. Miller, N. Understanding Psychological Man: Contribution. *Psychol. Today* 16(5):51, 1982.
13. Neisser, U. Understanding Psychological Man: Contribution. *Psychol. Today* 16(5):44, 1982.
14. Phillips, J. *The Origins of Intellect: Piaget's Theory.* San Francisco: W.H. Freeman, 1969.
15. Rogers, C. Toward Becoming a Fully Functioning Person. In Association for Supervision and Curriculum Development. *Perceiving, Behaving, Becoming,* Yearbook 1962, Washington D.C.: Association for Supervision and Curriculum Development. 1962. P. 27.
16. Skinner, B.F. Understanding Psychological Man: Contribution. *Psychol. Today* 16(5):48, 1982.

17. *The Human Body: The Brain: Mystery of Matter and Mind* Washington D.C.: U.S. News Books, 1981.
18. Tuckman B. A Four-Domain Taxonomy for Classifying Educational Tasks and Objectives. *Educ. Technol.* 12(2):36, 1972.

Suggested Readings

Archambault, R. (ed.). *John Dewey on Education.* New York: Modern Library, 1964.

Bloom B. (ed.). *Taxonomy of Educational Objectives: The Classification of Educational Goals.* Handbook I. Cognitive Domain. New York: David McKay, 1956. Handbook II. Affective Domain. New York: David McKay, 1964.

Bruner, J. *Toward a Theory of Instruction.* Cambridge: Harvard University Press, 1966.

deTornyay, R. and Thompson, M.A. *Strategies for Teaching Nursing* (2nd ed.). New York: Wiley, 1982.

Dunn, R. and Dunn, K. *Teaching Students Through Their Individual Learning Styles: A Practical Approach.* Reston: Reston, 1978.

Geschwind, N., Specialization in the Human Brain. *Sci. Am.* 241(3):180, 1979.

Guinee, K. *Teaching and Learning Nursing.* New York: Macmillan, 1978.

Hunt, M. *The Universe Within: A New Science Explores the Human Mind.* New York: Simon & Schuster, 1982.

Kolb, D.A. *The Learning Style Inventory: Technical Manual.* Newton: Institute for Development Research, 1976.

Maslow, A. *The Farther Reaches of Human Nature.* New York: Viking Press, 1971.

Phillips, J. *The Origins of Intellect: Piaget's Theory.* San Francisco: W.H. Freeman, 1969.

Rogers, C. *On Becoming a Person.* Boston: Houghton-Mifflin Co., 1961.

Schmitt, F.O., Dev, P., and Smith, B.H. Electrical Processing of Information by the Brain Cells. *Science* 193:114, 1976.

Skinner, B.F. *Beyond Freedom and Dignity.* New York: Bantam, 1971.

The Human Body: The Brain: Mystery of Matter and Mind. Washington D.C.: U.S. News Books, 1981.

Tuckman, B.W. A Four-Domain Taxonomy for Classifying Educational Tasks and Objectives. *Educ. Technol.* 12(12):36, 1972.

Part III

Strategies for Teaching

Chapter 5

Curriculum Development and Process

Suzanne Van Ort, R.N., Ph.D.

Study Questions

1. What is the relationship between institutional and program missions? Why are these missions important in designing a nursing curriculum?
2. In assessing needs and resources prior to development of nursing curriculum what service areas, constituencies, and support systems need to be considered?
3. What faculty characteristics are important in collegiate settings? How do these affect the curriculum?
4. What student characteristics are important in collegiate settings? How do these affect the curriculum?
5. What are the curricular patterns offered in basic nursing education?
6. What are the curricular patterns offered in graduate nursing education?
7. What steps are included in the curriculum process? What are the relationships among the components in the curriculum process?
8. What are the mechanisms for curriculum evaluation? What impact do these mechanisms have on curriculum revision?

Curriculum Development

In American higher education, the term, *curriculum*, has been defined in various ways by educators who use it in their work. For example, Bevis defines curriculum as "the learning activities that are designed to achieve specific educational goals" (3, p. 6). Conley describes curriculum as "the content and processes of relationships between students, teachers, and others, and the arrangement of the physical and social environment that facilitate the attainment of specified goals that are consistent with an integral part of the total school program" (4, p. 15). Guinee defines curriculum as "all the planned student learning outcomes stated in the behavioral objectives" (10, p. 89). Regardless of the specific definition of curriculum, each author refers to curriculum as a planned entity intended to achieve learning outcomes.

Curriculum in the collegiate setting is designed to provide learning experiences to prepare students in a given subject area or discipline. The mission of the institution provides direction to each educational program and, thus, to the curriculum. For example, in a research-oriented institution, courses in research methodology are built into the curriculum at all levels. In a church-related school with a religiously oriented mission, courses in philosophy, theology, and ethics are often inherent in the curriculum for all disciplines.

Institutional missions are determined by societal need as reflected in the constituencies served by the institution and the funding sources that support the institution. Missions that exist in American higher education institutions today are illustrated in Figure 5-1.

The framework illustrated in Figure 5-1 shows that

> In the first dimension, colleges concentrate on undergraduate instruction, with graduate instruction and research viewed generally as a secondary function if offered. A university, on the other hand, emphasizes graduate and advanced professional instruction and research. In the second dimension, application-oriented institutions emphasize occupational-professional major fields, interpretive scholarship, and applied programs of community and public service. Research activities are directed toward the solution of specific, immediate problems. In contrast, theoretically-oriented institutions stress basic theoretical knowledge, less specialized majors, and fundamental research. In this frame of reference, the outside vertical areas of the "educational universe" represent differentiated specialized institutions, one applied and the other theoretical. The larger middle area represents comprehensiveness with a varying emphasis on both theory and its practical application (11, p. 8).

As institutions and their missions respond to changes in society, the curricula of the institutions also change. For example, many institutions that were founded as teachers' colleges in the late nineteenth and early twentieth centuries expanded their missions in the 1950s and 1960s to become regional state colleges and

Curriculum Development

Figure 5-1 A two-dimensional framework for classifying higher educational institutions

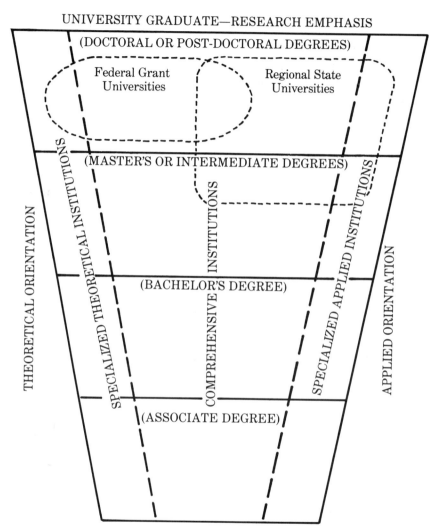

Source: Harcleroad, F.F., Molen, C.T., and Rayman, J. *The Regional State Colleges and Universities Enter the 1970s.* Iowa City, Iowa: The American College Testing Program, 1973. P. 8.

universities. During this expansion of mission, curricula were changed so that, in addition to teacher education and liberal arts, these schools offered degree programs in various disciplines and professions. Among these former teachers' colleges are many state universities that today offer baccalaureate and master's degrees in nursing.

Once the institutional mission is confirmed, the mission of programs within that institution is established. Nursing programs at the associate degree, baccalaureate degree, master's degree, and/or doctoral degree level may be offered by an institution. However, the type of degree program depends upon the institutional mission. If for example a research-oriented university decided to offer a doctoral program in nursing, this would be congruent with its institutional mission. However, it is highly unlikely that a doctoral program in nursing would be established in a small, private liberal arts college. Because of the research emphasis in doctoral education, research must be emphasized in both the institutional and program missions for the doctorate to be an acceptable program offering.

In the area of program mission, many graduate programs exist in health science centers where the diversity and complexity of nursing care provides ample learning experiences for graduate students. Conversely, one would not expect graduate programs to be located solely in rural communities that may offer minimal clinical opportunities for graduate student learning. However, rural clinical sites in combination with urban institutions offer special learning experiences not found in health science centers. Thus, the goals of the program are also important in determining the curriculum. Programs preparing family nurse practitioners for ambulatory care settings may well incorporate experiences in rural areas in order to offer students breadth of experience.

Before proceeding with program development, a feasibility study is done to assess program need and resources. The feasibility study involves administration, external constituencies, prospective students, faculty, and consumers. When designing a new program, educators are obliged to design a study that will assess the needs and resources of the area to be served.

Questions to be answered include:

1. What is the service area of the program? Is the service area geographically discrete, or will the program serve a large area in which travel is anticipated?
2. What constituencies will be served by the program? Are the

clients diverse in cultural background? educational background? age? socioeconomic status? Are the constituencies primarily families?
3. What support systems exist for the proposed program? Is it to be publicly or privately supported? Are there sufficient appropriate clinical facilities for the program to be offered?
4. What will be the relationship of the program to educational programs or nursing programs in the service area?
5. What will be the relationship of the nursing program to other educational programs within the institution? Who will provide the supporting courses for nursing students? Will the nursing program provide courses for other disciplines?

Data obtained from these questions are utilized for decision-making regarding the feasibility of offering a nursing program in a given institution. Additional feasibility data regarding faculty and student characteristics will be discussed in succeeding sections of this chapter. All feasibility data are summarized in report form for presentation to administrative authorities in order to validate (or refute) the need for a nursing program. At this stage of program development, administrative authorities will consider the feasibility data in relation to funding priorities and political considerations, then make a decision regarding program development and implementation. If a positive decision is made, curriculum development proceeds. A negative decision may lead to revision of planning strategies to submit a second request at a later date or abandonment of program development.

Concurrent with program development is the process of applying for state approval of the nursing program by the State Board of Nursing. Program developers must work within State regulations and cooperate with the State Board of Nursing requirements in order for program development to proceed toward State approval. Only if the program receives State approval will graduates be permitted to write the State Board examination for licensure. Also, criteria adopted by the councils for the National League for Nursing provide guidance in program development as they provide criteria to be used for accreditation by the National League for Nursing (15, 16).

Because data regarding faculty characteristics and student characteristics are so important to curriculum development, these categories have been isolated for specific discussion. In reality, both of these areas are included in the feasibility data discussed previously.

The characteristics of faculty for a nursing program determine, to a great extent, the viability and strength of the program. In order to provide a strong baccalaureate program, for example, faculty should represent a mix of demographic characteristics. Diversity of educational and experiential backgrounds provides students with a mix of knowledge bases and a broad range of experiences from which to learn nursing. Of course, a representation of clinical specialty areas is essential to provide depth of content in the specialty areas. A mix of doctorally and master's prepared faculty ensures that research content and research-based practice will be presented in the program. The goal of a totally doctorally prepared faculty is espoused by nursing education for the future. At present the insufficient supply of doctorally prepared faculty precludes attainment of this goal.

Student characteristics help determine the structure of the curriculum and the characteristics of curriculum content. If there is a large part-time student population, learning experiences in evenings or on weekends may be designed. Culturally homogeneous versus culturally heterogeneous student populations necessitate different curricular learning experiences. Urban student populations benefit from selected rural learning experiences to provide a breadth of experience.

Also, student populations that include students with prior academic degrees, students who have graduated from other nursing programs, or students who are returning adults may necessitate special consideration in curricular planning.

Admission requirements for students are based in part on the demographic mix of prospective students, the expected characteristics of the product of the program upon graduation, and the long-term expectations for graduates. Thus, the characteristics of a student population are inextricably linked to curriculum development and implementation.

Curriculum Patterns for Basic Nursing Education

Within nursing education, a variety of curricular patterns exists to offer education to diverse constituencies. As discussed in Chapter 1, the diploma model for providing nursing education in hospital schools of nursing was the original American model for nursing education. As nursing education moved into higher education, baccalaureate degree programs were developed. More recently, associate degree nursing programs were developed in community colleges and technical institutes. Each of these patterns will be discussed briefly in succeeding paragraphs.

Diploma Education in Nursing

The diploma model of nursing education typically incorporates three years of training in a hospital school of nursing. In some programs, the program includes one year of liberal arts and science education at an affiliated community college or local four-year institution. Emphasis in diploma programs is placed upon preparation of a graduate who can function in an acute care setting upon graduation. Clinical experiences are provided in the parent hospital so that students learn to apply the nursing process to a variety of patients in the hospital setting. Upon graduation, graduates of a hospital school of nursing receive a diploma indicating program completion and are entitled to take the State Board examination for licensure as a registered nurse.

Associate Degree Nursing Education

In the 1950s the associate degree nursing program was designed by Montag and her colleagues to prepare technical nurses (5). The two-year community college was selected as the setting for technical nursing education so that an associate degree program would be offered. Students in an associate degree nursing program focus upon care of patients with common, recurring nursing problems and application of the nursing process in caring for patients in acute and long-term care facilities (25).

Associate degree nursing programs now exist in two-year community colleges, technical institutes, and in selected four-year colleges and universities. Regardless of the institutional placement, the two-year program provides both liberal and technical education. According to the Division of Associate Degree Programs of the National League for Nursing,

> the practice for graduates of associate degree nursing programs:
> — Is directed toward clients who need information or support to maintain health.
> — Is directed toward clients who are in need of medical diagnostic evaluation and/or are experiencing acute or chronic illness.
> — Is directed toward clients' responses to common, well-defined health problems.
> — Includes the formulation of a nursing diagnosis.
> — Consists of nursing interventions selected from established

nursing protocols where probable outcomes are predictable.
— Is concerned with individual clients and is given with consideration of the person's relationship within a family, group, and community.
— Includes the safe performance of nursing skills that require cognitive, psychomotor, and affective capabilities.
— May be in any structured care setting but primarily occurs within acute- and extended-care facilities.
— Is guided directly or indirectly by a more experienced registered nurse.
— Includes the direction of peers and other workers in nursing in selected aspects of care within the scope of practice of associate degree nursing.
— Involves an understanding of the roles and responsibilities of self and other workers within the employment setting (7, p. 3).

Associate degree nursing graduates are prepared to function in the roles of care provider, communicator, client teacher, manager of client care, and member of the nursing profession (7). Flexible learning experiences are often provided in associate degree nursing programs to accommodate students from varying age groups, educational backgrounds, and socio-economic statuses.

Baccalaureate Degree Nursing Education

The third model of basic nursing education is the baccalaureate nursing program. Baccalaureate nursing programs are located in public and private four-year colleges and universities. Typically, the baccalaureate program provides four years of liberal and professional nursing education leading to the Bachelor of Science in Nursing degree. The majority of nursing content is offered in the upper division or the final two years of the program.

According to the Division of Baccalaureate and Higher Degree Programs of the National League for Nursing,

the graduate of a baccalaureate program in nursing will be able to:

1. Utilize nursing theory in making decisions on nursing practice.
2. Use nursing practice as a means of gathering data for refining and extending that practice.
3. Synthesize theoretical and empirical knowledge from the physical and behavioral sciences and humanities with nursing theory and practice.
4. Assess health status and health potential; plan, implement, and evaluate nursing care of individuals, families, and communities.
5. Improve service to the client by continually evaluating the effectiveness of nursing intervention and revising it accordingly.

6. Accept individual responsibility and accountability for the choice of nursing intervention and its outcome.
7. Evaluate research for the applicability of its findings to nursing actions.
8. Utilize leadership skills through involvement with others in meeting health needs and nursing goals.
9. Collaborate with colleagues and citizens on the interdisciplinary health team to promote the health and welfare of people.
10. Participate in identifying and effecting needed change to improve delivery within specific health care systems.
11. Participate in identifying community and societal health needs and in designing nursing roles to meet these needs (8, pp. 2–3).

Baccalaureate students practice in a variety of health care settings including acute care institutions, long-term care settings, and community health settings as they learn to provide health restoration, health promotion, and health maintenance of individuals, families, and communities. The Division of Baccalaureate and Higher Degree Programs of the National League for Nursing asserts that

baccalaureate programs provide students with an opportunity to acquire:

(1) Knowledge of the theory and practice of nursing;
(2) Competency in selecting, synthesizing, and applying relevant information from various disciplines;
(3) Ability to assess client needs and provide nursing interventions;
(4) Ability to provide care from groups of clients;
(5) Ability to work with and through others;
(6) Ability to evaluate current practices and try new approaches;
(7) Competency in collaborating with members of other health disciplines and with consumers;
(8) Understanding of the research process and its contribution to nursing practice;
(9) Knowledge of the broad function the nursing profession is expected to perform in society;
(10) Foundation for graduate study in nursing (8, p. 1).

Special Curricular Patterns

In addition to the generic associate degree and baccalaureate degree nursing programs, several unique curricular patterns exist to serve specific constituencies. For example, the *Second Step Program* (24) originally instituted at Sonoma State University in California, provides a "2+2" nursing program (9). In this program, registered nurse students from associate degree nursing programs are provided an opportunity to earn a baccalaureate degree in nursing within a two-year period of time. The Second Step model has been widely adopted and adapted to meet the needs of registered nurses who seek a baccalaureate degree.

Another unique model available to registered nurse students is the external degree program offered by the Regents of the University of the State of New York. The *Regents External Degree Program* incorporates assessment of prior learning and uses both clinical and theoretical examinations to measure current learnings by students who seek either an associate degree or a baccalaureate degree in nursing. The program involves self-paced learning by students in their home environment as no on-campus learning experiences exist. Examinations for proficiency are offered at various sites in the United States.

These two models exemplify educational program offerings designed to facilitate career mobility for registered nurse students. Additional information on career mobility is provided in Chapter 12.

A third unique basic nursing education model is the *nursing doctorate* (N.D.) *degree* offered by Case Western Reserve University in Cleveland, Ohio. The nursing doctorate program provides doctoral education as the first professional degree for individuals who have college background but no previous nursing education.

These education alternatives illustrate the diversity of basic nursing education and provide some basis for understanding the profession's quandary when nursing tries to explain its role to various constituencies within and outside the health care system.

Curriculum Patterns for Graduate Education in Nursing

Graduate education in nursing includes master's degree nursing programs, post-master's nursing specialist programs, and doctoral degree programs in nursing. Although master's degree education in nursing has existed since the 1940s, nursing specialist and doctoral programs in nursing are relative newcomers to the higher education arena.

The master's degree is the primary graduate degree in nursing in terms of numbers of students and diversity of program offerings. The purpose of master's degree education in nursing is to prepare leaders in nursing practice, nursing education, and nursing administration. According to the National League for Nursing,

the nurse in an advanced professional program:
1. pursues an area of clinical specialization;
2. elects an area of role development;
3. develops and tests nursing theories;
4. advances knowledge in the field through systematic observation and experimentation;
5. relates basic science theories to the development of knowledge in the clinical and functional areas;
6. identifies and implements nursing's leadership role within the health care delivery system; and
7. engages in a collaborative role with others interested in health care (14).

Based on a baccalaureate degree nursing education as a foundation, master's degree nursing education provides students with an opportunity to specialize in a clinical area as well as a functional area (teaching, practice, administration). In addition, opportunities are usually provided for a focused research experience involving a thesis or clinical research project. Also, advanced courses in liberal education are included to provide depth relevant to the area of specialization.

Typically, a master's degree program in nursing encompasses 36–48 credits and requires one to two years of study beyond the baccalaureate degree. Master's degree programs are offered in senior colleges and universities with a graduate education mission.

In order to provide increased clinical specialization at a postmaster's level, nursing specialist programs have been developed. These programs in areas such as pulmonary nursing, oncology nursing, and primary care nursing require one to two years of post–master's study. Nursing specialist programs emphasize depth of knowledge and development of clinical expertise in the specialty area. The nursing specialist program may incorporate a master's degree program and nursing specialist as one program. In this instance, the program includes the 36 units and thesis from the typical master's degree program plus the additional requirements of the nursing specialist degree. If the prospective student has completed a master's degree, the nursing specialist program usually requires one additional year of course work, a clinical research project, and a final comprehensive examination.

Doctoral degree programs in nursing emphasize clinical nursing research, advanced nursing practice, and the development and testing of nursing theory. Located in colleges and universities with a doctoral education mission, nursing doctoral programs prepare graduates to assume leadership positions in nursing education, nursing practice, and nursing research.

Degrees offered include the Doctor of Philosophy and Doctor of Nursing Science. At the present time, fewer than thirty doctoral programs in nursing are offered in the United States. Doctoral degree programs in nursing typically require three years of post-master's study and emphasize clinical nursing research. As in other disciplines, a dissertation involving original research is usually required.

Curriculum Process

Prior to initiating the sequential process of developing a curriculum in nursing, faculty make a decision as to the characteristics of the graduate (product) of their program. A description of the product will guide future curricular decisions regarding liberal education courses and nursing curricular content. Since this book focuses on teaching in collegiate schools of nursing, the generic baccalaureate nursing program will serve as the prototype for discussing the curriculum process. However, the process can be adapted to other curriculum structures.

According to Yura, nine beliefs form the basis of a description of the graduate of a baccalaureate nursing program:

1. Education makes a difference in nursing practice.
2. The generalist nursing practitioner prepared in the baccalaureate degree program in nursing is a well-educated person.
3. Nursing practice for the graduate of the baccalaureate program in nursing reflects the mastery of theory drawn from the sciences, arts, humanities, and nursing.
4. Nursing practice of the graduate of the baccalaureate program in nursing is heavily steeped in intellectual skills involving problem-solving, critical thinking, making nursing judgments, in interpersonal skills as interviewing, relating, conveying knowledge, information, interest, compassion, in technical skills—those needed to obtain data about the client and those designed to bring about prescribed behavioral health results in a preferred direction.
5. The baccalaureate curriculum focuses on the three processes which comprise professional nursing—the nursing process; the research process; and the leadership process. This focus is academically and experientially efficient and serves as a protection for the graduate against obsolescence in professional nursing practice.
6. The functions of the graduate of the baccalaureate program in nursing are independent and interdependent in nature.

7. The citizens of this country need and want a focus on the maintenance of wellness and support for an optimal level of health as well as sickness care.
8. The baccalaureate nursing student learns nursing theory in class through a variety of teaching–learning strategies and has an opportunity to apply this nursing theory with the client, the individual, the family, the community, and groups— whether well or ill, wherever the client is found.
9. Laboratory is a teaching method developed and utilized by nursing faculty to facilitate the student's ability to apply theory in an actual client situation (26, pp. 5–6).

These beliefs may change as nursing changes in response to societal need. However, each faculty must decide for itself the characteristics of the particular product to be prepared in the specific program.

Once a description of the product has been articulated, faculty need to decide on an overall curriculum structure. Institutional mission and requirements provide a framework for these decisions. Institutional requirements must be included in any nursing curricular structure. Curriculum structure includes a description of graduation requirements, upper and lower division major and supporting courses, and a decision regarding electives to be included in the program. Division of the nursing major into upper and lower divisions is also done at this time as faculty decide whether to offer any nursing courses in the lower division. Usually, the majority of nursing content is concentrated in the upper division so that professional nursing content is built upon a strong arts and science base. However, some baccalaureate programs offer nursing courses in freshman or sophomore years for economic reasons or to facilitate earlier entry of students into nursing courses. National League for Nursing criteria for accreditation also provide direction to curriculum structure. Although the overall curriculum structure may be altered or modified as the curriculum design is solidified, the initial structure provides guidance to both faculty and administration in specifying needs for the curriculum that is to be developed.

Once the overall structure is decided, the organizing structure for the nursing content must be developed. Historically, six approaches to curricular organization have been used in nursing: (1) Subject Matter, (2) Core, (3) Principles, (4) Behavioral Systems, (5) Concepts, and (6) Nursing Models (20, p. 39). Initially, curricula were organized by subject matter such as psychiatric nursing, obstetric nursing, or surgical nursing. Key nursing problems such as Abdellah's twenty–one nursing problems (1) provided a structure based on core concepts.

In the late 1950s, Nordmark and Rohweder (17) proposed scientific principles that could be used as a guide for nursing content. Johnson's behavioral systems approach typifies a systems model as an organizing scheme (12). Roy's adaptation model (23) illustrates the concepts approach to curriculum structure. Finally, some schools have adopted nursing models such as Roger's model of unitary man, (22) King's systems model, (13), or Putt's general systems model (19) as organizing approaches to curriculum.

According to a study by Quiring, (20, p. 42) concepts were a major choice for organizing baccalaureate nursing programs. Faculty tended to see concepts as a means of interrelating and unifying the many details in nursing content (20, p. 44). As nursing models became more clearly specified, the concepts model was interrelated with a nursing model or models. For example, Roy's adaptation model used the concept of adaptation as an organizing base for the nursing model.

During the 1960s and 1970s, the explication of nursing theory and nursing models led some nursing programs to adopt a nursing model as a guiding element in curriculum development. Nursing programs using a nursing model either adopt the work of one theorist or interweave the work of several theorists into one eclectic model. Nursing models initially evolved in three directions: developmental, interaction, and systems models (21). The work of Dickoff and James (6) provided guidance in generating nursing theory. Developmental theorists such as Peplau (18) used a growth and development approach as the basis for deriving a nursing model. Interaction theorists such as Riehl derived their models from symbolic interactionism (21).

Many nursing models have been based upon a systems approach. Johnson's behavioral systems model, Rogers' model of unitary man, Orem's self-care model, and Neuman's health-care systems model are derived from a systems orientation (21). Each systems model differs in specific conceptualizations, but the underlying theoretical base evolved from Bertalanffy's work in systems theory (2).

Although not all nursing programs use a nursing model, the proponents of nursing models assert the advantages of having a nursing theory base. Use of a nursing model allows the faculty to operationalize their own philosophy in a formal nursing model. This may facilitate student learning by moving from simple to complex within one model and clearly defined set of terms.

A primary advantage of using a nursing model is the influence of the model in facilitating internal consistency in the curriculum by providing a common language, common scientific base, and a conceptual framework that enhances the flow of the curriculum. For example, Roger's model of unitary man (22) has a base in the natural sciences, a language all its own, and a structure from systems theory. A disadvantage of adopting one single model may be the limitation imposed by the model itself. For example, Roy's adaptation model (23) limits the user to adaptation language and the adaptation–systems orientation. Thus, students are exposed primarily to only this one approach. This limitation may lead to a narrow view of the realm of nursing.

Regardless of the faculty's decision about a specific organizing structure or model, the faculty's beliefs and conceptualizations of nursing will be reflected in the nursing program's philosophy and conceptual framework as the faculty uses the curriculum process to operationalize the curriculum.

The curriculum process involves a sequential series of steps that build upon one another to reach a completed curriculum. The reader is referred to Figure 5-2 for an overview of the curriculum process.

As a first step in the curriculum process, faculty develop a philosophy that reflects the program goals and gives direction

Figure 5-2   Sequential steps in the curriculum process

and meaning to the curriculum. A philosophy contains two major components: (1) statements of belief about the major concepts in the curriculum such as man, health, society, nursing, and (2) statements of belief about nursing education, the teaching-learning process, and the roles of teacher and learner. The philosophy reflects the beliefs of a particular program's faculty. Therefore, development of the philosophy is a crucial step in curriculum development and gives the curriculum its uniqueness.

Once the philosophy is accepted by faculty, the program objectives are stated and related to the program goals and the philosophy. The conceptual framework provides overall structure for the major concepts in the curriculum. Each major concept in the curriculum (man, health, society, nursing, nursing process) is operationally defined as the faculty intends it to be used in the curriculum. The relationship between and among concepts is also described in the conceptual framework.

The conceptual framework and program objectives, sometimes called terminal objectives, relate back to the philosophy and goals so that the conceptual definitions flow from the faculty's belief about a given concept. Similarly, the program objectives describe a product that is philosophically congruent with the faculty's beliefs.

Figure 5-3 provides an example of how concepts (basic needs, nursing process) that are initially presented in the philosophy, become specified in the conceptual framework, are included in the program objectives, and are utilized as a vertical or horizontal thread when the curricular concepts are operationalized.

In addition, the conceptual framework and program objectives are used to organize the concepts and objectives into levels. For example, if nursing courses begin in the junior year of a four-year baccalaureate program, there might be four levels in the curriculum corresponding to the four semesters of nursing courses. Or the faculty may prefer to have two levels corresponding to the junior and senior years.

The conceptual framework and program objectives are used to identify curricular threads or strands. These threads provide a framework for the content at various levels of the curriculum. Vertical threads identify content that is presented periodically in the curriculum to add depth to content. Horizontal threads are presented sequentially in the curriculum at each level to build a concept continuously. For example, content on the concepts of stress or health might be vertical threads in the various levels of the curriculum. Content on the nursing process might be a horizontal thread beginning at the first level and building toward the final level.

Level objectives show progression of learnings—cognitive, affective and psychomotor—toward accomplishment of the terminal objectives. Thus, level objectives can be used by faculty to evaluate student learning and provide feedback to students. In addition, evaluation of level objectives can be used in program evaluation. Furthermore, level objectives show the relationship between curriculum threads and objectives.

Figure 5-4 shows the relationship between terminal objectives, level objectives, and curriculum strands or threads. At each level of this three-level model, the research and issues strands are operationalized in terms of specific level objectives and the overall

Figure 5-3   Relationship between philosophy, conceptual framework, program objectives, and threads

---

Philosophy

1. Man has basic needs.
2. Nurses use the nursing process.

Conceptual Framework

1. Maslow's hierarchy of needs is a schema used to categorize basic human needs.
2. Nursing process is a systematic method for organizing the delivery of nursing care.

Program Objectives

Upon completion of the program, the graduate will be able to:

1. Utilize the nursing process to assist individuals to meet their basic needs and promote, maintain and restore health.

Vertical Thread

One vertical thread at Level 1 would be presentation of content regarding Maslow's hierarchy of needs.

Horizontal Thread

A horizontal thread regarding the nursing process would be presented at Level 1 and expanded at the other curricular levels.

Source: Based on materials developed in collaboration with the faculty, School of Nursing, University of Wisconsin—Eau Claire.

Figure 5-4 An example of the relationship between curriculum threads, terminal objectives, and level objectives

---

Thread: Research Thread (Horizontal)

Terminal Objective: The student will be able to apply the research process in nursing.

Level Objectives: The student will be able to:
1. Demonstrate knowledge of the research process.
2. Use the research process in exploring nursing care alternatives.
3. Use the research process in validating nursing interventions.
4. Apply the research process in clinical decision-making.

Thread: Professional Issues (Horizontal)

Terminal Objective: The student will analyze current issues in the profession in terms of their historical and sociopolitical determinants and implications for the future.

Level Objectives: The student will analyze current issues in the profession in terms of their historical and sociopolitical determinants and implications for the future.

Level Objectives: The student will be able to:
1. Demonstrate knowledge of the evolution of nursing and current status of professional nursing.
2. Identify nursing issues and their historical and sociopolitical antecedents.
3. Apply knowledge of the sociopolitical process in analyzing current nursing issues.
4. Evaluate current nursing issues and predict outcomes for nursing in the future.

Source: Based on materials developed in collaboration with the faculty, School of Nursing, University of Wisconsin—Eau Claire.

content regarding research and issues. Faculty using this model could define specific content at each level that would provide the necessary breadth and depth to facilitate students' meeting of the level objectives. Thus, the level objectives and curriculum strands or threads are used together to guide faculty and students toward achievement of the terminal objectives.

As might be expected, course objectives are derived from the level objectives. Course objectives are specific and measurable so they can be used to evaluate student progress. Learning experiences are designed and selected by faculty to meet specific course objectives. Learning experiences can be used to meet more than one course objective. However, the selection of learning experiences is a critical step in the curriculum process and must not be minimized. The reader is referred to Chapter 6 for further discussion of this topic.

The final step in the curriculum process is evaluation. Faculty develop a plan for both formative (ongoing) and summative (outcome) evaluation of the curriculum. Since program evaluation is the topic of Chapter 11, the reader is referred to that chapter for a more thorough discussion of the evaluation process.

References

1. Abdellah, F.G., Beland, I.L., Matheney, R.V., and Martin, A. *Patient-Centered Approaches to Nursing.* New York: Macmillan, 1960.
2. Bertalanffy, L. *General Systems Theory.* New York: Braziller, 1968.
3. Bevis, E.O. *Curriculum Building in Nursing* (3rd ed.). St. Louis: Mosby, 1982.
4. Conley, V. *Curriculum and Instruction in Nursing.* Boston: Little, Brown, 1973. P. 15.
5. DeChow, G.H. *Curriculum Design for Associate Degree Nursing Programs: Factors in Program Direction.* NLN Publ. No. 23–1833. New York: National League for Nursing, 1980.
6. Dickoff, J., James, P., and Wiedenbach, E. Theory in a Practice Discipline. *Nurs. Res.* 17:415, 1968.
7. Division of Associate Degree Programs. *Competencies of the Associate Degree Nurse on Entry into Practice.* NLN Publ. No. 23–1731. New York: National League for Nursing, 1978.
8. Division of Baccalaureate and Higher Degree Nursing Programs. *Characteristics of Baccalaureate Education in Nursing.* NLN Publ. No. 15–1758. New York: National League for Nursing, 1979.
9. Galliford, S. Second Step Baccalaureate Programs in Nursing. *Nurs. Outlook* 28(10):631, 1980.
10. Guinee, K.K. *Teaching and Learning in Nursing.* New York: Macmillan, 1978. P. 89.
11. Harcleroad, F., Molen, C., and Rayman, J. *The Regional State Colleges and Universities Enter the 1970s.* Iowa City, Iowa: The American College Testing Program, 1973.
12. Johnson, D.E. The Behavioral System Model for Nursing in J. P. Riehl and C. Roy, *Conceptual Models for Nursing Practice* (2nd ed.) New York: Appleton-Century-Crofts, 1980.
13. King, I. *Toward a Theory for Nursing.* New York: Wiley, 1971.
14. National League for Nursing. *Characteristics of Graduate Education in Nursing.* New York: National League for Nursing, 1974.

15. National League for Nursing. *Criteria for the Appraisal of Baccalaureate and Higher Degree Programs in Nursing.* New York: National League for Nursing, 1977.
16. National League for Nursing. *Criteria for the Evaluation of Educational Programs in Nursing Leading to an Associate Degree* (3rd ed.). New York: National League for Nursing, 1973.
17. Nordmark, M.T. and Rohweder, A.W. *Science Principles Applied to Nursing.* Philadelphia: Lippincott, 1959.
18. Peplau, H.E., *Interpersonal Relations in Nursing.* New York: Putnam, 1952.
19. Putt, A.M. *General Systems Theory Applied to Nursing.* Boston: Little, Brown, 1978.
20. Quiring, J. and Gray, G. Organizing Approaches Used in Curriculum Design. *JNE* 21(2):38, 1982.
21. Riehl, J.P. and Roy, C. *Conceptual Models for Nursing Practice* (2nd ed.). New York: Appleton-Century-Crofts, 1980.
22. Rogers, M. *An Introduction to the Theoretical Basis of Nursing.* Philadelphia: F.A. Davis Co., 1970.
23. Roy, C. Adaptation: A Conceptual Framework for Nursing. *Nurs. Outlook* 19(4):254, 1971.
24. Searight, N.W. (ed.). *The Second Step: Baccalaureate Education for Registered Nurses.* Philadelphia: F.A. Davis Co., 1976.
25. Waters, V.H. *Distinguishing Characteristics of Associate Degree Education for Nursing.* NLN Publ. No. 23-1722. New York: National League for Nursing, 1978.
26. Yura, H. Who is the Product of the Baccalaureate Nursing Program? *Curriculum Process for Developing and Revising a Baccalaureate Nursing Program.* New York: National League for Nursing. NLN Publ. No. 15-1700, 1978. Pp. 5-6.

Suggested Readings

Anderson, E.H. *Innovative Approaches to Baccalaureate Programs in Nursing.* NLN Publ. No. 15-1804. New York: National League for Nursing, 1979.

Beare, P.Q., Daniel, E.D., Gover, V.F., Gray, C.I., Lancaster, J., and Sloan, P.E. The Real vs. Ideal Content in Master's Curricula in Nursing. *Nurs. Outlook* 28:691, 1980.

Dickerson, T.M. *Designing and Building a Curriculum.* NLN Publ. No. 16-1776. New York: National League for Nursing, 1979.

Dickoff, J., James, P. and Wiedenbach, E. Theory in a Practice Discipline. *Nurs. Res.* 17:415, 1968.

Ellis, L. Implementing a Conceptual Framework. *Nurs. Outlook* 27:127, 1979.

Fenner, K. Developing a Conceptual Framework. *Nurs. Outlook* 27:127, 1979.

Flaskerud, T.H. Utilizing a Nursing Conceptual Model in Basic Level Curriculum Development. *JNE* 22:224, 1983.

Fuhrman, B.S. and Grasha, A.F. *A Practical Handbook for College Teachers.* Boston: Little, Brown, 1983.

George, J.B. *Nursing Theories: the Base for Professional Nursing Practice.* Englewood Cliffs: Prentice-Hall, 1980.

Suggested Readings

Heller, B. Associate Degree Nursing: Preparation and Practice. *Nurs. Outlook* 30:310, 1982.

Johnson, D.E. The Behavioral System Model for Nursing, In J.P. Riehl and C. Roy, *Conceptual Models for Nursing Practice* (2nd ed.). New York: Appleton-Century-Crofts, 1980.

King, I. *Toward a Theory for Nursing.* New York: Wiley, 1971.

Kramer, M. Philosophical Foundations of Baccalaureate Nursing Education. *Nurs. Outlook* 29:224, 1981.

Lawrence, S.A. and Lawrence, R.M. Curriculum Development: Philosophy, Objectives, and Conceptual Framework. *Nurs. Outlook* 31:160, 1983.

Levine, A. *Handbook on Undergraduate Curriculum.* San Francisco: Jossey-Boss, 1981.

National League for Nursing. *Curriculum Development and its Implementation through a Conceptual Framework.* NLN Publ. No. 23-1723. New York: National League for Nursing, 1978.

National League for Nursing. *Curriculum Process for Developing or Revising Baccalaureate Nursing Programs.* NLN Publ. No. 15-1700. New York: National League for Nursing, 1978.

National League for Nursing. *Developing Nursing Programs in Institutions of Higher Education—1974.* NLN Publ. No. 14-1533. New York: National League for Nursing, 1974.

Norris, C.G. *Baccalaureate Nursing Education for RN's: Issues and Approaches.* NLN Publ. No. 15-1812. New York: National League for Nursing, 1980.

Notter, L.E. *The Open Curriculum in Nursing Education.* NLN Publ. No. 19-1799. New York: National League for Nursing, 1979.

Orem, D.E. *Nursing: Concepts of Practice.* New York: McGraw-Hill, 1971.

Peddiwell, J.A. *The Saber Tooth Curriculum.* New York: McGraw-Hill, 1939.

Pelczar, M.J., Jr. *The Value and Future of Graduate Education Leading to a Master's Degree: A National Perspective.* Washington, D.C.: American Association of Colleges of Nursing, 1980.

Putt, A.M. *General Systems Theory Applied to Nursing.* Boston: Little, Brown, 1978.

Quiring, J. and Gray, G. Organizing Approaches Used in Curriculum Design. *JNE* 21(2):38, 1982.

Riehl, J.P. and Roy, C., Sr. *Conceptual Models for Nursing Practice* (2nd ed.). New York: Appleton-Century-Crofts, 1980.

Rogers, M. *An Introduction to the Theoretical Basics of Nursing.* Philadelphia: F.A. Davis Co., 1970.

Roy, C. Adaptation: A Conceptual Framework for Nursing. *Nurs. Outlook* 19:4:254, 1971.

Slavinsky, A. and Diers, D. Nursing Education for College Graduates. *Nurs. Outlook* 30:292, 1982.

Smith, M.H. (ed.). *Graduate Education in Nursing: Issues and Future Directions.* Atlanta: Southern Regional Education Board, 1980.

Chapter 6

Development of a Single Course

Arlene M. Putt, R.N., Ed.D.

Study Questions
1. What contribution does each course make to the total program?
2. Of what use is a course description?
3. How is course credit determined?
4. How is credit allocated to a course?
5. What are the characteristics of behaviorally stated objectives?
6. What are the advantages of lesson plans?
7. How does one select learning experiences for students?
8. What factors facilitate learning?
9. What factors impede learning?
10. What criteria would you use to evaluate a student's achievement in a course?
11. How are course objectives linked to course grades?

In Chapter 5, the topics of curriculum structure and curriculum development were discussed. Then, to enact a curriculum, a series of single courses must be developed. In this chapter the process of developing a single course will be discussed, and the steps involved will be described. When the proposal for the course is completed, the usual process is to review and approve the material by the college curriculum committee and the university curriculum committee.

Contribution to the Total Program

Each course included in a nursing curriculum makes an obvious contribution to the total nursing program (2, 11). If the college utilizes a theoretical framework, the proposed course should fit that framework or model. For instance, several universities utilize a general systems framework (1, 10). Isaak (10) describes how a single course can be developed within the framework of general systems theory. Porth (14) uses another model, that of physiological coping, for her course development. One or more program objectives are addressed in each and every course. Some courses may address a few objectives while other courses may include multiple objectives. In well-developed nursing programs, each course is carefully articulated with other courses so that the entire collection of courses meets the sum total of the program objectives and contributes to the philosophy and conceptual framework of the program. In poorly developed programs, a single course may fill a single need with or without articulation of the other courses in the program. The net effect of such an ill-planned arrangement is akin to a patchwork quilt where one color and shape may not blend well with the next color and shape.

Not only should a single course address one or more than one objective, but the course should be in a sequence of courses ranging from basics to advanced concepts and skills. With the criteria of the program objectives and sequence in mind, the faculty can proceed to develop a single course using the format to be discussed. The process is summarized in Figure 6-1.

Course Description

Every course offered by an educational institution has a course description which is composed of several short sentences that can be included in the college catalogue. Many times the educational institution specifies how long a course description can be. This restriction is for the purposes of keeping the length of course descriptions consistent and keeping the costs of printing college catalogues reasonable. It is the responsibility of the faculty designing the course to communicate the nature and the extent of the proposed course as clearly as possible within the constraints of length imposed by the institution. Examples of course descriptions are as follows:

Nursing 600 A, Nursing Theory and Practicum, is the first in sequential series of three 3-unit courses on selected conceptual approaches to pathophysiology and nursing care of adults with medical-surgical problems related to cell proliferation, growth, body defenses, and neural transmission.

Figure 6-1 The ABC's of single course planning

A. WHERE ARE YOU HEADED?
B. HOW WILL YOU GET THERE?
C. HOW WILL YOU RECOGNIZE YOUR ACHIEVEMENTS?

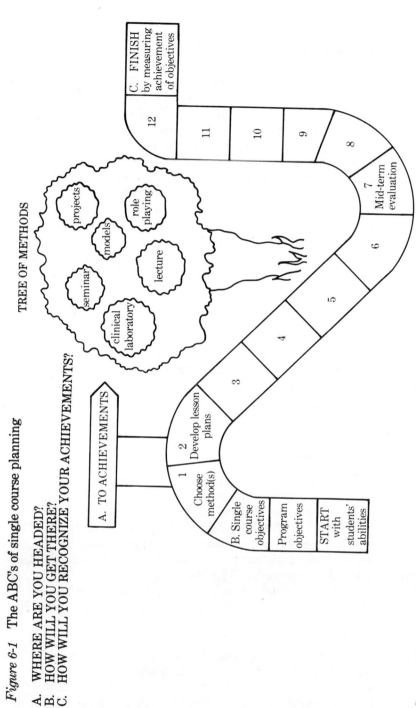

Source: Adapted with the assistance of Joseph H. Markle from "Write a Lesson Plan," Module B-4, *Professional Vocational Teacher Education Module.* Columbus: Ohio State University, 1974. P. 11.

92

Nursing 601, Physical Assessment, is a three unit course designed to develop skill in medical interviewing and physical examination for nursing assessment and for the development of a problem-oriented medical record (15).

From descriptions such as these the prospective and continuing students, the faculty, the transcript evaluator, and the public should all be able to determine the basic content and the focus of the course. This may be difficult if the course has integrated content from several content areas.

Allocation of Credit

Allocation of credit to a course may be predetermined by institutional patterns or may be decided by the faculty or the curriculum committee structuring the course. Most institutions have patterns such as the three-unit course as the basic allocation with heavier courses designed as multiples of three units. For some courses, the content is set first, and then the determination of credit is made. The problem with this latter approach is that the credit value derived may not fit into the total program, or it may not fit the semester or quarter pattern when concurrent courses are considered.

Also of concern in the allocation of credit is the distribution of credit hours to the various types of learning activities such as lecture, discussion, seminar, laboratory, and clinical practice. Most educational institutions have established ratios of time for each type of class. For instance, lecture classes are rated 1:1, one hour of lecture per week for one credit, while laboratory time is at a ratio of 1:3, three hours of laboratory experience equals one credit hour. This distribution of credit hours is a major decision that reflects the manner in which material will be presented. It is also a major factor in how well the course schedule will fit into the normal school week. Many compromises must be made at this point. There are only so many hours of credit possible and so many hours available in the week. Therefore, the best fit must be sought.

Prerequisites

Unless the course is a beginning course for which admission into the program is the only prerequisite, each course will have some restrictions defined as either prerequisite or corequisite courses to be taken prior to enrollment in this course or concurrently with the course. Usually the administrative officer or the instructor has a small amount of discretion in the manner of prerequisites to provide for the unusual student who appears to be qualified but who does not fit the usual pattern of student preparation.

Course Placement and Learner Level

As discussed in Chapter 5, where in a program the course is placed is of great importance. Is the course for the beginning student or the advanced student? Is the placement fixed or can the placement be flexible as in a choice between the sophomore and junior years? The answers to these questions will determine the level of the learner and the depth at which the course can be taught. The further along in the program that the course is placed, the more knowledge and skill are brought to the course by the students. If all of the students are at the same level, the instructor has an easier task of making the content fit the entering level of knowledge to build upon a common background. If the students represent several levels of background, the instructor must vary the approach so as to maximize the beginning level for the most students and try to make accommodations for the students with different backgrounds (7, 8, 13). In such a situation, younger students can benefit from the greater experiences of the more advanced students. More advanced students can add to their self-esteem by using their experiences to foster the learning of the younger students.

Of the various problems, one that poses a constant challenge for faculty is the placement of registered nurse students into a generic program (3, 7, 8, 13). Rarely is the fit a good one. How much is repetition and how much is new content for the nurse who has been practicing the profession of nursing? Many programs utilize competency examinations to determine the placement of registered nurse students (7). While this practice does allow some individualization of placement and allows some advanced credit, the examinations are stressful, costly, and time consuming. The registered nurse student usually achieves partial mastery of the material. If the registered nurse passes the examination, the expectation is that the material has been mastered in full, and progress to the next course is indicated. If the grade is a failure, the loss of self-esteem to the registered nurse is marked, and then the registered nurse is rerouted back through a course for which a segment must be repeated experiences with added loss of time and money. This ongoing problem has no adequate answer at the present time. However, one response to the registered nurse problem has been the development of special programs geared specifically for registered nurse students. These programs are discussed further in Chapters 5 and 13.

Behavioral Objectives

As identified in the Sequential Steps in the Curriculum Process, Figure 5-2, the behavioral objectives set for the course determine the learning experiences and the outcomes of the learning. Mager stated: "An objective is a statement describing an instructional outcome" (12, p. 7). He also declared a behavioral objective to be "what a successful learner can do at the end of the course" (12, p. 11). Mager further defined an objective as having three parts: *performance, conditions,* and *criterion* (12, p. 21). The performance part of the objective states what the learner can do; the conditions part, the conditions under which the learner can do the task; and the criterion part, the level at which the learner can perform. Thus, behavioral objectives define what active behaviors the learner will acquire. A key distinction is the word *active* behaviors as contrasted to passive behaviors. The verb, *understand*, is difficult to measure as understanding is a passive process in contrast to the verb, *demonstrate*, which is an active verb, the action of which can be observed. Because the end product of the learning must be measurable, the objectives should be stated in active verb format so the acquisition of that action can be easily measured. While the list of measurable action verbs can be rather lengthy, examples are: to list, to describe, to compare, to demonstrate, to solve, to apply, to plan, and to execute.

Examples of behavioral objectives for a course in physical assessment could include:

At the end of the course, the student will have the skill to:

1. Elicit a full medical history.
2. Perform a complete physical examination for a male or a female adult.
3. Describe findings in writing and diagram.
4. Develop a problem list for the patient.
5. Organize a problem-oriented medical record.

6. Describe each identified problem according to subjective and objective findings, assessment, and plan (15).

With this set of behavioral objectives, the student and the instructor can focus learning on one objective after another until all objectives have been met and weak areas identified for further practice and development.

How many objectives to include in any one course is a matter of choice and expediency. Generally, the number of objectives can vary from four to ten or more. The presence of many objectives is a good indication that main objectives have been subdivided into precise skills, or that the course may be overloaded with content. If there are a large number of objectives, the attainment of all of the objectives may be beyond the capabilities of the students in the time allotted for such learning. Clear thinking on the part of the faculty can avoid such pitfalls. The amount of material to be covered in the course leads to the next subject, content.

Course Content

The content of a single course revolves around the set of knowledge and skills that are needed in any one area of practice or with one or more broad concepts. If the course is in maternal and newborn nursing, then the content is focused upon pregnancy, birth, and the neonatal period. When the content is integrated so that concepts are used as focal points, the variations of the concepts as utilized in several areas of practice become the focal points. An example would be the concept of dependency as it relates to the infant, child, ill adult, and elderly person. With integrated patterns, the articulation of content from one course to the next is a delicate matter deserving very careful consideration or gaps appear in the learning, and essential content is omitted entirely with the other possibility of repeated coverage of other material. With the present high degree of specialization occurring in the health care delivery areas, it is far easier to cover and account for content specific to practice areas than to try to integrate everything and do it poorly. For this reason, the trend appears to be away from integrated curricula and back to clinical area patterns of content (16).

The other questions basic to decisions on content are how much content to cover and to what depth should the content be presented? How much to cover depends upon the credit value of the course and whether other opportunities exist for the student to learn the content at another time. If one has a short series of courses in an area such as medical-surgical nursing, the decision can be made as to which experiences to include in the first course and which experiences to delay until the second course. Another consideration may be access to clinical practice. If surgical experience can be obtained only in one part of the year, then the content is arranged to maximize this consideration.

The depth at which content is to be presented depends upon the background of the students and the time available for the presentation and the student learnings. Admittedly, an associate degree program cannot present content at the same depth as a baccalaureate program. With two years of scientific and social studies background, the baccalaureate student is able to relate more content at a greater depth than the associate degree counterpart can.

Teaching Methods

The choice of teaching methods may be made by the individual instructor or the area chairperson. As discussed by deTornyay and Thompson (4), there are many ways to present content ranging from lecture, seminar, discussion, role playing, debates, reports, audiovisual presentations, and models, to guest lectures, laboratory work, and clinical experience. Which method is effective for what content is a somewhat personal decision. Learning is facilitated if approaches are kept fresh and contain an element of newness. What works well for one student may not work nearly so well for the next. The reader is referred to Chapter 4 to the discussion of styles of learning and the tool for measurement in Figure 4-1. By choosing a variety of methods, the instructor is more likely to meet some of the needs of all of the students.

More important than just the choice of methods is the fact that certain types of content tend to lend themselves to certain types of presentations. For instance, debate is useful for comparing and contrasting. A film may be used to explore attitudes. A videotape is very useful for demonstrating step-wise procedures, and it can give every student a close look at the demonstration. Prior viewing of the videotape or the slides by the students allows the instructor time to discuss additional aspects. The basic questions are: What do you want to teach? How is the content best presented? What resources exist? How can you substitute for resources not available?

Handouts are very useful to students, freeing them to concentrate upon the information directly before them and reducing their need to spend the time trying to take an adequate set of notes. For ease of presentation, overhead transparencies are very useful, giving the advantages of an enlarged display upon which the instructor can point to successive features and upon which notations can be made. The matter of cost may dictate what methods may be utilized.

Time for good planning is essential. Good presentations require adequate thought and planning. If appropriate videotapes are not available, the instructor who has the resources of a video camera and video recorder can consider making an original production. If there are communications resources in the school, professional assistance can be obtained to aid in the planning and execution of the production. One caution to be noted is that good audiovisual productions require large amounts of time and considerable expertise. They do not become reality overnight.

In summary, the selection of teaching methods depends upon personal choice and the availability of various types of resources.

Lesson Plan

The lesson plan is the detailed description of each single class period for the course. The instructor arranges the content into logical and feasible segments and then describes in detail the way the content is to be presented and the activities to be engaged in by the instructor and the students. Lesson plans should be prepared well in advance so that attention can be given to having the supporting materials available when needed. Lesson plans can provide proof of the content that has been included in the course and can be a resource from which examination questions can be derived. Another advantage of well-prepared lesson plans is that they allow substitute teachers to take over classes on short notice without disruptions in the flow of material.

The format that the lesson plan takes can be varied, and the format is far less important than the detailed description of what should be occurring during the class time. Figure 6-2 shows a lesson plan for a class on cardiac sound assessment (15).

In conclusion then, the lesson plan is the way in which the course objectives are carried out and the content is presented.

Lesson Plan

The lesson plan may contain subobjectives for the particular session that together with subobjectives of other sessions may contribute to one or more course objectives. The course objectives tell where the content is going, and the lesson plans tell how to acquire that content. The next section will describe what vehicle is used to acquire the content.

Figure 6-2   Example of a lesson plan

Lesson plan: Topic: Cardiac Sound Assessment
Total time: 2 hours, class; 4 hours, clinical practice
Course objectives: At the end of the session, the student will:

1. Know where to auscultate heart sounds.
2. Recognize and describe normal heart sounds.
3. Identify abnormal heart sounds.

Instructor activity	Student activity	Time

Slide/sound presentation
    Nature of cardiac sounds
    Where to listen
    What to listen for:
        First sound (S_1)
        Second sound (S_2)
        Splitting of sounds
        Extra sounds:
            Third sound (S_3)
            Fourth sound (S_4)
        Clicks
        Snaps
        Murmurs
		30 min.

Questions		5
Summary		5
	Student practice	40
Discussion of findings		10
	Write up findings	15
Discussion of write-ups		15
	Clinical practice	4 hrs.

Selection of Learning Experiences

In the selection of learning experiences, the expertise of the instructor becomes very evident. The skilled instructor has a wide array of potential learning experiences from which to select and adapt to the present situation. The less experienced instructor has fewer skills in selecting and adapting learning experiences for students.

Learning is an active process on the part of the student. All the instructor should do is to organize and facilitate the learning by choosing experiences that are well within the abilities of the student. Selection of learning experiences that involve active participation on the part of the student helps the student to master the material in contrast to passive forms of learning in which the student is merely exposed to the material to be learned. For this reason, material presented as issues or problems for the student to practice solving involves a higher level of learning than the passive act of listening to material being presented. Lecture continues to have a place in the array of learning techniques, but less content is retained from lectures than from more active modes of learning (9). In addition to lecture, discussion, debate, role playing, student presentation, self-discovery sessions, group projects, audiovisual presentations, simulated practice, client interview, family interview, presentations by other members of the health team, sharing of experiences and feelings by the students, guided tours, partial clinical experiences, and extensive clinical practice highlight various aspects of the content. The selection of learning experiences to solidify the learning depends upon the creativity of the instructor, the resources at hand, and the time available.

Learning Evaluation

This topic will be discussed more fully in Chapter 9, Evaluation of Learning, but an overview is necessary at this point. Basically, evaluation of learning is determining if the course objectives have been met and to what degree they have been met. There are many ways to evaluate learning, none of which are perfect (6). Traditionally, course learning has been measured by examinations, usually by examinations of the objective, multiple-choice type. Sometimes, National League for

Nursing standardized examinations are utilized to determine how the students compare to national norms. Essay examinations, while more difficult to grade, do allow the student to organize and present material, thus demonstrating logical thinking. Other components of evaluation could include evaluation of projects, either individual or group in nature, and assessment of clinical performance. At best, evaluation techniques are but samples of aspects of learning that have occurred. The true measure of learning lies within the student in the way that the material is integrated, synthesized, and utilized. This composite of new knowledge and skills may not manifest itself until after the individual leaves the course and begins other experiences. Nevertheless, the instructor is faced with the problem of presenting some sort of challenge for the student to tackle at the end of the course for the purpose of assessing the growth of knowledge and competency during that single course. From the evaluation of the performance throughout and at the end of the course, a course grade is determined.

Grade Assignment

Assignment of grades is as easy or as difficult as the quality of the measurement upon which that grade rests (6). If the course objectives are clearly defined and the levels of expected performance have been communicated to the students, then the student and instructor should be in relative agreement as to the present level of performance of the student. One of the problems that arises is different interpretations of performance in the eyes of the student and the instructor. If objectives have been stated and discussed in advance, some of this difficulty can be eliminated.

One other stumbling block to the assignment of grades is the matter of how detailed expectations of performance should be made. If every detail is outlined, the student has only to follow the prescription to achieve a high grade. In such a system there is little room for individual judgment and growth of responsibility. On the opposite side is the situation where the expectations have not been defined and the student feels great anxiety at not knowing what is expected. Unfortunately, in the practice of nursing, there is always a large element of uncertainty as to what the best choice is at that moment, and expectations can only be defined in general terms of responsibilities. So as the student is being prepared to face reality, not every action can be defined in advance. Some things must be left to professional judgment—the development of which is one of the objectives of every nursing course.

Thus, the assignment of a course grade is far easier if the criteria for the grade have been thought out and spelled out for the students entering the course. Also at stake in the grading process is the level of mastery required for the successful completion of the course. Does the mastery have to be total or is a relative mastery of a stated percentage of the material adequate? This decision should also have been made at the beginning of the course.

If the course is a clinical one, then a determination should have been made as to how the theory and practice components are weighted or equated. The weight may be equal or assigned percentages in either direction. This topic will be discussed more thoroughly in Chapter 9. It is sufficient to conclude that the student should be aware of the conditions for satisfactory completion throughout the course and how the course grade will be determined.

Course Evaluation

The concept of students having the right and responsibility to evaluate each and every course they take has developed over the past ten years. Some systems require the students to complete a standard course evaluation form which is then computerized and the data distributed to the department, the instructor, and the educational research unit. In many systems these course evaluation summaries are utilized in decisions regarding instructor promotion, tenure, and merit increases. If this is the case, then results from several semesters should be averaged as opposed to the use of one set of evaluations from one semester alone.

Other ways to obtain feedback as to how the course went is to have the instructor fill out a self-evaluation or to have peer faculty assessments at different times during the course. One example of a guide for course evaluation is the author-constructed checklist found in Figure 6-3.

Figure 6-3 A guideline for course evaluation

I. Course placement, weight, and prerequisites

    A. Is the course classification as an upper or lower division appropriate?
    B. Is the course unit weight appropriate?
    C. Are the course prerequisites defensible?
    D. Is the course classification as "required" or "elective" defensible?
    E. Is the distribution of theory and practicum appropriate?

II. Course objectives

    A. Are the course objectives stated clearly in writing?
    B. Are the course objectives appropriate for the curriculum?
    C. Do the course objectives relate logically to the curriculum model?
    D. Are the course objectives reasonable?
    E. Are the course objectives described in terms of abilities to be acquired?
    F. Do the available facilities and resources permit the attainment of the course objectives?

III. Physical environment and material provisions

    A. Are the physical environments in which the course is taught conducive to effective teaching and learning?
    B. Does the course structure provide for economy of learning?
    C. Are audiovisual aids available when needed?
    D. Are laboratory facilities available when needed?
    E. Are the provisions for duplicated materials adequate for the needs of the course?
    F. Are the library facilities adequate?
    G. Are the areas utilized for student experience adequate for the attainment of course objectives?

IV. Teaching

    A. Are instructors with requisite abilities assigned to the course?
    B. Has the instructor selected content that is relevant?
    C. Is the instructor-student ratio adequate?

Source: Arlene M. Putt, R.N., Ed.D.

Figure 6-3 (continued)

    D. Are the teaching strategies appropriate to the content?
    E. Does the instructor attempt to individualize approaches to students?
    F. Does the instructor motivate students to want to learn?
    G. Is the instructor available to students when needed?
    H. Is there adequate dialogue between instructor and students?
    I. Is student opinion considered?
    J. Does the instructor encourage creativity in the students?

V. Assessment of student attainment

    A. Does the instructor attempt to identify the students' pertinent abilities?
    B. Are students informed about the basis for evaluation?
    C. Are pertinent cognitive skills assessed?
    D. Are pertinent psychomotor skills assessed?
    E. What provisions are made for assessing student attainment objectives?
    F. Are behaviors pertinent to the value systems related to course objectives assessed?
    G. If useful external instruments are available for measuring achievement, are they utilized?
    H. Are data of performance on state board examinations utilized for course upgrading?

VI. Teacher performance

    A. Is the instructor's knowledge in the field of of study adequate?
    B. Does the instructor organize learning experiences so as to foster learning?
    C. Does the instructor communicate clearly?
    D. Does the instructor provide time for individual student conferences?
    E. Is there evidence of mutual cooperative endeavors between student and instructor?
    F. Is the instructor attentive to student progress?
    G. Does the instructor give evidence of enjoying teaching?

VII. Outcome and impact

    A. How many students complete the coursesuccessfully per year?
    B. How well prepared are the students for the succeeding courses?
    C. How well prepared are the students for national examinations?

Some instructors prefer a simple open-ended questionnaire to elicit detailed suggestions from the students as to what in the course is good and what needs to be changed. However it is done, some form of course evaluation is advisable for every course taught. The information derived from the process of course evaluation is feedback for the instructor for purposes of self-improvement, feedback for the area chairperson for reconsideration of elements of the course and for teaching assignments, and feedback for the administrator as to how well the program is going and how satisfied the students are with their experiences. In the time of increasing educational accountability, course evaluations are here to stay. The process of evaluation will be discussed further in Chapter 9.

In this chapter the process of designing a single course has been described. This is but one approach to course design. Fuhrmann and Grasha (5) described alternative course designs. The reader will encounter others, but the fact remains: courses should be carefully designed and developed so as to fit well into the overall curriculum patterns and to provide the desired learning experiences.

References

1. Ball State University, Department of Nursing. *Descriptive Report to National League for Nursing for Accreditation of Programs in Nursing.* Muncie: Ball State University, 1982.
2. Connolly, A.C. and Van Hoozer, H. The Systems Approach: A Basic for Course Redesign. *Nurs. Outlook* 28:695, 1980.
3. Curran, C.L. and Lengarcher, C.A. RN Re-Entry Programs: Programmatic and Personal Considerations. *Nurse Educator* 7(4):29, 1982.
4. deTornyay, R. and Thompson, M.A. *Strategies for Teaching Nursing* (2nd ed.). New York: Wiley, 1982.
5. Fuhrmann, B.C. and Grasha, A.F. *A Practical Handbook for College Teachers.* Boston: Little, Brown, 1983.
6. Gentile, J.R. and Stevens-Haslinger, C.A. Comprehensive Grading Scheme. *Nurs. Outlook* 31:49, 1983.
7. Gross, L.C. and Bevil, C.W. The Use of Testing to Modify Curricula for R.N.'s. *Nurs. Outlook* 29:541, 1981.
8. Hale, S. and Boyd, B.T. Accommodating RN Students in Baccalaureate Nursing Programs. *Nurs. Outlook* 29:535, 1981.
9. Hayter, J. How Good is the Lecture as a Teaching Method? *Nurs. Outlook* 27:274, 1979.
10. Isaak, E.V. Design for a Clinical Nursing Course. In A. Putt, *General Systems Theory Applied to Nursing.* Boston: Little, Brown, 1979. P. 82.

11. Lawrence, S.A. and Lawrence, R.M. Curriculum Development: Philosophy, Objectives and Conceptual Framework. *Nurs. Outlook* 31:160, 1983.
12. Mager, R.F. *Preparing Instructional Objectives* (2nd ed.). Belmont: Pitman Learning, 1975.
13. Parlocha, P. and Hiraki, A. Strategies for Faculty Teaching the RN Student in a BSN Program. *JNE* 21(5):22, 1982.
14. Porth, C.M. Physiological Coping: A Model for Teaching Pathophysiology. *Nurs. Outlook* 25:781, 1977.
15. University of Arizona College of Nursing. Course Material. Mimeographed. Tucson: University of Arizona, 1982.
16. Welch, L.B. and Seagle, J.C. Does Integrated Content Lead to Integrated Knowledge? *JNE* 19(2):38, 1980.

Suggested Readings

Bevis, E.O. *Curriculum Building in Nursing: A Process.* St. Louis: Mosby, 1973.

Connolly, A.C. and Van Hoozer, H. The Systems Approach: A Basic for Course Redesign. *Nurs. Outlook.* 28:695, 1980.

Cross, K.P. Barriers to Adult Learning. *AAHE Bulletin.* 34:1, 1981.

Eble, K.E. *The Craft of Teaching.* San Francisco: Jossey-Bass, 1976.

Gagne, R. *Conditions of Learning.* New York: Holt, 1970.

Gross, L.C. and Bevil, C.W. The Use of Testing to Modify Curricula for R.N.'s. *Nurs. Outlook* 29:541, 1981.

Hale, S. and Boyd, B.T. Accommodating R.N. Students in Baccalaureate Nursing Programs. *Nurs. Outlook* 29:535, 1981.

Hayter, J. How Good is the Lecture as a Teaching Method? *Nurs. Outlook* 27:274, 1979.

Huckabay, L.M. *Conditions of Learning and Instruction in Nursing.* St. Louis: Mosby, 1980.

Lawrence, S.A. and Lawrence, R.M. Curriculum Development: Philosophy, Objectives, and Conceptual Framework. *Nurs. Outlook* 31:160, 1983.

McKeathie, W.J. (ed.). *Learning, Cognition, and College Teaching.* San Francisco: Jossey-Bass, 1980.

Miller, S.P. Clinical Knowledge: A Needed Curriculum Emphasis. *Nurs. Outlook* 23:223, 1975.

Muzio, L.C., Dhashi, J.P. The RN Student—Unique Characteristics, Unique Needs. *Nurs. Outlook* 27:528, 1979.

National League of Nursing. *The Challenge of Clinical Evaluation.* New York: National League for Nursing, 1979.

Norman, E.M. and Haumann, L. A Model for Judging Teacher Effectiveness. *Nurse Educator* 3(2):29, 1978.

Putt, A.M. *General Systems Theory Applied to Nursing.* Boston: Little, Brown, 1978.

Santora D. Conceptual Frameworks Used in Baccalaureate and Masters' Degree Programs Curricula. *League Exchange* 126:(6)3, 1980.

Suggested Readings

Sweeney, M.A., Hedstrom, B., and O'Malley, M. Process Evaluation: A Second Look at Psychomotor Skills. *JNE* 21:4, 1982.

Welborn, P. and Thompson, D. Strategies for Dealing with Students Whose Clinical Performance is Unsatisfactory. *JNE* 21(5):26, 1982.

Chapter 7

Teaching and Learning Modes

Arlene M. Putt, R.N., Ed.D.

Study Questions

1. What are the steps necessary to develop any audiovisual aid?
2. How do overhead transparencies, slide/sound productions, and videotapes compare as to ease of preparation, cost, and usefulness?
3. What is microteaching?
4. What are the advantages and disadvantages of learning to teach by microteaching?
5. How does microteaching compare with clinical practicum as a way to develop teaching competency?
6. What functions does the preceptor perform for the student teacher?
7. What are four classroom strategies that can be utilized by the teacher for group instruction?
8. What are the advantages and disadvantages of independent study?
9. What are the advantages and disadvantages of programmed instruction?
10. Self-pacing appears to be ideal for individual learning, but what problems develop when a curriculum is focused upon self-pacing?
11. How can the computer be utilized to assist instruction?

Learning to teach requires a large amount of planning and the use of a wide array of techniques and instructional materials. As discussed in Chapter 6, Development of a Single Course, each course is designed to have a course description, course objectives, course content, and lesson plans for each of the class sessions. The subject matter and course objectives sometimes dictate the use of certain basic materials and learning experiences and can suggest the use of other materials or leave the choice of materials to the instructor. There are usually multiple ways to approach the teaching of the same content from different points of views and with different instructional materials (2, 15). The teaching and learning modes to be discussed here are those of audiovisual materials, microteaching, preceptorship, and clinical student teaching, plus the classroom strategies of single instructor, team teaching, independent study, self-pacing, programmed instruction, and computer-assisted instruction.

Audiovisual Materials

In this section, the selection and the development of audiovisual materials will be discussed. Also the evaluation of audiovisual materials will be reviewed.

Selection of Audiovisual Materials

The process of selecting audiovisual materials begins with course objectives, funds available, facilities, instructor's ability, students' level of learning, constraints of time, equipment, and materials available. Instructional materials in written form include the course syllabus, textbook, supplementary readings, instructor's notes, periodicals, pamphlets, reference books, documents, clippings, and recorded data (11). Audiovisual materials include films, filmstrips, single-concept film loops, television, radio, records, audiotapes, slides, videotapes, pictures, drawings, transparencies, maps, globes, models, graphs, charts, diagrams, posters, specimen collections, actual objects, chalkboard, flannel board, magnetic board, actual equipment, and simulated models. Hardware for these materials includes projection equipment, tools, clinical equipment, and computers (7, 13). These materials are listed in Table 7-1.

Principles guiding the selection of instructional materials include assessing the aspects of

1. Availability
2. Suitability
3. Level of material
4. Accuracy of material
5. Currency of information

Table 7-1 Types of audiovisual materials

Written format	Audiovisual format	Hardware
Course syllabus	Films	Projectors
Textbook	Filmstrips	Tools
Readings	Film loops	Equipment
Notes	Television	Computers
Periodicals	Radio	
Pamphlets	Records	
References	Audiotapes	
Documents	Slides	
Clippings	Videotapes	
Recorded data	Pictures	
	Transparencies	
	Maps	
	Globes	
	Models	
	Graphs	
	Charts	
	Diagrams	
	Posters	
	Collections	
	Display boards	
	Equipment	

6. Logic of presentation sequence
7. Reality of situation
8. Accuracy of fit to course objectives
9. Size of group
10. Cost of material
11. Time to use material effectively
12. Equipment needed
13. Ability to preview material prior to use (5).

If not all of the criteria are met by the materials selected, the instructor may choose to utilize part of the chosen material and either supplement with other materials chosen or developed by the instructor or else develop instructor-made material for the entire topic. Development of materials will be discussed shortly.

Important questions to ask during the selection process are as follows:

1. What resources exist within the school?
2. What equipment and programs are readily available from local sources?

Audiovisual Materials

3. How easy is it to acquire commercially prepared materials?
4. Is there funding for rental or purchase?
*5. Are the materials desired compatible with the equipment at hand?
6. How far ahead of time do the materials have to be ordered?
7. How reliable is the delivery of the material?
8. Are free materials or free rental available from libraries, hospitals, industry, governmental agencies, or voluntary health agencies?
9. Is the selected mode of presentation appropriate for the size of the group?

Kemp (21) gives guidance on the types of materials that can be utilized for independent study, small group interactions, and large group presentations. As a general statement, the number of choices decreases to include amplified visual and audio presentations as the size of the group increases.

By now the reader should realize that the selection and acquisition of instructional materials is a complicated process which requires considerable time for exploration and selection of one particular instructional program to be utilized for one class session. Furthermore, there is no shortcut to this process. The time involvement is an ongoing commitment. Experience does make the process somewhat easier, but keeping instruction fresh and updated requires reinvolvement in the process each time that a course is taught.

While the use of instructional materials enhances the teaching of content, the overuse of these materials should be carefully avoided. Instructors should not depend upon instructional materials as substitutes for adequate preparation that should precede each class session. Instructional materials are not a replacement for a solid base of knowledge on the part of the instructor.

Much more can be said as to where and how to acquire instructional materials. Every school has its own list of materials and sources of supply. However, over a period of time, a prime responsibility of every faculty member is to develop a personal list of instructional aids of merit and a list of sources of availability. With each new course taught, the faculty member can extend this list, broadening the scope and extending the depth of material. Also, there is wisdom in developing a list of alternative aids that can be utilized to present the same content. This alternative list provides the instructor with a variety of approaches and second choices should the first choices be unavailable. When the selection of prepared materials is not an option, or the choice of prepared materials is poorly fitted to current need, the instructor may wish to develop materials.

Development of Audiovisual Materials

Before deciding to develop audiovisual materials, both advantages and disadvantages of the project should be considered. One big advantage of individualized creations is that they are tailor-made to fit the needs of the instructor and the students in that class. Another advantage is that the homemade production may be less expensive, but this is not always true. A third advantage is that the instructor-designed audiovisual materials are a form of creative endeavor that can be recognized by others, bringing acclaim to the instructor and to the school.

One disadvantage in making audiovisual materials is the cost in terms of time, media materials, equipment involved, and the technical assistance usually required. If good technical advice is not available or not utilized, the end production may have serious faults and appear very amateurish.

If the decision is to try to produce, several steps are necessary (5). To plan and to develop audiovisual material first requires a set of objectives. What is the production supposed to do? This is usually stated in behavioral terms. For example: At the end of this videotape, the student will be able to identify sources of contamination in a surgical dressing procedure and will be able to take measures to prevent contamination of the wound.

When one or several objectives have been determined, the content needed to achieve those objectives must be identified and outlined. After these steps are completed, the decision is made as to which media form is most appropriate, given objectives of the product, time, and money available.

When the media form has been selected, a script of the content is drafted, illustrations are chosen, and the text is put into storybook format, giving the text and the illustrations side by side (5). As a general principle, the text and the illustrations should relate as closely as possible to the stated objectives. The content of the script should be clear, concise, and parallel the illustrations shown. Wherever possible, the student viewer should be asked to participate by answering questions and making choices for which feedback is received in the form of validation of answers and explanation of the errors made.

Also important to include are credits for the origin of the program, the title, and the creator's name and affiliation. At the end of the program, a summary should be given, followed by credits to the sources utilized and the technical assistance given. Brown, Lewis, and Harcleroad (5) give detailed instructions on a wide variety of audiovisual modalities which will serve to increase the skill and expertise of the instructor developing individual materials.

The entire project is drafted in rough form and reviewed carefully for completeness and accuracy before final production is begun. When all of the steps of planning and drafting are completed, a production timetable is made as to when materials are to be available and the actual production process is to begin and to finish. The actual production may be done in segments and then edited into a desired sequence. This can also be done with videotapes.

If the product is to be one of good quality, the final production process cannot be hurried, or haste will take its toll. Estimating how much time any one project will require takes experience. The normal tendency is to underestimate the time required, thus making unrealistic deadlines. If time is short, the goal of the type of product must be downgraded accordingly. One solution to inadequate time is to use materials in trial format, evaluating the effectiveness of the material before greater time and effort are put into a larger production. If the production is a slide-sound presentation, it is an easy matter to put in certain slides, insert replacement material, and even to delete some audio portions, and replace them with new content of identical length. The making of audiovisual materials is a combination of art and technology in the truest sense of meaning.

Evaluation of Audiovisual Materials

Evaluation should be an ongoing part of the process of using audiovisual materials (5). If the material is instructor-made, the instructor and one or more knowledgeable peers should evaluate the product for its content and technical merit. If the audiovisual material is commercially prepared, evaluation of the appropriateness and the accuracy of the content is still required. The easiest way to evaluate such material is to have a checklist at hand while viewing the material. An author-designed checklist that can be utilized for most types of audiovisual material appears in Figure 7-1.

Figure 7-1 Assessment of audiovisual productions

Criteria	Excellent	Good	Poor	Not included

OBJECTIVES
  Stated
  Developed
  Clarity

CONTENT
  Level
  Amount
  Accuracy
    Verbal
    Visual
  Currency
  Illustrations
  Specificity
  Technology
  Audio
  Visual

ORGANIZATION
  Beginning
  Pacing
  Theme
  Body
  End
  Consistency
  Completeness

VIEWER ACTIVITY

ERRORS

TIME USAGE

OVERALL RATING
  Title of program
  Type of program
  Date
  Reviewer
  Comments

Microteaching

The philosophy of *microteaching* is the opportunity to practice selected teaching techniques in a microcosmic setting that is videotaped (1, 9, 10). The audience in this microteaching setting is a small group of student peers.

Some of the advantages of microteaching are the planned practice with repeated opportunities to perform, the instant feedback from peers and the instructor, and the ability to see immediately one's own performance on videotape.

Another advantage is that the microteaching serves to develop skills among peers as they see each other perform and relate their peers' performances to their own efforts. Finally, microteaching has the advantage of focusing upon a selected set of skills and the organization of presentation (10).

One disadvantage of microteaching is the artificiality of the setting. Microteaching does not take clinical setting into account, although there have been attempts to videotape actual student performance in certain clinical settings. Usually microteaching takes place in a classroom setting with a small group of student peers as the audience. Another disadvantage is that teaching a group of student peers is not as difficult as teaching a group of basic nursing students learning nursing content for the first time.

Numerous options exist for developing teaching skills through microteaching. These options include: inductive approach, deductive approach, discovery approach, gaming techniques, socratic approach, modeling, demonstration, planned practice, discussion, operant conditioning, cultural diversity, and social issues. Each instructor utilizing microteaching can choose which teaching skills are to be emphasized within the microteaching segment. Authors, deTornyay and Thompson (10), discuss the employment of reinforcement, the use of models, the techniques of asking questions, the creation of a set of background conditions, and finally the art of closure of the topic.

One schedule for microteaching that has worked well for this author is to have the students arranged into small groups where each student presents a short ten-minute segment for a series of classes designed to focus upon one selected technique for each of six weeks (29). The content of the series is the choice of the student and usually reflects the student's area of expertise. The student's peers serve as immediate sources of feedback to their colleague, who in turn will provide feedback for each of them. The instructor is present to see the performance and to evaluate the effort in terms of predetermined criteria and the assignment for that session. Armed with comments from peers and instructor, the student then visualizes his or her own performance via the videotape, integrating comments with observed performance. At the end of the microteaching segment, the students view their entire one-hour videotape as does the instructor. At this time progress over the six-week sessions can be readily noted along with strengths and weaknesses. Another use of these videotapes is that of a demonstration tape for future employers.

Skills identified as important to include in the microteaching segments are:

1. Presentation of objectives for each session
2. Organization of the material in a meaningful manner
3. Communication of the content in a clear and concise manner
4. Demonstration of good speaking characteristics
5. Appropriate pacing of material
6. Clear explanation of concepts
7. Adequate examples
8. Use of appropriate references
9. Encouragement of discussion
10. Encouragement of questions
11. Use of a teaching-learning approach
12. Utilization of learners' backgrounds
13. Appropriate level of presentation
14. Utilization of audiovisual aids
15. Summarization of important points
16. Evaluation of learning
17. Explanation of assignments
18. Estimation of overall performance (29).

The above areas are assessed by the faculty member and discussed with the student. Students are free to explain their choices and rationale. Commendation can be given for excellent performance and suggestions made for further improvement.

The overall strong points of microteaching are the simulated practice and the immediacy and completeness of the feedback. Seeing oneself as others do fosters much self-growth. Lacking full videotaping capabilities, a partially effective technique would be to audiotape presentations for the same type of review and also to photograph the presentor one or more times during the presentation. The audiotape and photographs provide less complete but useful feedback.

Clinical Student Teaching Under Preceptorship

One further step closer to the reality setting of teaching is practice teaching of basic nursing students under the guidance of a faculty *preceptor*. As part of courses in teaching techniques, master's students are frequently involved in an assignment of a period of time of practice teaching of undergraduate students in the clinical setting. In these assignments, the master's student is assigned on a one-to-one basis with a faculty member who is engaged in teaching a clinical course in nursing. In this assignment the student teacher functions along with the faculty member to work on course development, course presentation, selection and grading of assignments, and supervision of the undergraduate nursing student in the clinical practice of basic nursing skills. With the faculty member acting as a role model, the student teacher gradually develops skill and an increasing degree of responsibility for the supervision of a small number of basic nursing students in the clinical area. The student teacher selects the assignments, provides the direct supervision, and participates in the evaluation of the performance; all of the functions are performed in collaboration with the faculty member who gives direction and feedback to the master's student. At the end of the experience, the faculty member evaluates the performance of the master's student, noting strengths and weaknesses in performance which are shared with the master's student and the instructor in the teaching course.

Areas that can be evaluated are:

1. Assisting in orienting undergraduate students to clinical areas
2. Planning clinical goals with undergraduate students
3. Assigning suitable learning experiences for undergraduate students
4. Guiding the undergraduate students in the development of nursing skills
5. Supervising the performance of the undergraduate students
6. Planning seminars
7. Conducting seminars
8. Sharing information with the preceptor throughout the experience

9. Evaluating written reports of the students
10. Assisting the preceptor in writing evaluations for the students supervised
11. Participating in the evaluation conferences held by the faculty member
12. Constructing a test for undergraduate students
13. Administering the test
14. Evaluating the test results and interpreting them to the students
15. Participating in course and faculty meetings
16. Establishing and maintaining working relationships with preceptor, staff, students, and clients.

Comments are made upon the overall performance of the student teacher, and this is discussed with the master's student and the instructor in the teaching course.

By utilizing these types of experiences for the future teacher of nurses, a more realistic exploration of the faculty role can be obtained. With the one-to-one relationship of the master's student and the faculty member, many of the finer points of teaching and the individual expertise can be communicated. The success of this type of experience depends upon the relationship and interest between the faculty member and the master's student. Not all faculty members are adept at shepherding neophyte instructors through first experiences in the realm of teaching. Also occasionally, personality conflicts develop between students and their preceptors. In these situations, a change of assignment is often the best solution. Growth and performance suffer if there is not a trusting, respectful relationship between the student teacher and the preceptor. The logical extension of this type of experience is a mentorship for first-time faculty members in which the degree of responsibility is fully extended to the new faculty member, but the guidance and consultation needed to exercise that responsibility are readily available to the new teacher.

Classroom Strategies

While there are numerous *classroom strategies* available for use in the teaching-learning process, the discussion in this chapter will focus upon those strategies available to the single instructor, the team teacher, and the faculty member who is directing independent study and using the methods of self-pacing, programmed instruction, games, simulation, and computer-assisted instruction.

Single Instructor

Classroom strategies that can be utilized by the *single instructor* are many. For use with large groups, there are lectures, videotapes, films, filmstrips, overhead transparencies, records, radio, conference telephone, classroom discussion, debate, role-playing, demonstration amplified by television camera on closed-circuit television, group projects, question and answer, group problem-solving, reports, guest lectures, group interviews, sharing of student experiences, textbooks, and reference materials. Whatever modes are selected, the material to be presented must be carefully organized and displayed in sequential format large enough for all to see the details. Also, the material must be presented simply enough so that it can be understood by the student encountering the material for the first time. If the objectives of the class are stated at the beginning of the session, the student should be able to follow the logical development of the material. If the instructor stops periodically throughout the class to summarize the material and to encourage questions from the class, students missing part of the material can seek clarification before more material is added.

Strategies for use with small groups include those that can be utilized with large groups as well as several others. Seminar teaching works well with small groups. In this format the instructor can present material as in lectures, but there is more interaction with individual students. This interaction takes the form of dialogue between instructor and students or between several of the students themselves. Students participating in seminars have a greater responsibility for giving reports or contributions of individual thinking and outside readings. Because of the small size of the group, direct demonstrations work well as each student is close enough to see clearly each step of the procedure. With the small group size and much more informality, the use of any audiovisual aid will enhance the learning.

When the single instructor gives individual attention to students within a course setting, it is usually to explain further certain content, to give guidance for projects, or to plan and to review individual assignments and clinical assignments. It is customary practice for the instructor to maintain posted office hours to be accessible to students needing this kind of assistance.

In this aspect of the teaching role, the single instructor serves as a resource person for further assistance and for the exploration of individual special interests.

If the entire class is the responsibility of a single instructor, that instructor carries a heavy responsibility for decisions regarding the nature and depth of the content and the manner in which the material is to be presented. To provide advanced review of selected content and material, peer faculty members may be consulted. If there is an area chairperson, the single instructor should seek advice from this person. While there is no one best method of presentation and the effectiveness of any method depends upon the skill with which it is utilized, a variety of presentations will tend to keep the student alert to the change and novelty of the approach. The beginning instructor will want to try a number of techniques and will soon find that certain techniques are more easily incorporated into one's pattern of behavior. By conscious effort and repeated practice, additional skills can be acquired.

Not only does the single instructor have to choose the method and materials of presentation but must also choose how the learning will be evaluated. Maybe standardized examinations or previously developed examinations are in regular use, then the instructor has little or no choice. More likely, the instructor has full choice and must decide what is important to test and how to test the learning that has occurred. Test construction will be discussed in Chapter 9.

Team Teaching

This technique of teaching a course uses a team of instructors who work together, collaboratively developing and executing the course (17). This method of teaching developed along with the integrated curriculum. With several instructors jointly planning, teaching, supervising, and evaluating students in one course, the students have access to a wider range of faculty abilities and expertise and can benefit from being evaluated by more than one person. If the assigned instructors work well together and have abilities and expertise that are compatible, the *team teaching* can work very well. On the other hand, if the faculty members disagree on content or methods or have gaps in their expertise, student learning is likely to be disrupted and fragmented (14). Because the entire course is a shared responsibility, each instructor must share the outcomes, positive or negative. Also, each instructor receives only a share of the rewards for the endeavors put forth. Under team teaching, it is difficult for the instructor to receive direct feedback for the degree of effectiveness of individual efforts. Also, team teaching is time-consuming in that there is heavy demand for group work time which adds to faculty workload. The need for cohesion can be emotionally demanding and frustrating to many faculty members. For reasons such as these, many schools have tried team teaching but find it difficult to maintain through personnel changes (27).

Independent Study

Independent study is a form of special class arrangement set up between a faculty member and one student when the individual student desires content that is not covered in the usual course schedule (11, 12). Thus, by agreement between the faculty member and the student and with the approval of the institution, the student registers for a selected amount of independent study which entails stated individually written objectives, an outline of content to be covered, and a schedule of assignments and sessions with the instructor. During the time of the independent study, the student and the faculty member hold dialogues regularly to discuss the progress of the student. To give evidence of achievement, the student may complete a project, take an examination, or both. While the structure, pace, and content of the individual independent study are student-oriented, the use of faculty time is heavy and not cost efficient. Also, the superior student can benefit greatly from such an arrangement, but the average or slow student may miss the stimulation and shared experiences provided by contact with other students in the normal class situation. Hanson (18) discusses one student's view of independent study. However, each student will have a unique view of independent study.

Self-Pacing

As a classroom strategy, *self-pacing* has some interesting aspects (20). The idea basic to self-pacing is that if information to be mastered is set up in self-contained modules, the student can proceed through the modules at a self-determined pace and demonstrate mastery of the material at the end of each module (8). This arrangement provides for the fast and the slow learner. However, the faculty have little control over the pace that the students elect to take. Therefore, confusion may exist as to where the students are in their mastery, and there is a tendency for the students to lag behind and to become bunched together at some point. This erratic progress makes the scheduling of materials extremely difficult with the likelihood that a large number of the students will need the same materials at the same point in time. Another problem is the unpredictable completion time of the course. Several classes of students may end up together in the same module of content and not be ready to proceed to more advanced content. Such an arrangement leads to further difficulty in trying to schedule clinical assignments when the level of mastery is at widely different points. If self-pacing is modified to include a maximum time schedule in which to complete each module, the flow of students through the content can be controlled in part. The idea of setting up learning in modular format where each module has its own objectives, content, and evaluation does make good sense. Many of the ideas of self-pacing have been combined with programmed instruction and incorporated into conventional class schedules. The concept of mastery, while not always expressed in the same manner, is present to some extent in every course, and the student must demonstrate a certain preselected level of knowledge and skill before the course is considered successfully completed (4).

Programmed Instruction

Programmed instruction refers to a teaching technique that became popular during the early 1960s; content is broken down into very small increments and presented one fact and one concept at a time with immediate questioning to ascertain if the student grasps the content. The purpose of programmed instruction is to develop errorless learning (25). The student must answer correctly before proceeding to the next frame of content. These programmed instruction materials were either put into a slide/sound format or into an especially designed book in which the single concept or fact was isolated on one page with instructions to turn elsewhere in the book to check the answers to the questions presented at the end of the short segment of content. Another format that was utilized was a separate column of answers to the right-hand side of the page so that the answers could be covered and uncovered as needed.

Another feature of programmed instruction is the feedback given in case of a wrong answer. The student is immediately referred back to the material presented and is rerouted through the mastery questions again until the correct answers are given. One problem with books designed on these principles is that they lack indexes and are unwieldy as ready references.

Material is also presented in slow, tedious steps that is ill suited to the fast learner who wishes to scan material rapidly and find material concisely presented. One anonymous sage is to have said that a BOOK is the original programmed instruction tool.

Furthermore, programmed instruction texts are tedious to develop and expensive to print. In this day of computers, much of the material originally found in programmed texts can now be found in computer-assisted programs to be discussed later in this chapter.

Games

A relatively new strategy for teaching is the concept of presenting material in the form of games that the students can play while learning concepts, interaction of factors, and developing judgments (16, 28). The games are usually designed for use with small groups and frequently have a playing board with players taking turns and making choices. The consequences of the choices selected by the players depend upon the variables inserted into the game, the skill of the players, and the element of randomness. Decisionmaking, interpersonal relationships, and attitudes are some of the content for the games. There are a number of such games available commercially from publishers or mail-order catalogues. Instructors may wish to develop games of their own invention, but such creativity is time consuming, and many trials are needed to clarify rules and relationships of content and choices of action.

Simulation

Simulation refers to making materials and practice as closely approximate the real life situation as possible (19, 28). One common example of simulation is the disaster medical care drills in which, by moulage and acting, victims with varying degrees of injury are portrayed so that medical personnel can develop skill in triage and in caring for various types of traumatic and psychological injuries.

Simulation is a very valuable technique to teach complex care and decisionmaking in situations that cannot be encountered in reality or in advance as disaster settings. Simulation on a lesser scale is useful in teaching appropriate action in selected clinical settings such as the operating room, the delivery room, the emergency room, and the special procedure areas. While the concept of simulation is useful in presenting challenges of reality without the pressures of reality, simulation is still short of reality and the complexity that reality always presents. The use of simulation does require careful advanced planning and practice. Cardiopulmonary resuscitation is an example of this. Like fire drills, the simulation should be repeated frequently enough to assure smooth performance.

Computer-assisted Instruction

A rapidly growing area of teaching is *computer-assisted instruction* in which the student interacts with a computer software program designed to present content, pose problems, and assist the student in reaching solutions to the problems posed (22, 24). With the advent of graphics on cathode ray tubes, the content need not be just verbal, it can be diagrams, charts, drawings, models, three-dimensional relief drawings, and other art forms. The student need only have the ability to spell, read, and type basic letters into the terminal in order to operate computer programs. Familiarity with computerware is frequently found to a great degree in the present day student (26). Many students have learned to interact with computers via video games. Children as young as kindergarteners are learning their alphabets, math skills, and problem-solving via computers.

Nationally oriented computer-assisted programs exist for engineering, mathematics, and other sciences. One example is PLATO where students log on to the computer terminal in a special room of the library or classroom and do their homework on the computer (3). This work is then available to the instructor to check. A well-designed computer program will serve the role of the instructor functioning in a one-to-one relationship with the student, sitting next to the student, and guiding the student's actions. Feedback is given for correct answers as words of praise appear on the screen. Also, mistakes are called to the student's attention, and the reason for the error is explained and followed by words of encouragement to try again. Such programs allow the student the freedom of proceeding at his or her own pace, the freedom to make errors, and to explore the consequences of those errors as well as to get immediate positive feedback for the accuracy of the action taken (19). Another advantage of computer-assisted learning is the ability to compress time so that the student can see long-term effects of decisions in real time and in this way learn to make professional judgments (19).

Computers are obviously the most important tool now available to the present-day instructor. Nursing instructors are familiar with microprocessors that record clinical data from clients and with computer analysis of research data. The further extension of the computer use to the average nursing classroom and in clinical nursing practice is the next step in the technical enhancement of teaching and learning (23).

References

1. Allen, D. and Ryan, K. *Microteaching.* Menlo Park: Addison-Wesley, 1969.
2. Bauman, K., Cook, J., and Larson, L.K. Using Technology to Humanize Instruction: An Approach To Teaching Nursing Skills. *JNE* 20(3):27, 1981.
3. Bitzer, M.D., Boudreaux, M., and Avner, R.A. *Computer-based Instruction of Basic Nursing Utilizing Inquiry Approach.* (CERL, Report X–40). Urbana: University of Illinois, 1973.
4. Block, J.H. (ed.). *Mastery Learning: Theory and Practice.* New York: Holt, 1971.
5. Brown, J.W., Lewis, R.R., and Harcleroad, F.F. *AV Instruction Technology, Media, and Methods* (6th ed.). New York: McGraw-Hill, 1983.
6. Burke, R.L. *CAI Sourcebook.* Englewood Cliffs: Prentice-Hall, 1982.
7. Center for Vocational Education. *Professional Vocational Teacher Module: Select and Obtain Student Instructional Material.* Module B-5. Columbus: Ohio State University, 1974.
8. Corona, D.F. A Continuous Progress Curriculum in Nursing. *Nurs. Outlook* 18:46, 1970.
9. deTornyay, R. and Searight, M. Micro-teaching in Preparing Faculty. *Nurs. Outlook* 16(3):34, 1968.
10. deTornyay, R. and Thompson, M.A. *Strategies for Teaching Nursing* (2nd ed.). New York: Wiley, 1982.
11. Dick, D.J. Teaching Health Assessment Skills: A Self-Instructional Approach. *JNE.* 22:355, 1983.
12. Duane, J.E. (ed.). *Individualized Instruction—Programs and Materials.* Englewood Cliffs: Educational Technology Publications, 1973.
13. Duane, N.F. An Audiovisual Overview. *Nurse Educator* 4(4):7, 1979.
14. Floyd, G.J. Team Teaching: Advantages and Disadvantages to the Student. *Nurs. Res.* 24:52, 1975.
15. Fuhrmann, B.C. and Grasha, A.F. *A Practical Handbook for College Teachers.* Boston: Little, Brown, 1983.
16. Girard, N.L. A Game-Oriented Strategy for Teaching Surgical Terminology. *Nurse Educator* 6(5):16, 1981.
17. Griffith, J.W. Team Teaching: Philosophical Considerations and Pragmatic Consequences. *JNE* 22:342, 1983.

18. Hanson, K.H. Independent Study: A Student's View. *Nurs. Outlook* 22:329, 1974.
19. Hubert, C. Medical Students Learn from 'David' Tucson: *The Arizona Daily Star*, 3 January, 1984.
20. Huntsman, A. and Thompson, M.A. Self-paced Learning Requires Careful Planning. *Cross-reference* 7(2):1, 1977.
21. Kemp, J.E. *Planning and Producing Audiovisual Materials*. New York: Crovell, 1975.
22. Kirchoff, K. and Holzemer, W.L. Student Learning and a Computer-assisted Instructional Program. *JNE* 18(3):22, 1979.
23. Oliveri, P. and Sweeney, M.A. Evaluation of Clinical Learning by Computer. *Nurse Educator* 5(4):26, 1980.
24. Schleutermann, J.A., Holzemer, W.L., and Farrard, L.L. An Evaluation of Paper-and-Pencil and Computer-assisted Simulations. *JNE* 22:315, 1983.
25. Steven, B. The Teaching-Learning Process. *Nurse Educator* 1(1):9, 1976.
26. Strange, J.H. Adapting to the Computer Revolution. *1981 Current Issues in Higher Education*, No. 5:14. Washington, D.C.: American Association for Higher Education, 1981.
27. Tarpey, K.S. and Chen, S-P. Team Teaching: Is It for You? *JNE* 17(2):36, 1978.
28. Ulicone, M.S. Simulation Gaming in Nursing Education. *JNE* 22:349, 1983.
29. University of Arizona College of Nursing. Course Materials. Mimeographed. Tucson: University of Arizona, 1982.

Suggested Readings

Boocock, S.S. and Schild, E.O. (eds.). *Simulation Games in Learning*. Beverly Hills: Sage, 1968.

Brown, J.W., Lewis, R.B., and Harcleroad, F.F. *AV Instruction Technology, Media, and Methods* (6th ed.). New York: McGraw-Hill, 1983.

Bundy, R.F. Computer-assisted Instruction—Where Are We? In R.A. Weisgerber (ed.), *Perspectives in Individualized Learning*. Itasca: Peacock, 1971.

Burke, R.L. *CAI Sourcebook*. Englewood Cliffs: Prentice-Hall, 1982.

Chapman, J.J. Microteaching: How Students Learn Group Patient Education Skills. *Nurse Educator* 3(2):13, 1978.

Clark, C.C. Teaching Nurses Group Concepts: Some Issues and Suggestions. *Nurse Educator* 3(1):17, 1978.

Collart, M.E. Computer-Assisted Instruction and the Teaching-Learning Process. *Nurs. Outlook* 21:527, 1973.

Cooper, S.S. *Self-directed Learning in Nursing*. Wakefield: Nursing Resources, 1980.

Cross, K.P. *Accent on Learning*. San Francisco: Jossey-Bass, 1976.

deTornyay, R. Up and Running. *JNE* 22:365, 1983.

deTornyay, R. and Thompson, M.A. *Strategies for Teaching Nursing* (2nd ed.). New York: Wiley, 1982.

Suggested Readings

Eaton, S., Davis, G.L., and Benner, P.E. Discussion Stoppers in Teaching. *Nurs. Outlook.* 25:578, 1977.

Eble, K. *The Craft of Teaching.* San Francisco: Jossey-Bass, 1976.

Erickson, E.H. and Borgmeyer, V. Simulated Decision-Making Experience via Case Analysis. *J. Nurs. Adm.* 9(5):10, 1979.

Fuhrmann, B.C. and Grasha A.F. *A Practical Handbook for College Teachers.* Boston: Little, Brown, 1983.

Hogstel, M.D. and Ackley, N.L. Making Team Teaching Work. *Nurs. Outlook* 27(1):48, 1979.

McKeathie, W.J. (ed.). *Learning, Cognition and College Teaching.* San Francisco: Jossey-Bass, 1980.

Pittman, P.R. Videotaping: A Technique for Teaching Basic Communication Skills. *Nurse Educator* 2(6):16, 1977.

Chapter 8

Clinical Instruction: Viewpoints of a Faculty Member and Agency Administrator

Study Questions

1. What is the value of clinical instruction?
2. What is the value of simulated experiences as preparation for clinical experience?
3. What are the objectives of clinical instruction?
4. How much clinical experience should there be in a baccalaureate program? In an associate degree program?
5. What are the essential clinical experiences for a baccalaureate student? For an associate degree student?
6. What factors must be considered in making student assignments?
7. What are acceptable faculty-student ratios for clinical instruction?
8. What are the legal responsibilities of a clinical instructor?
9. How should the clinical instructor handle the following situations?
   The patient's condition changes very rapidly
   The student cannot cope with the assignment
   Service staff hostile to the student
   Clinical situations beyond the faculty member's experience
   Questionable ethics
   Different expectations for baccalaureate and associate degree students
   Divergent research and care interests
   Incorporating research into care
   Normative error

10. How should clinical performance be evaluated?

Introduction

In this chapter, various aspects of clinical instruction will be viewed from two points of view: the viewpoint of a faculty member responsible for clinical instruction and the viewpoint of a nursing administrator of an acute care agency in which the clinical instruction is enacted. These viewpoints, which are personal ones, will be compared and contrasted. The goal of this presentation is for the reader to understand that clinical instruction is a multifaceted topic which should be viewed from more than one perspective.

From a Faculty Viewpoint

Arlene M. Putt, R.N., Ed.D.

The Value of Clinical Instruction

One of the aspects of teaching nursing that differs from teaching many other subjects is the aspect of clinical instruction. Basic to the practice of nursing is the concept of learning by doing. This time-renowned concept goes back to the days of Kaiserworth Hospital and Florence Nightingale when nursing curricula contained a few hours of lecture and many hours of practice. Through the intervening years, the amount of nursing knowledge has grown exponentially, and the time allotted to learning by doing has contracted steadily. In recent years, numerous nursing groups have attempted to determine effective combinations of theory and practice.

The basic value of clinical instruction is uniformly recognized and accepted in the profession of nursing. The question has not been: Should there be clinical instruction? but rather How much and What kinds of clinical instruction should there be? Every nursing program includes some amount of clinical instruction and clinical practice, but the amounts vary greatly. It is recognized that in clinical practice, the theoretical knowledge and skills learned receive repeated testing. The student has the challenge of pitting this knowledge and skills against a real situation. Since

129

the goal of nursing education is to prepare future practitioners of nursing, the proof of that preparation lies in the competencies that can be demonstrated with real clients in a real health care setting. Every experienced nursing instructor has encountered the difficulties that arise when nursing students have excellent theoretical backgrounds and are unable to perform satisfactorily in clinical practice. Likewise, these instructors also have experienced students who do very well intuitively in the practice setting but have not mastered the necessary knowledge and judgment. Thus, the questions really are: How much and what kind of clinical instruction does each individual student need to become a competent practitioner of nursing? The value of clinical instruction is in the development of a competent nursing practitioner who has enough guided learning experiences so that the new experiences can be integrated successfully as the experiences are encountered in professional practice.

The Value of Simulated Experiences

One approach to bridging the gap between classroom instruction and clinical instruction is to expose the students to a series of laboratory simulations that in many ways parallel the problems the student is likely to encounter in the real setting. These simulated experiences, which take the forms of working with artificial models, mock physical set-ups, sample equipment, role-played scenes, computer-assisted instruction, and gaming, were discussed in Chapter 7.

With the wide variety of ways simulations can be presented, simulation techniques do provide a stepwise progression for the nursing student, allowing the student to concentrate on the practice of the skill without the added anxiety of knowing the situation is reality where certain mistakes must not be made.

The disadvantage of simulation is that the scene lacks reality and complexity. The final learning must occur in the real setting where the multitudinous factors surrounding the client and the health care problems are all interfacing at the same time. In the real situation, in addition to concentrating upon the skill required, the student must also focus upon the interaction with the client to whom the service is being rendered, while in many instances performing the skill for the first time. Both simulation and clinical experiences require the presence of an instructor to guide, reinforce, and correct behaviors.

Another form of simulated experiences that is gaining much momentum is computer-assisted instruction as discussed in Chapter 7. While this type of exercise is of great value in developing logical thought patterns, there is no assurance that the student who can solve complicated problems on a computer can then transfer that learning to the real setting where answers and judgments are not as clearly right or wrong. For mastery of material, processing patient information, and the development of basic judgments, the computer-assisted exercise is definitely the teaching tool of the present.

Objectives of Clinical Instruction

The objectives of clinical instruction are twofold. The prime objectives are to provide opportunities for the nursing student to:

1. Encounter reality in the practice of nursing
2. Synthesize learning
3. Practice activities described in course objectives
4. Practice activities described in program objectives.

The second objective is to provide opportunities for the faculty member to evaluate the performance of the student in a real setting.

Factors in Planning Clinical Instruction

While the factors to consider in planning clinical instruction are many, those to be discussed here include:

1. Amount and arrangement of clinical instruction
2. Time constraints
3. Cost
4. Facilities available
5. Faculty-agency arrangements
6. Selection of learning experiences
7. Supervision of learning experiences
8. Evaluation of learning.

Amount and Arrangement of Clinical Instruction

The amount and arrangement of clinical instruction can depend upon a number of factors acting in concert. The final decision of how much and what arrangement of clinical instruction will depend upon:

1. Philosophy of the school
2. Educational policy of the number of hours of laboratory per credit hour
3. Course objectives
4. Nature of the clinical facilities and their constraints
5. Faculty—student ratios
6. Various cost factors
7. Availability of blocks of appropriate time.

Many of these factors can be influenced by the attitudes of the faculty members regarding the nature and desirability of clinical practice, resulting in wide variance in the number of clinical hours. For example, in the various programs throughout one state (6), the clinical hours range from 600 to 1500. With such diversity of time spent in the actual practice of nursing skills, the graduates of these programs continue to take the same examination for licensing as registered nurses.

The amount and arrangement of clinical instruction should reflect careful thought on the part of the faculty members responsible for that instruction. There should be clear objectives for the instruction with experiences planned so that students do have opportunities to achieve the stated objectives. In this respect, the course syllabus should state what kind and how much clinical practice is included in the course. Then the student has the right to expect to have opportunities for such experiences to the extent stated.

Time Constraints

Two ongoing problems with clinical instruction are the placement and the length of the time segments. Most frequently, students have assigned clinical hours during the day or early evening, because these are the normal college hours, the normal hours for daily health care activities and departmental services. However, certain activities and experiences may not follow these hours: the delivery of babies and family visiting hours, for example. Also, certain selected experiences tend to overrun the allotted clinical time. Operations and special diagnostic procedures may not be completed according to the student's scheduled hours. While some variation of hours may be individually planned, it is difficult or impossible for an instructor to supervise an entire group of basic students on variable schedules of hours.

Other time constraints may also be present. Maybe the facility provides experiences for more than one group of students but restricts access to only one group at any one time. In this case, the access is limited to the allotted time, and this can further restrict the type and nature of clinical practice that may be available.

Cost

Clinical instruction is costly in terms of faculty time, student time, supplies, and staff involvement. The basic cost of one hour of clinical instruction per student will vary with each clinical setting, the number of students involved, and the faculty member's salary. One cost factor also involved is the time faculty need to make assignments. This means either a separate time to plan assignments on the day before the clinical experience or an early arrival on the day of the experience. The amount of time needed for this process of selecting assignments is a minimum of one-half hour and may be one hour, depending upon the degree of activity transpiring on the unit at that particular moment. Usually this process of selecting assignments is completed in consultation with members of the service staff who may have reasons why certain selected experiences are not feasible or desirable for students. Some schools pay travel expenses for faculty travel to make assignments. If the school does not reimburse the faculty member, the added costs of time and travel for assignments are at the faculty member's expense.

Other costs of clinical instruction include:

1. Agency staffing costs so staff have time to work with students
2. Cost of slowdown in work pace due to the slower pace of students
3. Cost of extra supplies utilized by and for students
4. Cost of extra forms and records used by students.

A definite increase in communication occurs when students are involved, for communication must precede, occur during, and follow actions. There is much reporting back and forth so everyone concerned is kept abreast of changes and accomplishments.

Emergency care for students who become injured or exposed to contagious disease is one more cost of nursing education. In times of shrinking economic support, each cost factor must be identified and assessed for its value. Cost containment policies may have to be established.

Facilities

Depending upon its location, the school or college of nursing may be fortunate enough to have a choice of clinical facilities from which to choose. Other nursing programs must utilize those facilities that are available or within range. In any case, the faculty must assess the facility to determine the nature, the extent, and the appropriateness of the clinical practice that the facility can provide. Graham and Gleit (8) report that most baccalaureate programs use a variety of agencies to prepare students for professional practice. In their sample of 90 programs, the range in the number of facilities utilized was 6 to 16. The types of facilities utilized by 75 to 95 percent of the programs in the sample included secondary care settings, homes, health departments, out-patient clinics, tertiary care settings, schools, community mental health agencies, day-care centers, and home health agencies. To a lesser extent, rehabilitation centers, physicians' offices, industries, community action programs, health maintenance organizations, prisons, and even summer camps are utilized. The trend was to use multiple sites rather than one or two agencies exclusively. Because associate degree programs have a narrower scope than baccalaureate programs, fewer facilities are needed to provide clinical experience for these programs. The facilities selected for associate degree programs are likely to be secondary or extended care facilities.

The facility selected for student experience should be large enough to accommodate several students at one time. If the facility is too small, there may be inadequate or restricted ranges of experiences for students.

The philosophy of the facility is very important. Not all health care facilities are attuned to teaching and the needs of students. Teaching functions require extra time and commitment on the part of staff members. Not every staff member is able or willing to invest this time in students' learning. Students have a right to have positive rather than negative role models.

Location of the facility is also important. In urban areas, there may be several choices for experiences while in rural areas, there may be one or no facilities within a wide area. If facilities are too far away, arrangements must be made to transport students and faculty to centers where experiences are available. Lengthy travel imposes hardships on students and faculty alike and is disruptive to the program.

The best mix of these factors must be weighed and chosen to provide access to clinical practice settings that are in line with program objectives. This mix will vary with each program.

Faculty-Agency Arrangements

After faculty have explored what facilities are available and have assessed the suitability of these facilities, contractual agreements are developed between the school and the health agency. These contractual agreements state what each side will provide, what policies will be adhered to, and the number of students who will use which parts of the facility for which hours. These finalized agreements are sent from the administrative level to boards of directors for final approval.

As part of the contractual agreement, faculty coverage is defined in terms of when an instructor is to be present with the students in addition to the amount and type of faculty orientation that is needed. Faculty responsibilities then include receiving an adequate orientation to the institution and its policies, following those policies while in clinical instruction, and providing communication with the staff regarding the objectives of the clinical experience, the nature, and the extent of student involvement.

The faculty member has a threefold responsibility:

1. To practice adequate safe competent nursing.
2. To supervise students during assignments.
3. To instruct students in those aspects of care necessary to adequate completion of the assignment.

Legally, the faculty member can be liable for negligence in any or all of the three areas (4). Therefore, the faculty member must understand the care requirements and have the skill to provide that care or communicate a need for assistance to the staff, must instruct the student in the nursing care skills required, and must supervise the students in the actual doing of the care, giving the students reassurance and direction as needed. Supervising eight to ten students caring for at least one client each, the instructor must communicate clearly and frequently with students, staff, and other health team members. For clarification of the legal responsibilities of the faculty member, the reader is referred to sources such as Cazalas (4) and Creighton (7).

Faculty orientations are usually arranged several days before the beginning of the term. These orientations may include a demonstration of the physical set-up and practices utilized by the agency. A time may be established for the faculty member to work in joint assignment with a staff member. Matters not clearly covered in the policy book should be discussed with the unit administrator before an issue arises. Faculty returning to units where they have worked at prior times still need a short period of orientation.

Selection of Learning Experiences

The success of clinical instruction hinges upon the selection of appropriate experiences to enhance student progress. There are many factors which influence the selection of these experiences. These factors will be identified and discussed in turn.

Course objectives are the primary factor in guiding the selection of learning experiences. Each nursing course should have its own set of objectives defined in behavioral terms so that the student knows what knowledge and skills are to be acquired during that course. With course objectives as a guide, the instructor seeks experiences that will insure the student an opportunity to practice the skill defined in the course objectives. For each separate experience, subobjectives are set. The use of nursing diagnoses may facilitate the selection of learning experiences to meet course objectives. If a discussion of nursing diagnosis is desired, the reader is referred to Carlson (3) and Kim (10). Rambo and Wood (15) discuss those skills necessary for clinical practice.

The level of the learners is a crucial consideration in the selection of learning experiences. If the learners are at or near the beginning level, simple experiences are desirable. If the learners are advanced students with greater experience, more complex clinical situations are appropriate. Tarnow (17), in working with adult learners, has identified what is important to adult learners. Adult learners are more clearly focused than their younger counterparts. Adult learners want specific knowledge to solve specific problems. Adult learners prefer to have material relate to their experiences and to practical problem solving. Because they have more experience in life than some of their younger classmates, adult learners may contribute greatly to the learning of other classmates. Regardless of the age of the learners in the group, the clinical instructor must assess each student individually, taking the level of learning of that student into consideration when selecting clinical experiences.

Availability of experiences is a constant concern for clinical instructors. Because of shifting case loads and changing clientele, health care agencies cannot guarantee that certain types of problems are readily available at all times. Some problems tend to run in clusters while others appear rarely or irregularly. This uncertainty makes the scheduling of learning experiences a constant challenge, one that requires frequent adjustment. If the most desirable experiences are not available, the instructor must select from those experiences that are available to fulfill learning objectives. Sometimes alternative arrangements can be made to delay the experience, substitute experiences of a parallel nature, simulate the experience, or have students share the limited experiences that do exist.

One daily problem that is encountered is the somewhat divergent nature of learning needs of students and care needs of clients. While learning for students is important if they are to develop into professional practitioners, the care needs of clients cannot be compromised. If the care needs of clients conflict with the learning needs of students, then the needs of the students must assume a secondary priority. This situation should be recognized by the clinical instructor but may have to be identified by the agency staff and communicated to the instructor. Sometimes a compromise can be reached so that elements of client care can be delegated to the students while other essential features of that care remain the responsibility of the agency staff. If the potential conflicts of interest cannot be resolved at the unit level, then higher levels of administrative involvement must be sought.

In many instances, the areas that are utilized for learning experiences are also utilized for learning experiences of other health professionals such as medical students, pharmacy students, respiratory therapy students, and physical therapy students. There are many advantages to students of varying backgrounds having experiences in common areas. Students who learn together, learn to work together, forming relationships that facilitate their work with other members of the health care team in later professional practice. However, because students have skills which are still in the formative phase, extra supervision is required to see that the students in nursing and the students in the other disciplines are proceeding in a positive direction and that the care given does not suffer from lack of mature skills. Cooperative arrangements can be evolved with the supervisors of the other types of students with these arrangements being mutually beneficial to all of the students in the area.

Time constraints are a constant problem. Only agreed-upon blocks of time are available for students. The timing of these allotted slots may be by design, convenience, or even default. Clinical instructors are left to plan the use of that time to the best advantage. This means selecting experiences or parts of experiences which can be accomplished within the time frame allotted. To accomplish this, maybe only one or two facets of care can be assigned. To assign too much means great frustration for the instructor and defeat for the student who cannot possibly accomplish all of the assignment.

One consideration in selecting learning experiences is whether the assignment is for an associate degree student or for a baccalaureate student. The two types of programs do have different objectives with some common knowledge bases. In comparing one associate degree program with one baccalaureate program, the following differences were noted (16). Terminal objectives differed with the associate degree program preparing a nurse to function in a structured setting under supervision, while the baccalaureate program prepares a nurse to function in both structured and unstructured settings. For this reason the strands of content are presented in less breadth and less depth in the associate degree program where the primary emphasis is on the individual patient instead of upon the individual, the family, groups, and the community as a whole. Other differences are that the baccalaureate program includes perioperative care, crisis intervention, counseling, and greater depth in physical assessment, research, community health, group teaching, legal implications, and patient advocacy.

Joint assignment is one approach that is utilized when the assignment is too heavy for one student or the experience is an unusual one. By sharing the assignment, two students have an opportunity instead of only one student. If joint assignments are utilized, the instructor has to communicate clearly the delegation of responsibility and accountability.

Attitudes of staff and physicians greatly affect the selection of learning experiences and the success of those experiences for the student learner. If positive attitudes abound on the part of the staff and the physicians, then the student's learning is enhanced. The opposite is also true. By explaining the learning objectives

From a Faculty Viewpoint

and the student's capabilities, the instructor can turn these attitudes to a positive direction.

Research is one area of the curriculum that can and should be incorporated into clinical practice. Research can be included in a variety of ways such as having the students collect data for selected clinical problems or studies or using the findings of other studies to guide and direct the giving of nursing care. One can also have the students contrast two ways of doing certain aspects of care and encourage the students to find and discuss studies that apply to the clinical problems that they are encountering in the clinical areas.

A high degree of situational flux exists in clinical assignments. At no time can the clinical instructor assume that the assignments will materialize as planned. There are many fluctuating variables in any one clinical situation. The patient may have a crisis of one nature or another. The patient may require immediate services outside of the purview of the agency or department. The patient may be discharged or the physician's plan of therapy may change abruptly. All of these occurrences require adjustments in the assignment at the time of the happening. Therefore, the clinical instructor must constantly monitor the progress of the assignment and make prompt adjustment when sudden or unexpected changes develop. To expedite such changes, close communication is needed with the agency staff.

Other resources for the development of clinical objectives exist in most agency settings. These resources take the form of special conferences, meetings, grand rounds, physicians' rounds, and special medical procedures in other departments. While the predictability of these resources being available when desired may be difficult to determine, these opportunities are worthy of consideration as learning experiences and may assist in the attainment of course objectives.

While Chase (5) claims that clinical experiences can be made easier, the success or failure of clinical experiences rests in large measure upon the abilities of the faculty member. Each faculty member will structure clinical assignments in a highly individualized manner depending upon the personal beliefs, strengths, and limitations of the faculty member. In the very complex environs for modern medical care, no one faculty member can have a high degree of expertise in a wide variety of areas. It behooves each faculty member to assess carefully personal strengths and weaknesses, using this knowledge to create good learning situations for the students. Where personal weaknesses or unfamiliarity with procedure exist, the faculty member should assume responsibility to compensate for deficits by seeking additional information or by practicing additional skills. Another approach is to acquaint the agency staff with these areas of weaknesses and have the agency staff supplement the weak areas of practice. Sharing areas of strength and weakness with the students is realistic. Students will then be able to see the faculty member in a more realistic light and conclude that if the faculty member does not know everything, then the student cannot be expected to have full mastery. If the faculty member chooses not to share such information with the students, the students will deduce for themselves the strengths and weaknesses of the faculty member, share their impressions with each other, and proceed with the awareness that the instructor has been less than fully honest with them. This jeopardizes the trust in the instructor-student relationship.

Supervision of Learning Experiences

Supervision of clinical experiences falls into several phases: the selection of learning experiences as reflected in the assignments, the pre-experience conferencing with the student, the actual overseeing of the enactment of the assignment, and the concluding conference or summary of the experience. Instructors have different styles of supervision. Some instructors supervise very closely, expecting every activity to be communicated or discussed prior to enactment. Other instructors allow students more independent action so that the quality of the students' judgment can be assessed more accurately. This greater freedom involves more risk-taking for the instructor. The ideal position is for the instructor to allow enough freedom for the students to problem solve to a point where the care of the patient does not suffer. Students must have freedom to make mistakes as long as those mistakes are not big ones that jeopardize the care of the patient. This is a fine line that is difficult to discern and one that is affected by experience on the part of the faculty member. New faculty members can utilize more experienced instructors to help them develop this perspective. Experience is the best teacher, and both student and instructor will make mistakes before a sense of an appropriate level of supervision is evolved.

Clinical instructors have a responsibility to help students reduce their anxiety in the clinical situation. It is very normal for nursing students to be very anxious when they are engaging in an act of actual nursing for the first or second time. It is the responsibility of the instructor to recognize the strengths and the weaknesses of the students' performance, to use that assessment to reassure the students, and to guide fledgling professional behaviors (5). Because many situations in nursing can be embarrassing for the beginner, the instructor can also serve as a role model on how to handle such aspects of care as privacy, perineal care, enemas, catherizations, and pelvic examinations. Another approach to assist students to feel more comfortable with intimate aspects of care is to discuss feelings before and again after the experience, thus allowing the students to work their way through situations that are potentially uncomfortable for them. This allows the students to accept that their emotions and feelings are important to consider in the giving of nursing care. O'Shea and Parsons (13) discuss effective and ineffective teacher behaviors in clinical instruction.

A final function involved in supervision is for the instructor to accept the fact that students perceive situations differently than the instructor. The students may have different views about the instructor—student relationship or the care they have seen. The instructor has a responsibility to listen to the students' viewpoint and to deal with any complaints as sincerely and constructively as possible.

Evaluation of Learning

While the topic of evaluation of learning will be discussed in detail in Chapter 9, it is important to emphasize here the evaluation of student learning in the clinical area should be by established criteria. Phillips (14) discusses faculty plans for evaluation of students in the clinical setting.

The students should know what is expected and how the grade will be determined. Criteria for evaluation, ideally, are derived from the course objectives plus such considerations as the safety of the patient, the quality of the care given, and the demonstrated levels of competence and professional judgment. These factors may be itemized on a checklist or a statement of expected end of course behaviors that can be marked superior, good, satisfactory, or unsatisfactory performance. Data are obtained by direct observation, diaries, staff reports, medical records, anecdotal notes, and other tools.

Technical error is an indication that the student lacks specific knowledge. Normative error is an error of judgment and may indicate that the value system of the student is different from that of the professional person. The management of medical failure in terms of technical and normative error is discussed by Bosk in *Forgive and Remember* (1) and has many parallels for nursing education. Failing performance must be recognized and addressed by the instructor (12). To report errors made, an incident report is made to the agency, and, if necessary, corrective measures are instituted. If criteria for satisfactory performance have been clearly identified, the deficiency of performance should be very evident. Students are entitled to have warning that their performance is in jeopardy and what measures are necessary to bring the performance to a satisfactory level. Instructors need detailed notes of student performance so that the decision on that performance may be justified. Subjective judgment alone will not suffice. Also, the instructor must supervise the failing student very closely so that the quality of nursing care given does not become unsafe. A student who is giving unsafe care should be removed from the clinical situation until improvement is seen in knowledge and judgment. Both instructors and the agency can be liable for mistakes of negligence or malfeasance that a student makes (7). In the final analysis, the student does have a right to fail (9). In the final phases of clinical instruction, the information gathered is converted into a grade by the method of grading that has been determined for the course. A summary of performance is written by the instructor, and a final conference is held between the student and the instructor. If both agree as to the level of performance, the grade is recorded. If there is disagreement, the student is free to add comments to the evaluation and, if necessary, submit a grade appeal. Carefully worded criteria and defined expectations along with adequate recording of performance make the likelihood of grade appeals an infrequent occurrence. However objective the instructor strives to be, there always remains the element of subjectivity in clinical performance. Interpretation remains in the eye of the beholder. Observations by two or more people can validate interpretations. Input by the agency staff can make a valuable contribution to the evaluation process. In the final analysis, the evaluation should be an accurate reflection of the learning and the progress that the student has made in relation to the objectives outlined for the course.

From an Agency Point of View

Karen Ehrat, R.N., M.S. Doctoral Candidate

The clinical component of nursing education serves as a medium for translating nursing theory into observable and definable student behaviors and client outcomes. To be certain, a balance must be struck between classroom and clinical instruction. That balance, however, may be unique for each individual.

The Value of Clinical Instruction

The value of clinical instruction hinges on both the quality of clinical learning experiences made available and the expertise of those providing formal and informal instruction and direction. The student's task is to integrate the application of the theoretical knowledge and skill with the norm of practice in any given clinical setting. It is prerequisite that the sites for clinical instruction be selected carefully and that students' objectives and clinical offerings be synchronous.

The end product of effective clinical instruction is practitioners who are competent in the fundamental aspects of nursing practice and well grounded in the nursing process. Employers of graduate nurses expect a certain baseline competency in these two areas.

The Value of Simulated Experiences

The value of simulated learning cannot be overstated in either the academic or service setting. Simulation tools provide for learning while controlling the various distractor variables found in the real situation (11). This mode of teaching places emphasis on incremental learning without discounting the broader scope of reality. Demonstrated competency in a simulated situation is the highest order of a proficiency that can be obtained in other than a real-life event. The limitations of laboratory simulations are simply that they fail to capture the multivariate nature of reality. Thus, simulated learning cannot stand alone as a methodology for imparting nursing knowledge or skills. It can, however, serve as an effective adjunct to both teaching and learning.

Beyond assisting theory and skill acquisition, computer-assisted simulation can be utilized to teach the components of the decisionmaking process. Algorithms can be developed to guide the student through basic clinical decisionmaking (2). Although the algorithms may change, given variable clinical situations, the analytic approach to decisionmaking stays constant. The result is that students learn to develop a rationale to support their clinical decisions and subsequent actions.

The utilization of computer-assisted simulation has positive ramifications beyond the imparting of knowledge. The student becomes familiar with both computer logic and computer hardware. Given the growing complexity of health care, computers are becoming a vital component in health care delivery systems. Thus, the student with computer experience can approach the changing health care system with a higher level of confidence.

Factors in Planning Clinical Instruction

From a clinical agency perspective, there is a separate set of planning variables to be jointly considered by agency personnel and faculty. It is important that clinical experiences be structured in a fashion to promote maximum student learning and to complement unit operations. Factors to be considered include:

1. Philosophy and mission of the health care agency
2. Organizational network
3. Patient acuity
4. Census variation and bed capacity
5. Staffing patterns, patient care modality, nurse-patient ratios, staff mix, and unit stability
6. Unit operations
7. Faculty orientations
8. Interface with agency orienting staff
9. Student to student interfaces
10. Role of agency staff in student learning.

Philosophy and Mission of the Health Care Agency

The written philosophy and mission statement of a health care agency can provide faculty with a conceptual orientation to the institution. Specifically, the agency's view on student learning, clinical research, and ongoing employee education are important elements for faculty to consider when selecting clinical instruction sites. Student learning is optimized in situations where there is congruence between the philosophies and missions of the health care institutions and the academic program. A supportive posture toward higher learning and multidiscipline education serves as an indicator in institutional receptivity to clinical instruction programs.

Organizational Network

The table of nursing organization within the health care agency can provide faculty with an overview of the formal nursing structure and the appropriate channels for communications flow. It is important that faculty understand the formal organizational network in order to deal effectively within the system. During the initial clinical planning stages, resources to assist faculty in problem-solving and conflict resolution should be clearly identified by the host agency. In most organizations, those resource persons will interface closely with the assigned clinical areas. When consensus of problem resolution cannot be effected at that organizational level, a secondary resource should be designated by the health care agency.

The communications flow within an organization is of fundamental importance to faculty. Procedural changes, policy revisions, inservice continuing education announcements, and other key communications follow a designated pathway through an organization. It is important that faculty identify that pathway and interface with that flow of information

Patient Acuity

The selection of a given clinical area for student learning should be a joint decision between the clinical agency representatives and the faculty. Though the construction of student objectives falls within the domain of the academic program, those objectives must be clearly translated and understood by agency personnel. It is critical that the student objectives be matched to appropriate patient populations. That matching process is facilitated by considering patient acuity classifications. In essence, a patient acuity classification scheme is an agency mechanism for rating the intensity of nursing care requirements in various clinical areas. The inappropriate meshing of student objectives and acuity parameters may result in both suboptimal student learning experiences and nursing staff-nursing student conflicts. The appropriate selection of a clinical area is fundamental to the students' meeting the course objectives. It is useful for involved faculty to become familiar with the acuity rating scheme utilized by the clinical facility prior to a joint planning session.

Census Variation and Bed Capacity

Another key consideration for both faculty and agency personnel has to do with the consistency of the patient census and the overall bed capacity of any given clinical area. To the degree possible, students should be assigned to stable census units that can support an entire learning group. In order to maximize student learning and facilitate unit operations, numbers must be considered. The complexity of student objectives, previous student experience, instructor proficiency, staff proficiency, patient acuity, census, and bed capacity are all variables that influence the number of students to be accommodated on any given clinical unit. In general, a 40-bed unit with an average patient acuity of 85 percent can comfortably support eight basic students. As student expertise increases and as higher order objectives are incorporated, the number of students who can be comfortably accommodated decreases. In other words, the number of students to be accommodated tends to vary inversely with student expertise and program expectations.

Staffing Patterns, Patient Care Modality, Nurse-Patient Ratio, Staff Mix, and Unit Stability

Effective integration of student clinical learning experience into unit operations necessitates the consideration of various staffing and staff-related variables.

Staffing patterns of eight-, ten-, twelve- or variable hour assignments may impact on student learning. As an example, if a ten-hour staffing pattern is utilized, student hours may need to be adapted so that students can be present for the nursing report and other valued activities.

Likewise, the patient care modality in operation may contribute to or hinder the students' meeting their objectives. If course objectives require team leading experience, it would be inappropriate to place students in a clinical area utilizing a primary care modality. A more liberal interpretation of that same objective of leadership focus could be satisfied on a unit utilizing this care delivery methodology.

The nurse-patient ratio is also a factor which contributes to student learning outcomes. An overabundance of staff may compromise the students' learning opportunities, while a staffing deficiency may limit the resources available to assist the learning process. It may be useful for faculty to compare budgeted with actual staffing and to review other staffing parameters. The hours of direct nursing care provided per patient are data that can serve as a reasonable indicator of staffing when compared with acuity measures.

Equally as important as the nurse-patient ratio is the staff mix. In an acute care facility, it is generally true that a minimum of 60 percent of the caregivers are licensed as registered nurses and practical nurses. There is a direct relationship between patient acuity and the percentage of licensed caregivers. As the acuity increases, the percentage of licensed nurses increases, and the greater the number of registered nurses. Depending upon the degree of teaching support desired or expected by faculty, the staff mix may be an important variable to consider.

The final staffing variable that influences the success of student learning has to do with unit stability. Turnover statistics can provide pertinent information regarding unit stability, and should be considered along with other staffing variables when selecting appropriate clinical areas for student learning.

Unit Operations

Unit operations is a generic term that encompasses such things as report time, method for giving report, distribution of personnel assignments, dietary arrangements, supplies, replenishments, charting methodology, drug distribution system, and other services. It is useful in the clinical planning phase to consider how students will interface with these activities.

Of paramount importance is the methodology utilized within the clinical area for making patient care assignments. An agreed-upon system for selecting student assignments should be decided in the planning phase. To the degree possible, that system should complement rather than disrupt the established method for making unit personnel assignments.

It is useful for faculty to establish an informal channel of communication with unit personnel for the purpose of identifying clients with care needs congruent with students' objectives. Learning can be facilitated when unit personnel have a clear understanding of procedures and nursing care routines with which students need experience.

Perhaps one of the more useful approaches for ensuring the

successful integration of unit operations with student learning activities is for the faculty to meet on a routine basis with unit personnel. This may be accomplished independent of, or in conjunction with, scheduled staff meetings. The purpose of this routine meeting is to provide a vehicle for both collaborative problem solving and future planning. It is also a means for providing feedback to unit personnel regarding their interactions with students. Just as performance feedback is critical to student performance, feedback to staff influences future student interactions.

Faculty Orientation

It is the expectation of health care agencies that affiliating faculty will practice competent nursing and will be proficient in the clinical area in which they are assigned to teach. Health care agencies accept the responsibility for providing faculty with varying degrees of facility and clinical area orientation as outlined in the contractual agreement.

It may be valuable for faculty new to any given agency to participate in portions of the new employee orientation. Commonly, employee orientation provides a philosophic overview of the institution, identifies key administrative personnel, and reviews critical policies and procedures. Participation in select orientation sessions may assist faculty in becoming familiar with the agency.

Prior to bringing students into a given clinical area, faculty may wish to be involved in the patient care routines specific to that area. This involvement serves three main purposes. It allows the faculty member to become familiar with patient care standards, unit operations, and management styles. It provides faculty time for any necessary skill review. Perhaps most importantly, this involvement contributes to building effective rapport between agency staff and the faculty member. Clearly, a collegial relationship positively influences student clinical learning experiences.

During the faculty orientation, it is important that the following parameters regarding student practice be established:

1. Students' role in fire or disasters
2. Students' role in medical emergency
3. Students' role in taking and transcribing physicians' orders
4. Protocol to be followed in the event of patient incident or error

From an Agency Point of View

5. Students' role in reporting real or suspected infections
6. System for double-checking students' preparation of medications
7. Protocol to be followed in the event of student injury
8. Method for students to obtain patient care assignments
9. Protocol for student access to medical records
10. System for students to notify clinical area of nonattendance during scheduled hours
11. System for contacting students or faculty during unassigned hours
12. Primary responsibility for supervising procedure and tasks unfamiliar to students.

New technology and treatment regimes tend to grow exponentially within acute care clinical facilities. This growth makes it difficult for even the most experienced nurse to stay abreast of current practice. Within the academic setting, new theories of nursing are explicated, and research contributions are commonplace. A useful tool for assisting the development of effective collaborative service-education relationships is to structure cross-sharing sessions, tapping the expertise of both groups.

Interface with Agency Orienting Staff

Historically, the ebb and tide of available nursing manpower has defied scientific prediction. Yet, with certain precision, one can forecast that large groups of newly hired nurses will have an impact upon a health care agency at the beginning of student clinical rotations. Thus, preplanning and a spirit of cooperation is necessary between faculty and agency personnel.

Inexperienced nurses are frequently viewed as competing with students for clinical learning experiences. In most instances, the health care agency prioritizes those learning situations in favor of the new employee, owing to orientation cost factors. Various creative solutions can be jointly planned to ensure adequate learning for both groups. Sample solutions may be to rotate new employees to similar clinical areas for beginning experiences or to arrange brief alternative student learning experiences. It is critical that both faculty and agency leadership personnel participate in this problem-solving process. The end objective is to provide meaningful learning experiences for both students and orienting nurses.

Student-to-Student Interfaces

Multiple nursing programs within a geographic region may necessitate those programs sharing clinical space provided by a single health care facility. To the extent possible, the health care agency attempts to make clinical space available on an equitable basis among programs. The numbers of students involved may require the use of a single clinical area for various levels of student experience. In order for the area to accommodate students at different levels, it is critical that nursing personnel clearly understand the objectives of each student group. It may also be useful for the various faculty members to establish a cooperative working relationship.

In any given clinical area, the greater the number and variability of the caregivers, the greater the need for overall patient care coordination. The literature is replete with evidence that continuity of care is a factor influencing both patient recovery and satisfaction. It may also be an index for monitoring patient risk. To ensure the ongoing provision of quality patient care, it is important that continuity be structured into that care.

Quality-oriented health care agencies may have policies regulating continuity, particularly sequential student assignments. For example, it may be against agency policy for a particular patient to be sequentially and repeatedly cared for by students. Owing to students' lack of familiarity with physicians' routines, long-range care goals, unit operations, and other such factors, the likelihood of omission or commission errors is thought to increase if students are sequentially assigned. Faculty sharing a clinical area can assist in the provision of care continuity by observing all student group assignments and selecting patients accordingly. An ordered interspersing of agency personnel in patient care delivery is easily achieved when a cooperative planning process is utilized.

Role of Agency Staff in Student Learning

Student growth and learning is either fostered or hindered by role models in the clinical agency. To a large degree, the posture assumed by the agency nurses hinges upon their understanding of the role the academic program desires them to assume. In all instances, agency nurses are accountable for the care rendered within their area and to their assigned patients. It is, therefore, fundamental to articulate clearly the scope of faculty supervision of students and the scope of agency nurse supervision of care.

In most instances, faculty assume responsibility for supervising new clinical procedures the students perform. It is less clear who assumes responsibility for supervising repeated procedures and the course of action to be taken when the faculty member is unavailable to assist with new procedures. There is no prescriptive method for resolving these concerns. Rather, these issues must be addressed and resolved in the planning phase of the clinical experiences and then clearly communicated to the nursing staff. There are certain procedures or care routines that may be best supervised by agency personnel with the faculty member providing student support. These procedures might include experimental therapeutic measures, intra-aortic balloon-assisted circulation, or other new and complex procedures that may be beyond faculty expertise.

The key to providing meaningful student learning and coordinated unit operations is collaborative planning and problem-solving between the faculty member and the leadership of the clinical area.

References

1. Bosk, C.L. *Forgive and Remember.* Chicago: University of Chicago Press, 1979.
2. Burke, R.L. *CAI Sourcebook.* Englewood Cliffs: Prentice-Hall, 1982.
3. Carlson, J.H., Craft, C.A., and McGuire, A.D. *Nursing Diagnosis.* Philadelphia: Saunders, 1982.
4. Cazalas, M. *Nursing & the Law* (3rd ed.). Germantown: Aspen Systems, 1978.
5. Chase, B.M. Clinical Experiences Made Easy. *JNE* 22:347, 1983.
6. Clock Hours of Clinical Experiences in Schools of Nursing. Mimeographed. Phoenix: Arizona State Board of Nursing, n.d.
7. Creighton, M. *Law Every Nurse Should Know* (4th ed.). Philadelphia: Saunders, 1981.
8. Graham, B.A. and Gleit, C.J. Clinical Sites Used in Baccalaureate Programs. *Nurs. Outlook* 29:291, 1981.
9. Hill, J.R. The Right To Fail. *Nurs. Outlook* 13(4):41, 1965.
10. Kim, M.J. *Pocket Guide to Nursing Diagnoses* (3rd ed.). St. Louis: Mosby, 1984.
11. Lange, C.M. Simulation for Teaching Clinical Competencies. In *Utilization of the Clinical Laboratory for a Baccalaureate Nursing Program.* New York: National League for Nursing, 1978.

12. Meisenhelder, J.B. Clinical Evaluation—An Instructor's Dilemma. *Nurs. Outlook* 30:348, 1982.
13. O'Shea, H.S. and Parsons, M.K. Clinical Instruction: Effective and Ineffective Teacher Behaviors. *Nurs. Outlook* 27:(6)411, 1979.
14. Phillips, M.K. Faculty Plans for Evaluation of Students in the Clinical Setting. NLN Publ. No. 16-1763:38, 1979.
15. Rambo, B.J. and Wood, L.A. *Nursing Skills for Clinical Practice* (3rd ed.). Philadelphia: Saunders, 1982.
16. Statement from Pima College and the University of Arizona Nursing Faculties. Mimeographed. Tucson: University of Arizona, 1982.
17. Tarnow, K.G. Working with Adult Learners. *Nurse Educator* 4(5):34, 1969.

Suggested Readings

Bevil, C.W. and Gross, L.C. Assessing the Adequacy of Clinical Learning Settings. *Nurs. Outlook* 29:658, 1981.

Carpenito, L.J. and Duespohl, T.A. *A Guide for Effective Clinical Instruction.* Gaithersburg: Aspen Systems, 1981.

Council of Baccalaureate and Higher Degrees. *Arrangements Between an Institution of Higher Education and Agencies Which Provide Learning Laboratories for Nursing Education.* NLN Publ. No. 15-776. New York: National League for Nursing, 1973.

Cross, K.P. Barriers to Adult Learning. *AAHE Bulletin* 34:1, 1981.

Curran, C.L. and Lengarcher, C.A. RN Re-Entry Programs: Programmatic and Personal Considerations. *Nurse Educator* 7(4):29, 1982.

Dale R. Contracting for Student Clinical Experience. *Nurse Educator* 1:22, 1976.

deTornyay, R., and Thompson, M.A. *Strategies for Teaching Nursing* (2nd ed.). New York: Wiley, 1982.

Eble, K.E. *The Craft of Teaching.* San Francisco: Jossey-Bass, 1976.

Gross, L.C. and Bevil, C.W. The Use of Testing to Modify Curricula for RN's. *Nurs. Outlook* 29:541, 1981.

Hale, S. and Boyd, B.T. Accommodating RN Students in Baccalaureate Nursing Programs. *Nurs. Outlook* 29:535, 1981.

Haukenes, E. and Mundt, M.H. The Selection of Clinical Learning Experiences in the Nursing Curriculum. *JNE* 22:372, 1983.

McKeathie, W.J. (ed.). *Learning, Cognition, and College Teaching.* San Francisco: Jossey-Bass, 1980.

National League for Nursing. *Considerations in Clinical Evaluation: Instructors, Students, Legal Issues, Data.* NLN Publ. No. 16-1764. New York: National League for Nursing, 1979.

Olivieri, P. and Sweeney, M.A. Evaluation of Clinical Learning: By Computer. *Nurse Educator* 5(4):26, 1980.

Smith, D.W. *Perspectives on Clinical Teaching* (2nd ed.). New York: Springer, 1977.

Tumminia, P.A. Teaching Problems and Strategies with Male Nursing Students. *Nurse Educator* 6(5):9, 1981.

Chapter 9

Evaluation of Learning

Arlene M. Putt, R.N., Ed.D.

Study Questions

1. When writing objective test questions, what principles are useful in constructing discriminating test items?
2. What are the characteristics of good essay questions?
3. How is the difficulty index of test items determined?
4. How is the reliability of a test calculated?
5. What are the component types of validity? Define each.
6. How does grading on a curve compare with normalized scores?
7. Under a percentage system, what percentage is passing? What percentage is superior? Defend your choices.
8. What are the merits of a pass-fail system of grading? What are the disadvantages?
9. What is contract grading?
10. How can an instructor avoid a large number of grade appeals?
11. What constitutes dishonest scholarship? How should an instructor deal with the students involved?

Learning Domains

Throughout this book, learning has been the topic of discussion. As described in Chapter 4, Bloom (2) categorized learning into cognitive, affective, and psychomotor domains—each of which is further divided into varying types. But how do we know when learning has occurred? Learning results in changes in behavior. Thus, can we say that the student has learned if there is a change of behavior between pre and post exposure to content? Maybe, but is the learning of the specific type and format that is desired?

153

Is the learning the result of experience provided in the course? Learning that is the product of a course of study must be specific to the content and to the objectives of that course of study. In short, learning resulting from a course of study is manifested by the fulfillment of the course objectives. Performance trials and examinations can be devised to measure the degree to which the course content and the course objectives have been mastered. Evaluation of learning requires measurement of learning in an organized and systematic manner (5). If one utilizes Bloom's taxonomy as a basis for the types of learning that occur in the learning of nursing knowledge and skills, one is then confronted with the evaluation of that learning in terms of the cognitive, affective, and psychomotor domains. While there are probably many other ways to organize nursing content and nursing skills, Bloom's taxonomy is a useful framework because of its breadth of modes of learning and its depth of the types of learning. This discussion will be focused upon test development utilizing Bloom's framework (2).

Test Development

The topic of test development includes the design of the test, the types of questions to be utilized, the level of learning to be tested, the test items and their reliability and validity (7, 12, 13, 14). By taking Bloom's taxonomy and making a grid of learning domains and course objectives, one can design a model of the types of learnings and the level of the learning to be evaluated. For example, one can consider each important segment of content and decide in which domain and at what level that content should be tested. A skeleton of such a grid appears in Figure 9-1.

Test Design

The design for a test includes the plan for the coverage of the content to be tested. The instructor has decisions to make on the specific content, the emphasis to place on each area, and the type of questions to ask.

Coverage of content   How to design the test to cover the content of the course is a prime consideration. One can randomly sample aspects of the content, or one can design a plan to test the content

Test Development

Figure 9-1 Course objectives in grid with Bloom's domains of learning

	Domains		
	Cognitive	Affective	Psychomotor
Course Objectives			
1.			
2.			

at selected points and at selected depths of understanding (2, 4, 5). One plan for this was described in Figure 9-1.

Types of questions The type of questions asked becomes an equally important aspect of evaluation of learning. The choices of question types are these.

Essay questions
Processing information
True-False questions
Five-option questions
Listing
Labeling
Multiple choice questions
Matching questions
Simulation (14).

The merits and disadvantages for each of these types of questions will be discussed in turn.

Essay questions have these merits.

1. Essay questions allow students the opportunity to organize and to express their own thinking on the topic.
2. Essay questions are excellent ways to test for application, analysis, synthesis, and evaluation of information.
3. Essay questions must have specific points included in the answer to warrant credit.
4. Essay questions discourage cheating.

Disadvantages of essay questions are as follows:

1. Essay questions are time-consuming to grade.
2. Unless the inclusion of specific points is adhered to, the grading of essay questions is open to criticism of subjectivity on the part of the instructor.
3. Unless the wording is carefully considered beforehand, essay questions may be open to more than one interpretation.
4. Because of their limited number per examination, essay questions weigh heavily in test scores.

Processing of information is a variant of the essay question. The processing of information is a higher order of learning in which the examinee is asked to take a set of information and to order a sequence of action, or to make a judgment on the basis of that information. Often the answer requires setting up a priority of actions to be taken to reach a desired outcome. The task does require thinking one or more steps beyond the input of the information given. Determining the priority of patient care activities is an example of this type of question.

True-false questions require a yes or no answer only. The advantages of true-false questions are these.

1. The statements are either true or false. If any part of the statement is false, the entire statement is considered false.
2. True-false questions are excellent for testing knowledge and comprehension.
3. True-false questions are easily graded.
4. True-false questions are concise statements, each of which is considered on its own merits.

Disadvantages of true-false statements are as follows:

1. True-false statements require careful reading. One word can falsify the statement.
2. True-false questions are poorly adapted to testing judgment.
3. True-false questions require the examinee to think in polarized fashion.
4. True-false questions may be difficult for the superior student to answer because of the limited range of thinking required.

Five-option questions are a variant of the true-false statement. The five options questions consists of two paired statements and the examinee has the problem of determining:

1. If both statements are true
2. If both statements are false
3. If one is true and the other false
4. If the second statement is logically derived from the first statement.

While designed to test higher order learnings, the fact remains that students have difficulty in determining what constitutes a logical relationship between statement one and statement two. For this reason this form of testing has lost support.

Listing is a form of recall of information and organization of the material. It is a test of knowledge and comprehension but not a test of utilization of material.

Labeling questions test recognition and association but do not test usage of information. Therefore, this type of question tests lower levels of learning.

Multiple choice questions consist of a stem composed of an incomplete sentence or a question stating the basic problem, followed by four or five options from which the examinee must choose a correct answer. The options presented must be plausible answers so that the examinee has equal likelihood of choosing any of them. Thus, the element of guessing the correct answer is equal in all questions. To discourage sheer guessing, one format that can be used is to weight incorrect answers more heavily than one so that, if the student is not certain of the correct response, guessing may decrease the score.

In reality, the options are themselves true-false statements. The item as a whole should have one clear-cut answer. Care must be taken to use language that is clear and to avoid catch questions. Answering should not depend upon vocabulary or reading skills but upon knowledge and judgment derived from that knowledge. The items should be concise and at a level of difficulty appropriate to the examinee's ability.

Multiple choice questions do present the instructor with the possibility of testing at various levels of knowledge from fact to understanding, application, analysis, synthesis, and evaluation. Multiple choice questions can be utilized with any level of learner. They also are easily arranged into alternative formats for parallel examinations to discourage cheating by students.

Disadvantages of multiple choice questions are several. Good items are time consuming to construct and may require repeated editing to develop reliable and discriminating questions. Also, the questions may be used singly without any relationship to the previous questions.

Since the advantages of multiple choice questions and the range of their possibilities are great, they remain the mainstay of the standardized examination. Sources of information on multiple choice examinations are the Educational Testing Service and the National League for Nursing (4, 13). Another source of information is the National Council of State Boards of Nursing which oversees the state board tests for the profession of nursing.

Simulation situations in mock format or videotape also provide a technique for presenting information from which questions testing knowledge and judgment are derived (15). Any of the above types of questions can be utilized with simulation questions.

Levels of Learning

When designing a test one prime consideration is determining the level of learning at which the test is to be constructed (4, 12, 13). Is the instructor satisfied to know that the student recognizes or recalls the information, or does the instructor require proof that the student can actually apply the information or analyze it or even synthesize it? If the goal of the course is to develop competency, then some measure of performance of that skill is needed in evaluating the outcome of the course. As discussed above in consideration of the various types of questions, certain types of questions are better adapted to testing certain types of intellectual abilities. In a high performance profession such as nursing, it is important to test for higher levels of cognitive functioning as a prelude to the reality of the working arena where higher levels of decisionmaking are a normal requirement. The situation of a student who has ample amounts of knowledge but who does not know how to use that knowledge is a very real experience for many nursing instructors. To avoid this dilemma, the instructor can give careful attention to the level at which the test questions are asked. To prepare students for higher order questioning, the instructor also must utilize such questions in the class sessions and in the class assignments so as to provide students with the opportunity to practice higher order thinking.

Also important is the testing for the level of learning of RN students who are either challenging or enrolling in a basic course. An accurate evaluation of their knowledge and judgment is needed (14).

Construction of Test Items

Taking the test design in hand, the instructor plans what content to cover and at what level to pose the question. A course outline of the content can be useful to determine adequate sampling of the major points of content in that outline. Then the decision is made as to the level at which the question should be asked. The instructor then decides how many and what types of questions to utilize. For instance, the instructor decides that the care of patients with hypertension is a major understanding and a skill that students should be acquiring. Therefore, the instructor allots six questions to the care of patients with hypertension. The instructor can ask six separate questions or construct a concise patient care problem involving the treatment and care of a patient with hypertension, and then ask six questions that relate to that situation. The use of patient care situations more closely simulates the reality of health care and thus allows the student to think through an entire sequence of events involved in the care of one common health care problem.

Some thought needs to be given as to the construction of the stem of the questions (4, 9)) The stem holds most of the necessary information of the question so the stem must be short and clearly worded. Caution should be heeded regarding the use of negative statements. They tend to confuse the examinee and must be read very carefully for clarity. It is also helpful to underline key words in such instances. The use of double negatives should be avoided entirely.

Options should be grammatically correct in relation to the stem. The options should also be homogenous, plausible, and provide no clues to the correctness of the answer. If options are a sequence of numbers or dates, they are best arranged in the logical order. The items should not be interdependent; that is, the answer to question two should not depend upon a correct answer to question one. Furthermore, the location of the correct answer should be randomized and not set into a predictable pattern (13).

The overall length of the test should be that three-fourths of the class can complete it without difficulty in the time allotted. The instructor should plan an appropriate amount of time for the test. Speed tests put added stress upon the students. Higher blood pressure readings are commonly found in students undergoing testing. Thus, the stress levels upon the students may be much greater than the stress anticipated by the instructor. The wise instructor will not develop tests that are marathons. All that is required of a test is to sample the achievement level of the knowledge and skill of the student at several points along the line of content in the course. The sampling should be free of bias and be fair to all students (4, 13).

How does one know how good a test item is? First, one can make a prediction as to what percentage of the students will answer the item correctly. Frequently this prediction is grossly in error. The only valid way to assess the usefulness of any item is to analyze the results of a test after a group of students answer that item. For this analysis there are two useful measurements: the *index of difficulty* and the *index of discrimination* (8).

The index of difficulty is the percentage of students who get the item correct (8). The index of difficulty can be calculated by taking the number of students who got the item correct, dividing by the total number of students taking the test, and multiplying by 100 to convert the answer to a percentage (8, p. 211). Actually the higher the index of difficulty, the more students who got it correct and the less difficult the item really is. While every test should have a few easy items, items with high indices of difficulty serve little purpose in discriminating the high achievers from the low achievers. For that function the index of discrimination is needed.

The index of discrimination is the degree to which the item separates the high scorers from the low scorers (8). To obtain this value, the entire range of scores is ranked from high to low and the upper third of the scores is sorted from the lower third of scores in the range. Then the index of discrimination for any one item is the number of students in the upper third of the class who got the item correct minus the number of students in the lower third of the class who got the item correct, divided by one-half of the total number of students taking the test (13). If an equal number of students in both the high and the low scoring groups get the item correct, the index of discrimination for that item is zero. It is also possible for an item to have a negative index of discrimination—the result of a greater number of students in the lower group getting the item correct. If this is the case, there is something wrong with the item. There are several reasons for negative discrimination.

1. The key is not correct.
2. There is more than one correct answer.
3. The question is ambiguous.
4. The intended answer is flawed.
5. The students are guessing.
6. The item is either difficult or different in context (13).

Items with low or negative discrimination should be revised or discarded.

While we have talked about individual items, how does one evaluate the test as a whole? The entire test should be tested for *reliability* and *validity*. What does test reliability mean? What is test validity?

Reliability

Reliability in a test is the consistency with which a test measures the same thing (6, 8). It should be a stable measurement over time. Reliability is a statistical concept, expressed as a correlational coefficient between testing number one and testing number two. This coefficient can be obtained by any one of several methods: test-retest method, equivalent forms methods, split-half method, or the Kuder-Richardson 20 or 21 formula. The KR 20 formula is based upon the proportions of persons passing each item and the standard deviation of the total test scores. The KR 21 is easier to compute and is based upon the number of correct answers. These formulas and their explanations are to be found in any statistics or measurement text (8, p. 83). The standard error or measurement, the estimate of the variation to be expected in the scores, is also a type of measurement of reliability.

The reliability coefficients tend to increase with the length of the test because greater test length gives more sampling of knowledge and tends to decrease the effects of guessing. Measurement textbooks can be consulted for discussions of desirable levels of reliability coefficients for various types of tests.

Validity

Validity pertains to the results of a test and the purpose for which that test is given. Validity is a matter of degree (6, 7, 8).

There are four types of validity: *content validity, predictive validity, concurrent validity,* and *construct validity.* Content validity is how well the test measures the subject matter and the behaviors sought. Predictive validity is how well the test predicts future performance. Concurrent validity is how well the test results compare to some other measure. Construct validity is how well the test results can be interpreted in relation to some abstract psychological concept such as reasoning or logical inference which is derived from indirect evidence. The aim of construct validity is to explain all factors influencing performance on a test. Thus, construct validity is an important concept in all types of testing (8, p. 61).

There are many factors that affect both the reliability and the validity of test results. However, a test first must be reliable before it can be evaluated as valid. The essence of validity is to express to what extent the test results will serve the particular use for which the test was intended. For methods of determining the validity of a test, consult a measurement textbook.

Scoring and Grading Systems

There are several ways to score a test (8). One can grade on the basis of *raw scores*, the percentage of correct answers, a weighted score, or a standard score. Also, a decision must be made as to whether the scores obtained will be compared to norms obtained by other groups, a *norm-referenced method*, or compared to a criterion level of mastery, a *criterion-referenced method* (3, 6, 10). The decision of which way to score a test involves the competency level desired (1) and the philosophy of testing of learning (9).

If one utilizes raw scores for grading, one is likely to rank papers in order, to look for natural breaks in the sequence, and then to base the grades on the occurrence of natural breaks. The problem with this method is that there is no criterion measure for what constituted an A or a B grade. It is an arbitrary method. The breaks in the range occur by chance alone and are not likely to be statistically significant. Gentile and Stevens-Haslinger (6) argue that if scores are not statistically significantly different, the grade should be the same.

Grading on the curve is another much utilized method in which the instructor decides that a certain percentage of the grades will be A, another percentage will be B, and so on. Then the scores are ranked from top to bottom, the predetermined percentage calculated, and grades assigned. This is a norm-referenced method (6). The problem with this grading system is that it is also arbitrary. Before the test is given, it has been determined that there will be a set number of A, B, and C grades, regardless of the achievement level of the students. Different groups can be expected to perform differently. A letter grade does not really tell how the student scored. The students then have to compete against each other so as to get into the top percentage getting A grades. This encourages behaviors aimed at getting high grades at the expense of learning.

A variant of grading on the curve is to use the *mean and standard deviation* of the scores of the group (8). With this system, those students scoring 1.5 standard deviations, (sd) above the mean get a grade of A, those 0.5 to 1.45 sd above the mean get a grade of B, and those students scoring from 0.49 sd above the mean to 0.5 sd below the mean get a grade of C. This system does not determine in advance how many A's, B's, and C's there will be. However, the grade of any student is still a matter of that student's score in relation to the scores of the groups as a whole. One further step is to take the scores and convert them into standard scores by taking the mean and adding a value for the amount of the standard deviation that that score has from the mean. For example, the mean is 50 and the standard deviation is 10, so a standard score of 65 means that the student scored one and one-half standard deviations above the mean for the group. This is also called a T score. This then shows how one student compared to a large group of students who took the test (8).

There are three methods of mastery or criterion-referenced grading (6, 11). One method employs the *percentage grade*. The student is scored on the basis of the percentage of material that was correct. Under such a system the level of passing can vary but by common usage is frequently 60 percent. If that is the case, then 90–100 percent is A, 80–89 percent is B, 70–79 percent is C, and 60–69 percent is D. Sometimes in nursing, D grades are considered unsatisfactory and eliminated from the system, then the student must achieve 70 percent or higher to be considered as passing the material. The percentage system does allow the student to compete against self rather than other students. Achievement is related to the amount of material mastered, but the true amount of material to be mastered is still a concept in the eye of the instructor, and so the standard is more relative than

163

absolute. As argued by Gentile and Stevens-Haslinger (6) there really is no statistical difference between a 79 and an 80; therefore, the grade should be the same.

A variation of the percentage method is the *contract-for-grade method* in which a student understands that if all course objectives are achieved at a high level of performance, the course grade will be A (11, 16). If the major objectives are achieved and some of the minor objectives are obtained, the grade will be B. If most of the objectives are obtained, the grade will be C. This method requires clear communication beforehand as to what behaviors constitute an A or a B level of achievement.

A third method is the *pass-fail system* where the only distinction that is made is whether the performance was at a satisfactory level or not. While the pass-fail system takes pressure off of the grading, there is no way to reward students for superior performance or to indicate the relative level of that performance. Pass-fail systems also create problems for transfer of credit as the grade point average cannot be calculated.

Clearly, by now the reader should be aware that there is no perfect system for grading. All systems have arbitrarily defined limits that the students are expected to meet. Unfortunately, a grade of A does not mean the same thing to different classes, different instructors, or to different education systems (17). Each instructor has a responsibility to clarify what material is to be mastered to what degree. The grade should reflect, as well as possible, the relative mastery of the content and skills of the course. If all scores are converted to standard scores, weighted, and summed before grades are assigned, partial values can be retained to give the student credit for finer points. Standard scores do reduce the subjectivity and the tendency to be influenced by conditions other than measurement of learning (8).

Grade Appeals

The process by which students can appeal their course grades is formalized in many educational institutions. The first and obvious step is to discuss the grade with the instructor. The instructor should be able to justify to the student the way in which the grade was determined and how that derivation was consistent for all students in the class. If the student cannot accept this reasoning or has evidence of unfairness, the next step is to appeal to the course chairperson, the department head, or the dean. Many colleges have committees to hear student grade appeals and to recommend further action.

The procedure for grade appeal is long and tedious and produces stress for both the instructor and the student (14). Many potential grade appeals can and should be handled on a one- to-one basis with calm, considered discussion between the student and the instructor. Grade appeals are less likely to arise if the students have a statement in writing at the beginning of the class specifying how the final grade will be determined. The instructor has a basic right to determine how a course will be graded as long as the instructor's policy does not conflict with that of the college as a whole. No pressure should be brought to bear upon an instructor to change a student's grade. If the instructor's method of grading is out of line, the matter can be referred to the administrative person in charge to work out a compromise for future use.

Dishonest Scholarship

Unfortunately, while instructors prefer to view all students as honest, cases of dishonest scholarship do arise from time to time. Most educational institutions have prescribed penalties for dishonest scholarship. What constitutes dishonesty may vary somewhat from one institution to another, but it invariably includes:

1. Cheating on a test.
2. Handing in another's work as one's own. This includes having another person write the paper or lifting passages from printed works of others without credit or permission.
3. Altering grades or work submitted (18).

To avoid later confrontations, students should be made aware at the beginning of the program or course as to what the acceptable rules of scholarship are. When infractions of the rules do occur, the instructor should ask the student to explain the behavior, and then the matter should be referred to the course chairperson or dean. Again, many institutions have a formal system of hearing committees and trial boards to investigate such matters. In such procedures, the rules of due process apply. The student must be informed of the charges and have a chance for self-defense. The instructor must have evidence of such a serious charge of misconduct as the consequences for the student are severe. The student can lose credit, lose respect, and may even be suspended from the program. To avoid undue pressure on students, the instructor can clarify alternatives such as incomplete grades or make-up opportunities. In the end, the instructor must evaluate the students' achievement as fairly as possible and transcribe those evaluations into grades that bear evidence of the level of achievement in that course of study.

References

1. Benner, P. Issues in Competency-Based Testing. *Nurs. Outlook* 30:303, 1982.
2. Bloom, B. (ed.). *Taxonomy of Educational Objectives: The Classification of Educational Goals.* Handbook I. Cognitive Domain. New York: David McKay, 1956. Handbook II. Affective Domain. New York: David McKay, 1964.
3. Bower, F.L. Normative- or Criterion-referenced Evaluation. *Nurs. Outlook* 22:499, 1974.
4. Educational Testing Service. Making Your Own Tests: A Work Kit. Princeton: Cooperative Test Division, Educational Testing Service, 1967.
5. Fuhrmann, B.C. and Grasha, A.F. *A Practical Handbook for College Teachers.* Boston: Little, Brown, 1983.
6. Gentile, J.R. and Stevens-Haslinger, C.A. Comprehensive Grading System. *Nurs. Outlook* 31:49, 1983.
7. Glaser, R. and Nitko, A.J. Measurement in Learning and Instruction. in R.L. Thorndike (ed.), *Educational Measurement.* Washington, D.C.: American Council on Education, 1971.
8. Gronlund, N.E. *Measurement and Evaluation in Teaching.* New York: Macmillan, 1965.
9. Jernigan, D.K. Testing—A Learning not Grading Process. *Nurs. Outlook* 28:120, 1980.
10. Krumme, U.S. The Case for Criterion-referenced Measurement. *Nurs. Outlook* 23:764, 1975.
11. Kruse, L.C. and Fager Barger, D.M. Development and Implementation of a Contract Grading System. *JNE* 21(5):31, 1982.
12. MacAvoy, S. and Welch, L.B. Tips on Test Construction. *JNE* 20(3):15, 1981.
13. National League for Nursing. *Developing Tests to Evaluate Student Achievement in Baccalaureate Nursing Progress.* NLN Publ. No. 15–1761. New York: National League for Nursing, 1979.
14. Office of Institutional Research and Development. *How To Avoid A Grade Appeal.* Tucson: University of Arizona, n.d.
15. Richards, A., Jones, A., Nickols, K., Richardson, F., Riley B., and Swinson, R. Videotape as an Evaluation Tool. *Nurs. Outlook* 29:35, 1981.
16. Schoolcraft, V. and Delaney, C. Contract Grading in Clinical Evaluation. *JNE* 21(1):6, 1982.
17. Spray, C.O. Meaningful Grade Reporting. *Clearinghouse* 43:338, 1969.
18. University of Arizona. *Code of Academic Integrity.* Tucson: University of Arizona, 1983..

Suggested Readings

Aleamoni, L. *Technical Report: Kinds of Examinations.* Urbana: Office of Instructional Resources, University of Illinois, 1968.

Anastasi, A. *Psychological Testing.* New York: Macmillan, 1976.

Astin, A.W. Let's Try a 'Value Added' Approach to Testing. *Chron. Higher Educ.* 24(22):40, 1982.

Bloom, B.S., Hastings, J.T., and Madaus, G.F. *Handbook on Formative and Summative Evaluation of Student Learnings.* New York: McGraw-Hill, 1971.

Bondy, K.N., Criterion-referenced Definitions for Rating Scales in Clinical Evaluation. *JNE* 22:376, 1983.

Crancer, J., Maury-Hess, S., and Dunn, J. Contract Systems and Grading Policies. *JNE* 19(3):44, 1980.

Dash, E. *Contract for Grades.* Washington, D.C.: ERIC Clearinghouse on Higher Education, 1970.

Erickson, B. and Todd, C. In Quest of the Perfect Test. *Nurs. Outlook* 29:579, 1981.

Fowler, G.A. and Heater, B. Guidelines for Clinical Evaluation. *JNE* 22:402, 1983.

Glass, G.V. Standards and Criteria Bibliography. *J. Educ. Measurement.* 15:237, 1978.

King, E.C. Constructing Classroom Achievement Tests. *Nurse Educator* 3(5):30, 1978.

King, E.C. Determining and Interpreting Test Validity, Reliability, and Practicality. *Nurse Educator* 4(3):6, 1979.

Lenburg, C.L. *The Clinical Performance Examination.* New York: Appleton-Century-Crofts, 1979.

Magnusson, D. *Test Theory.* Reading, Mass.: Addison-Wesley, 1967.

Miller, P., Sr. Facilitating Student Grade Appeal Hearings. *Nurs. Outlook.* 29:186, 1981.

Mueller, D.J. Mastery Learning Partly Boon, Partly Boondoggle. *Teacher's College Record* 78:41, 1976.

Niedringhaus, L., and O'Driscoll, D.L. Staying Within the Law—Academic Probation and Dismissal. *Nurs. Outlook* 31:156, 1983.

Nunnally, J.D. *Psychometric Theory.* New York: McGraw-Hill, 1967.

Osborn, W.P. and Thompson, M.A. Variables Associated with Student Mastery of Learning Modules. in M.A. Batey (ed.), *Communicating Nursing Research* Vol. 9:167. Boulder: Western Interstate Commission for Higher Education, 1977.

Rezler, A.G. and Lee, R.W. Hope for that Hopeless Essay Test. *JNE* 16(11):5, 1977.

Ross, G.R. and Ross, M.C. Using the Computer to Prepare Multiple Choice Examinations: A Simplified System. *JNE* 16(5):32, 1977.

Schneider, H.L. *Evaluation of Nursing Competence.* Boston: Little, Brown, 1979.

Smeltzer, S.O. The New State Board Exam. *Nurs. Outlook* 30:312, 1982.

Westwick, C. Cultural Fair Testing. *JNE* 17:(1):35, 1978.

Whitley, T.W. Some Common Flaws in Multiple Choice Exam Questions. *Nurs. Outlook* 27:466, 1979.

Chapter 10

Evaluation of Teaching

Suzanne Van Ort, R.N., Ph.D.

Study Questions

1. What are the goals and objectives of a system for documenting teaching effectiveness?
2. What are the common characteristics of effective teaching?
3. What are the common models for a teaching effectiveness system?
4. What is included in each of the components of teaching effectiveness evaluation: student, peer, administrative, and self-evaluation?
5. What are three alternative measures for evaluating teaching effectivenesss?
6. What is a typical process for evaluating teaching using a developmental model?

The evaluation of teaching is essential in order to demonstrate that nursing's educational goals are being met in an effective, efficient manner. Teaching in collegiate schools of nursing involves the acquisition, transmission, and expansion of knowledge. These three functions are carried out by faculty in classroom and clinical settings with a diverse student population and a heterogeneous client population. Thus, the evaluation of teaching in nursing is a complex process that is continually being refined.

Teaching is always being evaluated, whether by formal or informal means. This chapter discusses the implementation of formal mechanisms within a faculty evaluation system.

Evaluation of teaching effectiveness is an important part of

This Chapter is reprinted, in part, from the *Journal of Nursing Education* October, 1983, Vol. 22, No. 8, pp. 324–328. Published by Slack Incorporated, Medical Publishers, copyright 1983. Used with permission.

faculty evaluation and must be viewed in that context. Any teaching effectiveness system should blend with the faculty evaluation system of the institution or program. Thus, teaching effectiveness, research productivity, and community service work will form a composite of faculty endeavor that is documented in a faculty evaluation system.

The purposes of faculty evaluation are to evaluate the institutional and program goals, identify individuals for rewards and personnel decisions, promote faculty growth, and maximize individual talent (1). Seldin (8) states that faculty evaluation has four primary goals: (1) improve faculty performance, (2) provide data for personnel decisions, (3) provide guidance to students in selecting faculty, and (4) provide data to outsiders.

In this context, there are two basic assumptions that underlie a faculty evaluation system. First, overall evaluation is inevitable (7). The current trend toward accountability mandates the utilization of a system for evaluating teaching. Also, there is no foolproof way to evaluate teaching; every evaluation system can be improved (3).

Regardless of the type of evaluation system that is designed, the system must reflect the institutional mission and goals, the program goals and expectations, and the faculty's level of educational preparation and experience. For example, in a research degree-granting institution, the emphasis upon the research mission will have an impact upon the teaching mission. Institutions with doctoral or master's degree programs in nursing have a research-oriented mission within which teaching and service may be of secondary importance in the reward system. If research and publication are the primary requisites for promotion and tenure, faculty will need to concentrate their faculty growth efforts in those areas. Consequently, the teaching improvement efforts may receive lower priority. Thus, the designers of evaluation systems need to consider the institutional and program missions and the structure of rewards available to faculty.

Characteristics of Effective Teaching

Characteristics of effective teaching have been validated in the literature and are useful in an evaluation system since they can be used as evaluative criteria. Irby (5) conducted several studies dealing with medical students' perceptions of clinical teachers in which he isolated six factors of clinical teaching effectiveness: (1) organization/clarity, (2) enthusiasm/stimulation, (3) instructor knowledge, (4) clinical competence, (5) clinical supervision, and (6) group instructional skill. Administrators' perceptions of effective teaching were demonstrated in Seldin's (8) study of 410 academic deans' views of effective teaching. Five factors described by academic deans included: (1) being well-prepared for class, (2) motivating students to do their best, (3) communicating effectively to the level of student, (4) demonstrating comprehensive knowledge, and (5) treating students with respect. These characteristics indicate that both students and administrators expect faculty to be knowledgeable, well-organized, sensitive to the needs of students, and able to communicate effectively.

One primary ingredient for success in evaluating teaching is an understanding of the teaching styles of the faculty and their educational experiences. An evaluation system should allow for individual faculty teaching styles to be evaluated equitably within the program goals and expectations.

Mann and his colleagues (6) describe six teaching styles that can be used to identify an individual's teaching style. Although most teachers are eclectic in nature, some characteristics may predominate. Mann's typology includes styles of expert, formal authority, socializing agent, facilitator, ego ideal, and person.

These teaching styles also need to be considered in the context of the predominant learning styles of the students. Using a nonstructured teaching style for teaching structure-dependent learners contributes to teaching-learning stress that impedes the learning process. Conversely, a structured teaching approach with flexibly oriented learners can be equally deleterious.

In addition, the characteristics of effective teaching may differ depending upon the setting. Four primary settings are used in nursing education: the classroom, the clinical laboratory, seminar or small group meetings, and the on-campus skills laboratory. All of these settings are educational environments; however, the environmental variables differ. For example, the teacher has control over and can manipulate the classroom environment. In the clinical setting, the number of variables increases and the teacher's control or ability to manipulate the learning environment varies. Also, events in the clinical area are unpredictable, and the teacher must be flexible in order to assist the students to learn while adapting to clinical events as they occur. Teaching effectiveness evaluation must consider the setting and variables affecting the teaching-learning interaction.

Evaluation Models

In a recent National League for Nursing publication, Applegate (1) discussed several evaluation models for documenting teaching effectiveness. The three models are not necessarily mutually exclusive; combinations can be used depending upon the program goals and expectations. A developmental model utilizes an open system in which data are collected on an ongoing basis for both faculty growth and personnel decisionmaking. The author emphasizes the need to separate growth and personnel data so that risk-oriented growth data do not have a deleterious effect on personnel decisions.

The personnel decision model provides for data collection only as needed for personnel decisions. This model would be useful to institutions that evaluate faculty only when data are needed for reappointment, promotion, tenure, or salary decisions. Data in this model are used to compare faculty with each other and with predetermined evaluative criteria.

The focus of the faculty growth model is on change to meet the individual's goals. This model may utilize a criterion-based or an objective-based system. Formative data are used to indicate growth or progress towards the individual's goals. In a criterion-based system, the faculty set standards by which they are evaluated. An objective-based system is predictive and outcome-oriented as faculty develop individual contracts for their own professional growth.

From these alternative models, it is possible to select an evaluation model to document teaching effectiveness in a given program. Some combination of models is also useful depending upon the program goals and faculty preferences (2).

Components of Teaching Effectiveness Evaluation

The most common components of teaching effectiveness evaluation are student evaluation, peer evaluation, self-evaluation, and administrative evaluation. Rating scales are the typical instruments for measuring teaching effectiveness.

Potential participants in teaching effectiveness evaluation include students, peers or colleagues, consumers, and nursing staff. Each setting needs to be examined and the contribution of each type of evaluator weighed. In the clinical area, teaching effectiveness evaluation by students, nursing staff, colleagues, and consumers may be possible. Selection of appropriate participants is crucial to obtaining accurate and realistic data.

Student Evaluation

In terms of reliability and validity of teaching effectiveness instruments, much research has been published about the various components of evaluation. In particular, student evaluation of teaching has been the subject of research for many years. Several systems are standardized and have been utilized with large numbers of students. The IDEA System at Kansas State University, the CIEQ at the University of Arizona, and the Purdue Cafeteria System are examples.

In terms of validity, the central issue is whether effective teachers are also rated highly by students. A high correlation between student evaluations of teaching effectiveness and student learning is desirable. However, the evidence here varies in consistency. Also, the influence of student level of learning is difficult to measure because of confounding variables. For example, the student's motivation to learn as well as the student's interest and ability may contribute at least as much to learning outcomes as does teaching effectiveness.

In addition to reliability and validity, several other correlates with student ratings have been the subject of research. Class size has been found to have a minimal effect on student ratings of teaching effectiveness (3). Instructors of classes under fifteen students often receive very high ratings, but beyond that the relationship between class size and student ratings of teaching effectiveness is minimal (3).

Sex composition, class level, academic rank of faculty, whether the course is required or elective, and student grade average have all been thought to affect student evaluation of teaching effectiveness. However, no consistent, replicable findings have been reported.

Finally, the teacher's personality is an important factor, and some believe that personal magnetism is essential to achieve high student ratings. Numerous studies conclude that teachers who have the highest student ratings are "substance" teachers and not merely entertainers. Furthermore, the positive effect of personal magnetism, when seen as enthusiasm for the subject matter, is also well-documented.

Thus, the reliability, validity, and correlates of student evaluations of teaching effectiveness have been the subjects of much research. When used appropriately, student evaluations of teaching are an important component in the overall evaluation of teaching.

Peer Evaluation

Peer or colleague evaluations constitute a second component for evaluating teaching. The definition of peer or colleague must be made before evaluation is planned. Is a fellow faculty member a peer or colleague? Must a peer be similarly educated or have similar clinical expertise? Should a colleague have the same academic rank? Each program's faculty must be explicit in defining these terms so that confusion is prevented and validity of data is assured.

Once the terms peer and colleague are defined, three types of evidence are desirable in peer evaluation: examination of instructional materials, observation of teaching through classroom visitation, and validation of student achievement. Instructional materials to be examined may include the course syllabus, course objectives, student assignments, examinations, teaching methods, textbooks, handouts, reading lists, course content outlines, or lecture notes. Evaluators may also scrutinize clinical assignments and their rationale, student evaluation criteria, and feedback mechanisms for student progress. Any or all of these instructional materials may be evaluated by peers or colleagues.

Classroom visitation is a controversial issue in nursing education. Some faculty believe that classroom visitation is threatening to their interaction with students. However, if the visitation is appropriately conducted, useful data can be obtained. First and foremost, the interaction between the teacher and evaluator must be preplanned and objective criteria used. The teacher and students need to be as comfortable as possible with the evaluation visit. A follow-up session should be planned after the visit to discuss with the evaluatee the outcome of the evaluation and any recommendations made by the evaluator.

A third type of peer evaluation may be a validation of student achievement. Evidence regarding students' learning, achievement on examinations, performance in the clinical area, and achievement in subsequent courses can be utilized to document effective teaching. Evidence that the teacher is fair and reasonable in evaluating student achievement is also important. These student progress indicators can be very useful as one component for evaluating teaching effectiveness.

In order to validate the usefulness of colleague evaluation, researchers have compared colleague ratings and student ratings of instructors. Centra (3) studied colleague ratings based on classroom visitation compared with student ratings. He found colleague ratings to be generous and higher than student ratings.

Furthermore, the effect of colleague bias is a serious issue which must be considered in peer evaluation. Repeated visits and observer training may decrease the effects of colleague bias and increase the reliability of the peer evaluations.

Self-evaluation

Self-evaluation as a component for evaluating teaching is a controversial method that is growing in popularity. As a method to improve teaching performance, self-evaluation is widely accepted. Its value in personnel decisionmaking is often questioned because of the subjectivity of the evaluation.

A study of 300 teachers in five colleges compared instructor self-evaluation with student ratings of the instructor (3). The highest correlations occurred in factual items and the lowest correlations on subjective items. Overall, only a modest correlation between self-evaluation and student ratings resulted.

In general, the literature suggests that of the uses for self-evaluation its use in personnel decisionmaking is less well validated or accepted than its use in improving faculty performance and instruction.

Administrative Evaluation of Teaching

Finally, the component of administrative evaluation needs to be considered. Essential to this discussion is the definition of administrator. Does the dean assume a role in evaluating faculty? Are course chairmen and/or department chairmen identified as administrators for purposes of evaluating teaching? Is administration's role one of final decisionmaking based on submitted data? These questions must be answered before an administrative component is included in evaluating teaching.

Measures for Evaluating Teaching

Dressel (4) discussed *input, process*, and *outcome measures* that are used in academic program evaluation. These can be adapted to teaching effectiveness evaluation as indicated in succeeding paragraphs.

Input measures are those characteristics that the teacher and learner bring to the learning environment. Input measures may include the teacher's educational background and clinical expertise, instructional materials, the students' grade averages or class level, characteristics of the learning climate, and any organizational variables affecting the learning environment.

Process measures are those factors which promote or inhibit teaching-learning interactions. The teacher's teaching style, the teacher-student interaction, or environmental variables such as time of day, weather, learning climate, or time of year may affect the learning outcomes. Processes bring together inputs and environment.

Output or outcome measures are those factors which indicate the results of the teaching-learning interaction. Student achievement, teacher self-evaluation, student progress, success of graduates, evaluation by outsiders, or measures of the quality of care delivered to patients are all measures of the educational outputs or outcomes.

Input evaluation is concerned with use of appropriate resources in relation to goals or objectives. Process evaluation involves assessing the move from inputs to outputs. Output evaluation documents success or acknowledges discrepancies between intent and actuality. The overall role of these evaluations is to provide evidence on the exact state of affairs and to suggest needed adjustments or changes.

Figure 10-1 has been developed (9) to show relationships between the categories and components in an evaluation system. Examples of items in each category are provided in Figure 10-1. When using this categorization system, one must keep in mind that the categories do not stand still, nor are the items mutually exclusive. That is, items may be inputs at one point and outputs at another. For example, a student's grade average may be an input at the beginning of a course and an output in terms of achievement at the end of the course.

Process for Evaluating Teaching

Although each program and/or institution determines its specific process for evaluating teaching, a general process can be described. The process will differ depending upon whether a developmental model, personnel decisionmaking model, or faculty growth model is used.

Figure 10-1 Model for teaching effectiveness evaluation

Elements in teaching effectiveness	Alternative categories		
	Input	Process	Outcomes
Student	Intellectual ability Grade average Class level	Learning style Motivation Class participation	Student Achievement State Board scores Student satisfaction
Learning environment	Faculty Funding Support services Organizational structure	Setting and facilities Climate (time of day) (time of year) Teacher-student interaction	Accreditation, audits Alumni evaluations Agency evaluations Placement of graduates
Teacher	Educational background Experience Clinical expertise	Teaching style Motivation, enthusiasm Creativity in methods	Faculty satisfaction Faculty growth Course goal achievement

Source: Dressel, P. *Handbook of Academic Evaluation.* San Francisco: Jossey-Bass, 1978. P. 18.

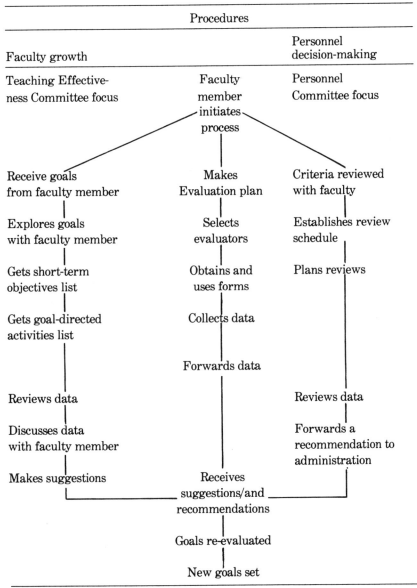

Figure 10-2 Developmental model for evaluating teaching in a collegiate school of nursing

Figure 10-2 illustrates a developmental model for evaluating teaching for purposes of faculty growth and personnel decisionmaking. The evaluation process begins with the faculty member who sets his/her goals, selects the participants in the evaluation process, and establishes an evaluation plan. The faculty member then administers (or arranges for administration of) the evaluation instruments.

The resulting data are submitted by the faculty member to the Teaching Effectiveness Committee and the Personnel Committee. The Teaching Effectiveness Committee works with the faculty member to facilitate faculty development and growth. The Personnel Committee evaluates all faculty evaluation data (teaching, research, and community service) and makes recommendations regarding reappointment, promotion, tenure and/or salary increases. Personnel Committee recommendations are forwarded to the program administrator and then through specified institutional committees to the university administration. The recommendation is forwarded to the governing board when appropriate, such as in decisions regarding tenure. Following action at appropriate levels, the faculty member is then notified of the outcome of the personnel decisionmaking process.

In a developmental model, it is important to recognize that both formative and summative data are useful for faculty growth, whereas summative data are typically used in personnel decisionmaking. Formative data may be obtained periodically or gathered at midsemester and at the end of a semester on a routine basis. Formative evaluations enable the faculty member to promptly change teaching behavior in response to the evaluation, if such change seems appropriate.

Thus, this chapter has discussed teaching effectiveness evaluation, its components, processes, and alternative models. In the future, it can be anticipated that evaluation of teaching effectiveness will become an increasingly important component of faculty evaluation of collegiate schools of nursing.

References

1. Applegate, M. *Faculty Evaluation In Higher Education.* NLN Publ. No. 23–1876. New York: National League for Nursing, 1981.
2. Aroian J., Cloutterback, J., Gilbert, J., Newton, M., and Williams, P.S. Renewal—A Positive Outcome of Faculty Evaluation. *Nurs. Educator* 7:33, 1982.

3. Centra, J.A. *Determining Faculty Effectiveness.* San Francisco: Jossey-Bass, 1980.
4. Dressel, P. *Handbook of Academic Evaluation.* San Francisco: Jossey-Bass, 1978.
5. Irby, D.M. Clinical Teacher Effectiveness in Medicine. *J. Med. Educ.* 53:808, 1978.
6. Mann, R., Arnold, S.M., Binder, J.L., Cytrynbaum, S., Newman, B.M., Ringwold, B.E., Ringwold, J.W., and Rosenwein, R. *The College Classroom: Conflict, Change and Learning.* New York: Wiley, 1970.
7. Miller, R.I. *Evaluating Faculty Performance.* San Francisco: Jossey-Bass, 1974.
8. Seldin, P. *Successful Faculty Evaluation Programs.* Crugers: Coventry Press, 1980.
9. Van Ort, S. Developing a System for Documenting Teaching Effectiveness. *JNE* 22:324, 1983.

Suggested Readings

Allbritten, D., Megel, M.E., Buckley, K.A., Scalone, R.C., and Panwar, S. Faculty Peer Review: An Evolving Process. *JNE* 22:296, 1983.

Applegate, M. *Faculty Evaluation in Higher Education.* NLN Publ. No. 23–1876. New York: National League for Nursing, 1981.

Aroian, J., Cloutterback, J., Gilbert, J., Newton, M., and Williams, P.S. Renewal—A Positive Outcome of Faculty Evaluation. *Nurse Educator* 7(2):33, 1982.

Berquist, W.N. and Phillips, S.R. *A Handbook for Faculty Development.* Washington, D.C.: The Council for Advancement of Small Colleges, 1975.

Brannigan, C.N. and Burson, J.Z. Revamping the Peer Review Process. *JNE* 22:287, 1983.

Centra, J.A. *Determining Faculty Effectiveness.* San Francisco: Jossey-Bass, 1980.

Dennis, C.M., Woodtli, A.O., Hatcher, B.J., and Hilton, A.M. Peer Evaluation: A Process of Development. *JNE* 22:93, 1983.

Dressel, P.L. *Handbook of Academic Evaluations.* San Francisco: Jossey-Bass, 1976.

Eble, K.E. *The Craft of Teaching.* San Francisco: Jossey-Bass, 1976.

Eble, K.E. *Professors as Teachers.* San Francisco: Jossey-Bass, 1971.

Fuhrman, B.S. and Grasha, A.F. *A Practical Handbook for College Teachers.* Boston: Little, Brown, 1983.

Highet, G. *The Art of Teaching.* New York: Knopf, 1950.

Kinsey, D.C. Implementation of Peer Review Within a Baccalaureate Nursing Program. *JNE* 20(5):29, 1981.

Lacefield, W.E. and Kingston, R.D. Relationships Between Faculty Evaluation and Faculty Development. *JNE* 22:278, 1983.

McKeachie, W. *Teaching Tips: A Guidebook for the Beginning College Teacher.* Lexington: Heath, 1978.

Miller, R.I. *Developing Programs for Faculty Evaluation.* San Francisco: Jossey-Bass, 1974.

Miller, R.I. *Evaluating Faculty Performance.* San Francisco: Jossey-Bass, 1972.

National League for Nursing. *Concepts and Components of Effective Teaching.* NLN Publ. No. 16–1750. New York: National League for Nursing, 1978.

National League for Nursing. *Evaluation of Teaching Effectiveness.* NLN Publ. No. 15–1680. New York: National League for Nursing, 1977.

National League for Nursing. *Faculty Evaluation in Higher Education.* NLN Publ. No. 23–1876. New York: National League for Nursing, 1981.

National League for Nursing. *Generating Effective Teaching.* NLN Publ. No. 16–1749. New York: National League for Nursing, 1978.

National League for Nursing. *Program Evaluation.* NLN Publ. No. 15–1738. New York: National League for Nursing, 1978.

Seldin, P. *Successful Faculty Evaluation Programs.* Crugers: Coventry Press, 1980.

Van Ort, S. Developing a System for Documenting Teaching Effectiveness. *JNE* 22:324, 1983.

Chapter 11

Program Evaluation

Alice Longman, R.N. Ed.D.

Study Questions

1. What are the goals and objectives of program evaluation?
2. Which commonly used types of evaluation strategies are appropriate for a nursing education program?
3. What measures are most appropriately labelled input measures and outcome measures?
4. Which aspects of the educational program should be considered in internal program evaluation?
5. Which aspects of the educational program should be considered in external program evaluation?
6. What are the future directions for program evaluation in nursing education?

The overall goal of nursing education is to prepare an individual for a definite career. The course of study is organized and consists of required and optional courses. Furthermore, the course of study is organized into lower division and upper division courses. The curriculum of a nursing education program is planned to provide learning experiences—both theoretical and clinical—which will move students toward the achievement of defined program objectives.

Educational evaluation is the appraisal of the worth of the educational program and its products (7, p. 1). Educational evaluation in nursing is a means by which collected data are used for decisionmaking about individuals and courses in a nursing education program and for judging how the educational system is functioning. Plans for the development and implementation of a curriculum should concurrently include plans for the evaluation of the nursing education program.

Program evaluation includes all of the internal and external forces and constraints that impinge upon a nursing education program (11, p. 186). An analysis of all facets of the program is implied. Thus, the purpose of program evaluation is to assist a nursing education program identify its needs, develop goals to achieve the needs, and implement the goals. According to Welch et al., the question to be answered is: "How is the educational program different and better today than it was before?" (11, p. 186). The evaluation process should identify what actions should be taken to improve a nursing education program. The method of evaluation selected should be objective and feasible within the limits of time and funding resources (5, p. 122).

There are several aspects of a program that need to be evaluated to furnish feedback for the ongoing process. Planned evaluation, according to Bevis, should do the following:

1. Reveal whether the behaviors of graduates are similar to the behaviors desired of graduates as specified in the objectives. If so, how? If not, how not?
2. Tell how graduates of the program compare with previous graduates.
3. Indicate how graduates of the program compare with graduates of other comparable programs.
4. Disclose whether the behaviors of graduates are those expected by the professional organization for the type of program. If they are different, in what ways are they different and is the difference an intentional one? (3, p. 247).

Types of Evaluation

Since the process of decisionmaking is inherent in evaluation, it is useful to have some knowledge of the types of evaluation. Four types of evaluation have been identified and program evaluation usually includes the procedures of these types. The four types are *planning evaluation, input evaluation, process evaluation,* and *output evaluation* (6, p. 15).

Planning evaluation is sometimes referred to as developmental and requires a systematic, organized approach. It involves both a review of the past practice and a prediction of future practice.

The following are included in planning evaluation: (1) describing the environment; (2) identifying unmet needs, unused opportunities, and both available and needed resources; (3) describing sources of deficiencies, as related to personnel, environment, and materials; and (4) seeking to predict deficiencies in the future by considering the relationships among the inputs, processes, and outcomes (6, p. 15).

Input evaluation deals in detail and depth with numerous alternatives to assist in making decisions about how to use resources to achieve goals. Included in input evaluation are the following: (1) describing the potential of individuals and agencies; (2) analyzing strategies for achieving goals; (3) designing implementation strategies; (4) estimating personnel, resource, and cost requirements; and (5) projecting the necessary requirements for personnel and resources (6, p. 15).

Process evaluation uses continuing or periodic feedback so that program planners can monitor and perhaps change earlier decisions. Several elements are inherent in process evaluation and include: (1) malfunctioning in procedures or their implementation; (2) identifying the sources of difficulty; (3) providing information for revision and improvement; (4) appraising communication patterns and adequacy in use of resources; and (5) projecting additional resource requirements not anticipated (6, p. 15).

Output evaluation refers to the assessment of goal attainment at appropriate stages or at the end of a program. It includes: (1) comparison of the original objectives with the actual attainment of the goals; (2) identification of unintended results and suggestions for the reasons; (3) provision of suggestions for decisions to replace previous planning, input, and process decisions; (4) provision for quality control; and (5) suggestions for continuing, modifying, or terminating the program (6, p. 15).

Two other terms have been used to describe the types of evaluation. *Formative evaluation* is the "gathering of data to use in the decision-making process that occurs during the planning, development and implementation of a program" (1, p. 6). Formative evaluation is frequent, periodic, and provides feedback to the program while it is ongoing to assist in making changes to achieve the goals of the program. The purpose is to refine and improve the processes to be used in the program.

The purpose of *summative evaluation* is to determine the effectiveness of a program after it has been completed. "Summative evaluation measures final outcomes or results and is divided into two stages: short-term and long-term evaluation" (1, p. 11). Short-term evaluation occurs periodically such as at the completion of a series of courses or a semester, and long-term evaluation refers to an assessment of the extent to which the desired outcomes or goals have been achieved. Both formative and summative evaluation refer to the finality of a decision. Since programs in nursing education are seldom eliminated, most evaluation is formative.

Input Measures

As a result of systematic program evaluation, specific changes in a nursing education program can and do occur. However, both tangible and intangible factors impinge upon the faculty's efforts at program evaluation.

Conrad identified environmental inputs as key variables which influence decisions about curriculum and over which faculty have minimal control (4, p. 23). Three areas were described as integral components of environmental inputs. These were *societal factors, institutional characteristics*, and *student clientele/culture* (4, p. 23).

Societal factors influence the broad goals of a nursing education program. These factors may include the needs of various institutions—for example, acute care hospital needs, long-term institutional care needs, continuing education needs of nursing personnel, or constraints imposed by state agencies such as the State Board of Nursing or by various certification agencies.

Institutional characteristics have to be understood to facilitate program evaluation. These can be described in terms such as characteristics of the institution, financial and physical resources, faculty resources, governance structure, and management style of both the institution and the program under review.

Finally, the characteristics of the student body and the faculty have to be known. For those students in a nursing education program, some of these characteristics are average age, working status, previous academic preparation, and expressed needs. The characteristics of the faculty include academic preparation, expressed needs related to research, service, and teaching, investment in the program, and the commitment to the institution's goals. As a means of stimulating professional and individual growth, evaluation is invaluable to faculty. Finally, a communication network is essential to the collection of this information for successful program evaluation.

Outcome Measures

Outcome measures usually correspond to the purposes and functions of higher education; namely, teaching, research, and service. Those measures related to teaching include an assessment of the knowledge base acquired by the students and how much is reflected in exit behaviors. External measures such as performance on state board examinations provide useful information for faculty. Faculty competence upon appointment to the program can be determined and then used as a standard by which to measure overall performance in the program. Measures also include the faculty's record in terms of publications, research endeavors, teaching ability, commitment to clinical practice, and professional activities such as participation in the American Nurses' Association. The mission of the university in relation to public service is used as a gauge by which to measure both student and faculty involvement in settings outside the institution. Such activities can be related to involvement with voluntary agencies such as the American Heart Association, the American Cancer Society, and the American Lung Association.

Overall Program Evaluation

The goal of overall program evaluation is to identify what needs to be done to improve a nursing education program. Program evaluation encompasses all aspects which relate to the operation of the program. The process is essentially one of self-evaluation and is not based on the record of another nursing education program. To be complete, program evaluation involves administrative aspects of the program including the budget and support services. Planning for the needs of the program, the faculty, and the students is also necessary for overall program evaluation.

There may be a tendency to focus only on those types of activities that can be more easily measured such as cognitive components. In addition to obtaining information on the acquisition of cognitive skills by the students, attention must be directed toward the development of skills, attitudes, and understandings in all areas. The broader view involves value judgments and is most often related to societal needs. Two aspects of program evaluation need to be considered: *internal program evaluation* and *external program evaluation*.

Internal Program Evaluation

The chief goal of internal evaluation is to assess the program's strengths and weakness and to provide periodic and continuous feedback to the faculty. In professional education, the specification of courses is important. Hours and types of clinical experience as they relate to the specified courses in the program are essential.

Three major areas should be addressed in internal evaluation. These are: the resources, both personnel and physical; the knowledge base to be acquired; and students enrolled in the program. The following sources, written materials, questionnaires, interviews, and observations provide information for the three areas.

In assessing the strength of the faculty for the task of program evaluation, it is important to gather information on abilities, interests, and teaching skills. Often, members of the faculty may not have too clear an idea of the strengths and abilities of their colleagues. The teaching strategies of colleagues in the classroom or in the clinical area may be known to all but a few of the faculty. An important aspect of beginning program evaluation is to identify and then use the strengths of each faculty member. To facilitate collecting this information, a questionnaire such as Figure 11-1, can be designed to determine nursing knowledge and expertise, special interests and skills in the clinical area, the teaching method in which there is the most skill, and the role best fulfilled in a group—be it facilitator, leader, or member.

A sampling of questions to be asked can be seen in Figure 11-2. The results are then tabulated and circulated. The information should be reassessed each year as interests and new skills are added. Through the systematic collection and dissemination of this information, those faculty who are most suitable for each aspect of the evaluation process can be readily identified.

Figure 11-1 Questions for evaluation of personnel

1. What are the overall abilities and interests of the faculty?
2. What are the desired abilities and interests of the faculty in relation to program evaluation?
3. How will the desired abilities and interests be developed in the faculty?
4. Who will evaluate these abilities and interests? Peers, superiors, students?

Figure 11-2 Questions for evaluation of teaching skills

1. What are the overall teaching skills of the faculty?
2. What are the desired teaching skills of the faculty in relation to program evaluation?
3. How will the desired teaching skills be developed in the faculty?
4. Who will evaluate these teaching skills? Peers, superiors, students?

Clinical learning settings are an integral part of any nursing education program's activity. The strengths and limitations of each agency involved with the program need to be determined to ensure that the program's objectives can be met. The available personnel in the agencies who are able to act as resources to faculty needs to be determined as ongoing professional relationships are necessary to the operation of the program. The expectations of the staff in the agencies in relation to the program, students, and faculty are necessary for an organized approach to evaluation.

Bevil and Gross (2, p. 658) described the development of an instrument for evaluating the adequacy of clinical facilities. The instrument includes general information about the agency and specific details about the units actually used. In developing the instrument, four essential requirements were identified. These were that the instrument (1) should meet the needs of all clinical courses in the program, (2) should be appropriate for traditional and nontraditional clinical facilities, (3) should be brief and easy to use, and (4) should elicit objective data (2, p. 659). In addition, the program and level objectives served as the basis for the development of the instrument to ensure the relationship between learning objectives and clinical agency selection. Available resources in the settings need to be appraised. Questions in relation to clinical facilities can be seen in Figure 11-3.

The physical resources of both the program in nursing and the total institution are necessary to conduct the program. The faculty has to assess the facilities to determine if the program's activities can be achieved. These facilities include space for both theoretical and clinical learning. While the structural components of the program are not under the control of the faculty, suggestions can be made for modifications within the constraints of time and money.

Other resources for consideration are the availability of learn-

Figure 11-3 Questions for evaluation of clinical agencies

1. What are the overall goals of the available clinical facilities?
2. What are the available resources in the clinical facilities?
3. What are the expectations of the personnel in relation to the program in the clinical facilities?
4. Who will evaluate the clinical facilities? Peers, superiors, students?

ing materials for students. An assessment of the current textbooks in nursing should be undertaken with the goal of providing the students the most current practice in nursing. The periodicals available and used by practicing nurses should be reviewed to determine if they are appropriate for students. The availability of periodicals to both faculty and students is important. The library holdings should be reviewed to determine if they are adequate for the program's needs. Other resources such as audiovisual equipment and software need to be reviewed to determine deficiencies. The use and availability of learning resources can be critical in deciding what content can most appropriately be learned and reinforced by these sources. Practice equipment needs to be reviewed, catalogued, and replaced as needed.

The knowledge base of the program includes the goals of the program, the content of the program, and the associated learning activities. Most curriculum endeavors center around the program objectives and student outcome measures. However, for a sound curriculum to be implemented, the faculty concurrently is concerned with the philosophy of the program and the conceptual framework as a basis for refining the program objectives and the courses in the program.

Most would agree that the faculty must be cognizant of the philosophy of the parent institution. The philosophy of the university is a statement of the mission of the institution and reflects three major thrusts: teaching, research, and public service. A unified picture of the nursing program should be reflected in the program's philosophy and should convey the beliefs and values of the faculty with respect to education, nursing education, nursing practice, and the goals of the program or programs. Developing a philosophy for a nursing education program is a time-consuming task and faculty need to reconcile their differences into a cohesive whole. The philosophy of the program is perhaps the most difficult to evaluate, yet there should be consensus among the faculty. It is important to communicate the philosophy to the administration of the college/university to be sure that the direction of the program is well understood. Suggested questions to evaluate the philosophy of the program are listed in Figure 11-4.

To organize nursing practice, graduates of nursing education programs must have some framework within which the theory for nursing practice is enveloped. Emanating from the philosophy, a conceptual framework provides the structure upon which the curriculum can be based. The major concepts around which most conceptual frameworks are developed are: man, society, health, and nursing (10, p. 4). These concepts are then clarified by identifying subconcepts and pertinent theories that are activated throughout the curriculum. These subconcepts and theories may then appear as horizontal or vertical strands throughout the curriculum. These in turn provide the direction for learning experiences and pertinent content. The uniqueness of the nursing education program is established by the identification, clarification, and development of the subconcepts and theories related to the major concepts. These concepts, subconcepts, and theories should be traced throughout the entire program. Selected questions for consideration can be seen in Figure 11-5.

Program objectives are usually developed in concert with the philosophy and conceptual framework. The following topics are usually included in program objectives: knowledge of the practice and process of nursing, knowledge of the function the profession serves in society, knowledge of the contributions of other disciplines, to the nursing profession, accountability for nursing practice, and the implementation of strategies to improve health care delivery. The program objectives are intended to serve as guides

Figure 11-4 Questions for evaluation of statement of philosophy

1. Is the statement of philosophy of the nursing program consistent with the philosophy of the parent institution?
2. Is the statement of philosophy of the nursing program a reflection of the faculty's current beliefs and values?
3. Is the entire faculty committed to the statement of philosophy of the nursing program?
4. Is the statement of philosophy of the nursing program clear to the students?

Figure 11-5 Questions for evaluation of the conceptual framework

1. Is the statement of the conceptual framework based on the statement of the philosophy?
2. Is there a clear statement of the conceptual framework?
3. Is there consistency among the concepts, subconcepts, and theories in the statement of the conceptual framework?
4. Are the concepts, subconcepts, and theories of the conceptual framework apparent in the content and learning activities of the nursing program?

for the development of course objectives. A system should be devised to relate the course objectives to the program objectives. Figure 11-6 illustrates such a series of questions.

The development of specific course offerings with specified learning activities is related to the conceptual framework and the program objectives. The decision for which course should be taught when should be made in concert with the activities that will ensure learning has taken place. Each course should assist the students in attaining the competencies stated in the program objectives. The courses should be developed in detail and should include objectives, content, and evaluation strategies to be employed. Time must be allocated so that the faculty can discuss the implementation plan and evaluation strategies for each course. Useful areas for course evaluation include the objectives, course content, pencil-and-paper tests, performance evaluation, and other techniques necessary for the conduct of the course.

The entrance characteristics of the students should be determined in relation to the proposed or existing program. An assessment of the students can then be made in relation to the program's objectives with consequent revisions in the objectives as necessary. The interim achievement of the student is made in relation to each course in the program and to each term or semester. Finally, exit characteristics should be determined in

Figure 11-6 Questions for evaluation of program objectives

1. Are the program objectives based on the statement of philosophy and the conceptual framework?
2. Are the program objectives stated clearly and concisely?
3. Are the program objectives used in planning the course objectives?
4. Are the program objectives used in planning the learning activities?

relation to the program's objectives. An inventory form is one mechanism that would be useful for annual assessment of students. Treated as consumer evaluation, these assessments can be useful in pursuing the program's activities.

Bevis (3, p. 249) identified four questions to be answered regarding students. These were:

1. How well do students meet these objectives on entry to the program?
2. How do they progress toward meeting the objectives of the program?
3. How well do students meet the objectives for graduation?
4. In what ways consistent with program expectations as expressed in the objectives do graduates function on the job after graduation?

Several instruments are available for internal program evaluation. The wider the variety, the more data can be retrieved. Some methods are student discussions, faculty sessions, and performance checklists. Content measures such as the National League for Nursing achievement tests, personal characteristics measures, and interpersonal relationship measures are also useful for program evaluation.

External Program Evaluation

The chief goal of external program evaluation is to assure the quality of the educational program and the quality of the product of the program. External program evaluation refers to "judgments made about an educational program by outsiders" (11, p. 187).

In nursing education, external evaluation is almost always synonymous with accreditation. Accreditation is defined as "a voluntary process of evaluation by which schools/programs are appraised in relation to predetermined criteria and are publicly recognized as being in compliance" (9, p. 35). There are two types of accreditation: institutional and specialized. *Institutional accreditation* refers to a review of the entire educational institution, and *specialized accreditation* refers to a specific program within the institution.

Specialized accreditation identifies for the public (including the educational community) programs which meet established standards of educational quality. Specialized accreditation stimulates improvement in educational standards and programs by involving faculty in self-evaluation, research, and planning (11, p. 187).

Nursing has been involved in voluntary efforts to raise its educational standards for over fifty years. Accrediting activities during the 1920s and 1930s were begun by many different organizations, including the National League of Nursing Education. In 1949 accrediting activities were centralized in the National Nursing Accrediting Service. In 1952 several national nursing organizations merged with the National League of Nursing Education to form the National League for Nursing. Accrediting in nursing education became the function of the National League for Nursing's Division of Nursing Education. Presently, accreditation activities of the National League for Nursing are conducted through four membership units of the organization: the Council of Associate Degree Programs, the Council of Diploma Programs, the Council of Baccalaureate and Higher Degree Programs, and the Council of Practical Nursing Programs. Each council has responsibility for the types of programs in its title. The Division of Accreditation Services administers the accrediting program and services the membership councils. In addition, the National League for Nursing is officially recognized as the national accrediting agency for nursing education by the Council on Postsecondary Accreditation and by the U.S. Department of Education.

The official criteria for the evaluation of each of the types of educational programs in nursing are available on request from the National League for Nursing. The school or program assumes the responsibility for initiating the process and seeks the appropriate documents since they serve as the basis for accreditation. All of the necessary information is available in the booklet *Policies and Procedures of Accreditation for Programs in Nursing Education* (9). Accreditation involves everyone within a program—the faculty, the students, and the administrators.

The process of National League for Nursing accreditation involves six stages: (1) determination of eligibility for National League for Nursing evaluation, (2) initiation of the process, (3) self-study process and writing of the self-study report, (4) accreditation visit, (5) evaluation, and (6) systematic program of ongoing evaluation (9, p. 7).

A program in nursing education may seek National League

for Nursing accreditation when the institution offering the program is legally authorized to grant the credentials to which the program leads and is accredited by the appropriate agency. Approval must also have been granted by the State Board of Nursing. Master's degree programs or programs admitting previously licensed nurses do not need approval from the State Board of Nursing. In addition, one class of students should be nearing completion of the program.

The National League for Nursing Division of Accreditation Services is available to faculty in programs of nursing education to answer questions and arrange office conferences in anticipation of applying for accreditation. Workshops are held periodically to provide the opportunity to learn about the processes, policies, and procedures. Since National League for Nursing accreditation is based on predetermined criteria, the faculty and the administrative officers of the program decide when the program is ready for the appraisal. Initial accreditation refers to programs not previously accredited by the National League for Nursing while continuing accreditation refers to those programs which have previously participated in the process. The dates for the scheduled visit are set in consultation with the program in nursing.

The self-study report is used as the primary document in the evaluation of the nursing program. The report is based upon the criteria currently in effect for the particular type of program. The systematic process inherent in the preparation of the self-study report provides a basis for:

1. identifying the strengths of the program,
2. diagnosing difficulties in the program, and
3. making decisions about needed improvements and program growth (9, p. 13).

While all faculty may not be involved in the actual writing of the report, faculty must be aware of the process and must contribute to the content included in the report.

When the self-study report is complete, one copy of it and one copy of the current catalogue is sent to each of the accreditation visitors. Fifteen copies of the report are sent to the secretary of the appropriate Board of Review. Prior to the accreditation visit, the faculty assemble materials for review by the visitors. The purpose of the visit is to provide an opportunity for the program to clarify, verify, and amplify program materials presented in written form. The visit usually ranges from three to five days, depending upon the size and complexity of the program, the location of the resources used for clinical activities, and the coordination of the visit with other agencies. All of the necessary information for the visit is contained in the previously mentioned National League for Nursing manual. Upon completion of the visit, the visitors read their report, give a Xerox copy to the administrator of the program, and send the original to the National League for Nursing for typing.

Each educational council of the National League for Nursing has the authority and responsibility to evaluate nursing education programs. The Board of Review is composed of ten members— nine peers from the same council, and one member from outside the interest of the council. The nine peers are currently active in the type of nursing education which is the interest of the council. These members are elected by peers to serve a three-year term. As the basis for evaluation, the Board of Review uses the self-study report, the school catalogue, and the report of the visiting team. The Board of Review decides the accreditation status of the program in relation to compliance to the criteria. Usually, programs accredited by the National League for Nursing are revisited for accreditation at eight-year intervals.

The final process is the systematic process of ongoing evaluation. It is the responsibility of the program to engage in systematic evaluation for continued improvement and compliance with accreditation criteria.

Judgments about programs are also made by State Boards of Nursing. These bodies establish minimum standards for schools/-programs in their jurisdiction. Application to the State Board is made by the institution, and representatives of the institution meet with the board to review the application. Usually, the results of a feasibility study indicating that the program is needed is required. Similar data to that included in a self-study report are required. Representatives of the board visit the institution, submit a written report, and notify the institution regarding granting or denial of approval. The program director is periodically requested to submit a summary report regarding the activities of the program.

Program evaluation is a complex yet vital process and identifies for the faculty what needs to be done to improve their nursing program. Thus, the worth of the program is appraised, and the students of the program are assured a quality education.

Suggested Readings

References

1. Bell, D.R. and Bell, D.L. Effective Evaluations. *Nurse Educator* 4(6):6, 1979.
2. Bevil, C.W. and Gross, L.C. Assessing the Adequacy of Clinical Learning Settings. *Nurs. Outlook* 29:658, 1981.
3. Bevis, E.O. *Curriculum Building in Nursing: A Process* (3rd ed.). St. Louis: Mosby, 1982.
4. Conrad, C.E. and Pratt, A.M. Making Decisions About the Curriculum. *J. Higher Educ.* 54:16, 1983.
5. Dixon, J. Developing the Evaluation Components of a Grant Application. *Nurs. Outlook* 30:122, 1982.
6. Dressel, P.L. *Handbook of Academic Evaluation.* San Francisco: Jossey-Bass, 1976.
7. Lynch, E.A. *Evaluation: Principles and Processes.* New York: National League for Nursing, 1978.
8. Munro, B.H. A Useful Model for Program Evaluation. *Nurse Educator* 8(1):35, 1983.
9. National League for Nursing. *Policies and Procedures of Accreditation for Programs in Nursing Education* (4th ed.) New York: National League for Nursing, 1982.
10. Torres, G. and Yura, H. *Today's Conceptual Framework: Its Relationship to the Curriculum Development Process.* New York: National League for Nursing, 1974.
11. Welch, L.B., Carmody, C., Murray, M., and Rafenski, L. Program Evaluation: An Overview. *Nurs. and Health Care* 1(11):186, 1980.

Suggested Readings

Clark, I., Goodwin, M., Mariani, M., Marshall, M.J., and Moon, S. Curriculum Evaluation: An Application of Stufflebeam's Model on a Baccalaureate School of Nursing. *JNE* 22(2):54, 1983.

Clayton, E.R., and Triplett, J.L. Measuring Effects of a Liberal Education. *Nurs. Outlook* 29(10):582, 1981.

Dean, P.R. and Edwards, T.A. A Multidimensional Approach to Evaluation. *JNE* 21(2):18, 1982.

Ediger, J., Snyder, M. and Corcoran, S. Selecting a Model for Use in Curriculum Evaluation. *JNE* 22(5):195, 1983.

Hawkins, J.W. Selection of Clinical Agencies for Baccalaureate Nursing Education. *JNE* 19(10):7, 1980.

Holzemer, W.L., Barkauskas, V.H., and Ohlson, V.N. A Program Evaluation of Four Workshops Designed to Prepare Nurse Faculty in Health Assessment. *JNE* 19(4):7, 1980.

Kissinger, J.F. and Munjas, B.A. Predictions of Student Success. *Nurs. Outlook* 30(1):53, 1982.

Koehler, M.L. Evaluating a Curriculum. *JNE* 21(1):32, 1982.

Malarkey, L.M. Sounding Board: Accreditation: The Tail That Wagged the Dog. *Nurs. Outlook* 29(4):237, 1981.

Meisenhelder, J.B. Clinical Evaluation—An Instructor's Dilemma. *Nurs. Outlook* 30(6):348, 1982.

Parsons, M.A., Collison, C.R. The Process of Change in Curriculum Evaluation. *JNE* 19(9):36, 1980.

Smeltzer, S. The New State Board Exam. *Nurs. Outlook* 30(5):312, 1982.

Stamper, J., Huerta, C. and Manilla, J. Evaluating for Accreditation: A Structured Approach. *JNE* 22(2):67, 1983.

Sweeney, M.A., Hedstrom, B. and O'Malley, M. Process Evaluation: A Second Look at Psychomotor Skills. *JNE* 21(2):4, 1982.

Waltz, C.F. and McGurn, W.C. An Approach to the Assessment of Programs in Nursing Education. *Nurs. and Health Care* 4(12):576, 1983.

Part IV

Issues in Teaching

Chapter 12

Education and Practice Issues

Norma J. Briggs, R.N., Ph.D.

Study Questions

1. What is the entry into practice issue and its potential impact on teaching in collegiate schools of nursing?
2. What is involved in the issue of career ladder-articulation? What are the major dilemmas in this issues? Who are the primary proponents and opponents of the issue?
3. What is the competencies issue? What is the current status of national efforts to develop competencies for two levels of nursing in the future? Who are the primary proponents and opponents of this issue?
4. What are primary issues in master's degree education in nursing?
5. What are primary issues in doctoral education in nursing?

Entry into Practice

The educational preparation of nurses in the U.S. has been the subject of discussion since the time of Florence Nightingale. Statements of how, where, and to what extent nurses should be educated are prolific in the nursing literature. While nursing has been studied by individuals and groups inside and outside the profession, the subject of educational preparation for the professional nurse still remains a hotbed of issues open to debate. Until there are collective, political decisions made by the profession with regard to many of the following topics, the debates will continue. Recently, more emphasis on educational preparation has occurred as some individuals believe resolution of this issue will resolve a large number of professional concerns. Thus, this material will focus on only the more recent aspect of the issues.

199

Historical Perspective

Three significant national reports relevant to this issue are the Goldmark Report of 1923 (7), the Brown Report of 1948 (5), and the American Nurses' Association *Position Paper* of 1965 (1). These reports are also discussed in Chapter 1. The Goldmark and Brown Reports recommended changes in the educational preparation of nurses. Some of the recommendations related to curricular content, faculty qualifications and facilities, and moving nursing into institutions of higher learning. The American Nurses' Association *Position Paper* of 1965 recommended two levels of nursing, professional and technical, and a clear delineation between the levels with regard to educational preparation. The *Position Paper* produced a very divisive response among members of the profession (see Chapter 1). Nurses were willing to work toward upgrading and improving the educational preparation of nurses in general. However, many nurses were not willing to accept standards or titles designed for the future, which they perceived as reflecting negatively upon themselves. The great debates began: professional versus technical; baccalaureate versus associate degree; diploma versus associate degree; diploma versus baccalaureate degree.

National Efforts in Response to the 1985 Proposal

Responses to the 1985 Proposal at the national level have been made by both the American Nurses' Association and the National League for Nursing. The American Nurses' Association has examined career mobility, competencies, and titling. The National League for Nursing has focused on the open curriculum model and competencies.

American Nurses' Association Actions

The impetus for action by the American Nurses' Association was generated at the 1978 American Nurses' Association Convention when the House of Delegates adopted three resolutions related to educational preparation of nurses. The first resolution to be discussed is Resolution #56, Identification and Titling of Establishment of Two Categories of Nursing Practice. This resolution in part recommended: (1) two categories of nursing practice be clearly identified and titled by 1980, and (2) by 1985 the minimum preparation for entry into professional nursing practice will be the baccalaureate degree in nursing. The content of this resolution became known in popular terms as the 1985 Proposal. The great debates continued and increased in scope. Professional versus technical versus nurse associate. What about the diploma-prepared nurse? What is a grandfathering clause? What about the supply of new graduates if there are no diploma programs to produce large numbers of graduates? The responses to some of these questions became emotion laden, and the strategies used became very political in nature.

The second resolution was Resolution #58, Increasing Accessibility of Career Mobility Programs in Nursing. This resolution proposed that the American Nurses' Association actively support increased accessibility to high-quality career mobility programs which utilize flexible approaches for individuals seeking academic degrees in nursing. The resolution was seen as supportive of and necessary to the implementation of the 1985 Proposal. The key terms *quality* and *flexibility* generated more questions: How flexible is flexible? What determines quality? How does one develop a flexible program/curriculum and maintain quality?

The third resolution was Resolution #57, Establishing a Mechanism for Deriving Competency Statements for the Two Categories of Nursing Practice. The American Nurses' Association was directed to establish a mechanism for deriving a comprehensive statement of competencies for two categories of nursing practice by 1980. A Task Force on Entry into Practice was established in 1979, with a subgroup to work on competencies.

In 1980 at the American Nurses' Association Convention, a motion was made to make the master's degree the minimum preparation for entry into professional nursing. The motion was defeated. One can only surmise the intent of the motion. Was it a sincere, well thought out idea and truly the belief of its supporters? Or was it a political move to try and get nurses to look at the entry into the profession issue with a more realistic or well-grounded approach? Consequently, the great debates continue and will do so until some resolve, some compromise, or some entirely new solution is agreed to by the profession. A solution that cannot be overlooked in this regard is time. Over time all things change, and over time these issues could all resolve themselves. The question is: Do we have the time to wait for this change to occur?

Is this the passive type of change that we want to occur? As a profession shouldn't we be taking a more active role in planning for the future, so that we can move on to other major issues related to the delivery of nursing services and the people we serve?

National League for Nursing Actions

The National League for Nursing has always had an active role in all aspects of nursing education. However, the National League for Nursing remains consistent in trying to support all levels of nursing and has published some competencies for all four levels of nursing. These competencies have been developed by the individual councils in the organizational structure. The reader is referred to Chapter 5 for additional information on competencies and characteristics of various levels of nursing.

Regional and State Actions

It is not possible to describe all the different endeavors put forth by the many creative people in nursing. Some examples of career mobility programs are presented to show the diversity of approaches to the issue.

The Agassiz Region Nursing Education Consortium (ARNEC) was formed in 1973 (2). Nursing institutions and nursing education programs involved in the project were located in Minnesota and North Dakota. The major goal of the Consortium was to develop a career mobility program that would serve the students of the region and at the same time pool faculty, educational facilities, and clinical agencies. The ARNEC Program encompassed four levels: nursing assistant, practical nurse, associate degree nurse, and baccalaureate nurse. The associate degree program was a missing link. The Curriculum Committee set about designing an associate degree program that would articulate with the other programs and allow for a progressive educational sequence.

In 1972, a career ladder project was begun in New Mexico with informal meetings of nursing educators. This three-phase project, ultimately funded by the W. K. Kellogg Foundation, became known as the System for Nursing Articulation Program, or the New Mexico SNAP Project (6). The facilitation of career mobility for graduates of nursing education programs at all levels of nursing was developed. The structuring of cooperative inter-relationships among all of New Mexico's institutions offering nursing programs allowed the graduates to further their education with a minimum amount of repetition of learning experiences. In order to accomplish this statewide cooperative plan, minimal behavioral expectations of new graduates of each type of nursing program in the state needed to be established.

In the development of career mobility programs, many descriptive terms for the programs came into usage. Such terms as second step, two-plus-two, upper two, and advanced placement are descriptors used by different institutions to describe the methods used to design professional curricula offered for nurses who are diploma or associate degree graduates.

The first second-step program was developed at California State College, Sonoma in the early 1970s (12). The program was designed on the concept of an "open curriculum," a type of "non-traditional study." The West Virginia University School of Nursing developed an advanced placement program for registered nurses in 1979 (3). Both programs are designed to facilitate the return to school of nurses seeking a baccalaureate degree in nursing.

While the National League for Nursing and American Nurses' Association have published competencies, many state nurses' associations or statewide groups have looked at or attempted to develop competencies which will meet their particular needs. Such is the case in Wisconsin, where a statewide task force on nursing competencies worked for two years to develop two levels of competencies. Published in 1982, the task force report includes competencies for baccalaureate degree/professional and associate degree-technical nurses (4). Competencies were categorized under care provider, teacher, investigator, manager, and member of the discipline. The task force membership was representative of both nursing service and nursing education. The task force also delineated the scope of practice for both levels of nursing.

In the early 1970s, Alverno College introduced competency-based education for the entire college. Located in Milwaukee, Wisconsin, this institution is a private, Catholic, four-year liberal arts school for women. The nursing program is an entirely competency-based educational program. The preceding examples of nursing curricula illustrate the attempts to respond to diverse needs for nursing education.

Career mobility questions are: How should such programs be organized? What content needs to be taught? Should credit be given for life experiences? Can a technician philosophy be the basis for learning a professional philosophy? How does one manage articulation? The concept of articulation in relation to curriculum development involves arrangements between education programs which allow the student to build upon previously learned content when moving into the higher level program. Stevens (13) discusses downward articulation, but this author suggests that in order to look at the totality of the concept, one needs to consider the pros and cons of upward articulation. In other words: Which program should determine what is to be taught where? Does the more advanced program determine what needs to be taught before the student can enter the program? or Does the less advanced program say, this is what we are teaching, now you adjust to accommodate our students? Stevens also believes that individuals who support the two-plus-two nursing curriculum in baccalaureate programs have an antiarticulation philosophy.

Dilemmas

In additional to the questions already generated by the concepts of career mobility, articulation, and competency-based education, there are other concerns related to education-practice issues. For example, in economically difficult times, the cost of education to the student becomes an even greater concern. Cost with regard to career mobility is not only cost in tuition but the cost in perceived time spent repeating content students believe they already know. Thus, how does an institution or a faculty determine what methods best evaluate the knowledge of the applicant? Does one give credit for life experiences, and, if so, how does one measure those life experiences in a consistent and fair manner? Does one try to be flexible and do an individualized type of evaluation of each applicant? How realistic is this process if 50, 100, or 200 students are applying? Where is the realistic point when a faculty has to go to standardized testing? Is standardized testing available that will provide the information faculty need? How valid or reliable are the results?

In attempting to provide for educational advancement for students in a nursing curriculum, several concerns need to be considered. Since a nursing curriculum has only one set of terminal behaviors/objectives which describe the end product of the program, how does one take two different populations of students, generic and registered nurses, and have them arrive at the same destination? Historically, some baccalaureate nursing programs had two separate paths for students to follow to reach the terminal behaviors. They had a generic curriculum and a registered nurse curriculum which was commonly referred to as a two-track program.

In the early 1960s, the National League for Nursing Department of Baccalaureate and Higher Degree Programs issued a *Statement of Beliefs and Recommendations* regarding baccalaureate nursing programs and the admission of registered nurse students (10). Subsequently there was a shift toward the integration of the registered nurse into the generic curriculum with a resultant one-track program. The intent was to have one curriculum and to move the registered nurse through the program with a diversity of strategies. Some courses could be challenged, some courses had to be taken, some courses were specifically designed to meet the needs of this student body, and some blanket credit was given. This one-track curriculum approach, unless the process is handled carefully, has produced many of the negative feelings registered nurses have about pursuing the baccalaureate degree. The potential for anger, frustration, and hostility toward nursing education on the part of the registered nurse student is enormous. While individualization of the course content and clinical experiences was proposed, the burden placed upon faculty teaching a heterogeneous group is time consuming, challenging, and unrealistic in some instances. The ideal resolution of this specific problem comes about when there is a large enough enrollment of registered nurse students that they can be placed in homogeneous groups.

In 1970, the National League for Nursing published a statement approved by the Board of Directors dealing with the open curriculum in nursing education (11). In the statement was a discussion of the pressures for re-establishing a baccalaureate program expressly for registered nurse students, which seemed to far outweigh the forces for restraining such a move. This statement, plus the cost and negative feelings generated by the one-track programs, began a trend of returning to the two-track approach for this educational dilemma. The two-track approach holds the potential for curricular modifications which will be most beneficial to both the faculty and the students involved.

Another dilemma is the recruitment/motivation of registered nurses into some type of baccalaureate program. While statistics show that the number of registered nurses applying to baccalaureate programs is increasing, the percentage of returnees remains small (8). Whether this small percentage of returnees is due in part to registered nurses' resistance to the one-track programs will remain to be seen.

Another dilemma is the baccalaureate competency issue. While characteristics of the baccalaureate graduate have been adopted by the National League for Nursing Council of Baccalaureate and Higher Degree Programs, no extensive set of baccalaureate competencies per se has been generated at the national level. The more common occurrence is for baccalaureate competencies to be generated at state/regional levels. Not only are the competencies and what they should include debatable, but when discussing psychomotor skills and how proficient/competent the baccalaureate graduate need to be, the famous Pandora's Box is opened. The diversity of expectations among nursing educators becomes very evident.

Other questions which have been raised are: Is competency-based education appropriate for institutions of higher education? Does competency-based education foster mediocrity? and How are transcripts with no grades evaluated?

One issue that may be settled through the development of competencies for associate degree graduate is: How much and how many concepts are to be taught in a two-year program originally designed to prepare a technician? Because of a failure on the part of nursing service to respond to differently prepared personnel with different job descriptions, and because of a failure on the part of nursing education to clearly delineate the differences in the two levels of nursing, in many settings all registered nurses, regardless of educational preparation, are hired as nurses under the same job description. In order to prepare the associate degree graduate to meet these present job expectations, many associate degree programs have begun to include community health nursing and leadership content in their curricula. Montag, who proposed the original concept of the associate degree program in nursing, questions whether we are losing sight of the intended function of the associate degree nurse and just how much needs to be included in the curriculum (9). Hopefully with more clearly delineated competencies for each level of nursing, nursing service will respond with different job descriptions utilizing each employee to his/her fullest potential.

While it is not possible to produce identical graduates from any specific nursing program, nursing educators must come together on key issues soon or time and unplanned change will lead us into more dilemmas. The only way to resolve many of these dilemmas is to come to a consensus and plan for change. We must begin to think about the survival of the profession while we are continuing to reconsider, reiterate, and re-evaluate these education-practice issues, many external forces are making decisions which remove from us nursing functions and nursing responsibilities and leave us with a smaller and smaller circumscribed area within which to function.

Education and Practice Issues

Suzanne Van Ort, R.N., Ph.D.

Graduate Education

There are many issues related to graduate education in nursing—its purpose, content, products, funding, and faculty. Two primary issues will be presented here to illustrate the dilemmas. Each issues will be presented and alternatives discussed where appropriate. For master's degree education, the issue of purpose and content focus will be discussed. The doctoral degree dilemma regarding type of degree and focus of content will then be described.

Master's degree education in nursing grew rapidly in the 1950s and 1960s as the need for nurses prepared for leadership roles was recognized. In that era, the purpose of master's degree education included the preparation of nurse leaders who were prepared in a functional area of role development such as teaching, administration, or clinical practice (4). A primary focus of master's degree programs was the preparation of teachers of nursing for the rapidly expanding baccalaureate programs. In 1969, the American Nurses' Association called for the preparation of nurse clinicians capable of improving nursing care through the advancement of both nursing theory and nursing practice (1).

This effort to focus on the advancement of nursing theory and clinical practice paved the way for master's degree education, based upon a generalist baccalaureate degree in nursing, that prepared nurse clinicians for advanced nursing practice.

In 1979, the National League for Nursing reaffirmed that master's degree education in nursing should provide for the preparation of nursing leaders. According to the National League for Nursing (7), master's education involves concentrated study in nursing and the application of research methodologies in the study of a nursing problem. Clinical specialization and functional role development are both included in the master's program.

The issue facing master's degree education in nursing now is whether the master's degree should prepare nurse clinicians in a specialty area, nurse leaders with functional role expertise, or a combination of both. Given the fact that most master's degree programs are one year in length, how should the master's curriculum be structured? Some educators assert that advanced nursing content should be the primary focus, with functional role preparation as a secondary focus (4, p. 5). Other nurse leaders suggest that advanced nursing content be concentrated in a one-year program with an optional second year offered for those desiring functional role preparation (3). McLane recommended preparation for dual roles as clinician and educator or other functional role (6).

Also, with the increasing availability of doctoral education in nursing, is the master's degree a preparation for doctoral study? If so, should a solid foundation in research, including a thesis requirement, be incorporated into master's degree programs? As baccalaureate and doctoral curricula evolve and change, master's degree programs will need to respond to change and define their unique role in nursing education. While national leadership in defining the purposes and scope of master's degree education is essential, faculty and administrators in each institution need to examine their mission and the congruence of their graduate program with that mission. Diversity, flexibility, and plurality in master's degree education for nursing are being encouraged for the future (4).

Doctoral education in nursing has as its purposes: (1) theory development and testing; (2) creation of more sophisticated research designs for studying nursing and health problems; and (3) expansion and application of knowledge relevant to the care of persons experiencing health-illness (2). Two related dilemmas exist for doctoral education: (1) Should the master's degree in nursing be a prerequisite for doctoral study? and (2) Should the product of doctoral education be an advanced clinician, a researcher, or both?

Lenz (5) asserts that master's degree preparation in nursing provides essential research experience and advanced clinical knowledge that can be used a foundation for doctoral work. She believes that the master's degree enhances the individual's insights into nursing practice and broadens the individual's horizons. Conversely, Waltz (8) argues that building the doctoral program directly upon the baccalaureate degree is most efficient when the goal is to prepare nurse researchers. Thus, her discussion focuses upon the Doctor of Philosophy degree. Waltz advocates immersion of the post-baccalaureate doctoral student in the research milieu to promote socialization into the researcher role. However, if the goal of the doctorate is clinical, she recommends a Doctor of Nursing Science program rather than the Doctor of Philosophy degree. In this instance, she suggests that master's preparation in nursing provides groundwork for doctoral study.

As in master's degree education, the focus of doctoral education in nursing is dependent upon both national and local forces. Nationally, doctoral education in nursing is emerging with two primary types of degree: (1) the Doctor of Philosophy (Ph.D.) with a major in nursing, and (2) the Doctor of Nursing Science (D.N.S.) with a major in nursing. Typically, the Doctor of Philosophy is a research-oriented degree while the Doctor of Nursing Science is more practice-oriented. Faculty and administrators in each program define their purposes and scope of doctoral education within the mission of their institution. At the present time, due in part to the evolution of doctoral education in nursing, the distinctions between the research-oriented and practice-oriented degrees are not always clear. However, in the future, educators will need to clarify the expectations of graduates of the doctoral programs and then define the content accordingly.

References

Entry into Practice

1. American Nurses' Association. *Educational Preparation for Nurse Practitioners and Assistants to Nurses: A Position Paper.* New York: American Nurses' Association, 1965.

2. Andrews, J.K. The Development and Demonstration of an Articulation Model. *Nurs. and Health Care* 3(4):181, 1982.
3. Borgman, M.F. and Ostrow, C.L. An Advanced Placement Program for Registered Nurses. *Nurs. Educ.* 20(5):2, 1981.
4. Briggs, N.J. *Report of Statewide Task Force on Nursing Competencies.* Eau Claire: University of Wisconsin, 1982.
5. Brown, E.L. *Nursing for the Future.* New York: Russell Sage Foundation, 1948.
6. Ferrell, M.J. and Maloney, J. *Final Report of New Mexico SNAP Project.* Albuquerque: University of New Mexico, 1980.
7. Goldmark, J. *Nursing and Nursing Education in the United States.* New York: Macmillan, 1923.
8. Lenburg, C.B., Johnson, W.L., and Vahey, J.T. *Directory of Career Mobility Opportunities in Nursing Education.* NLN Publ. No. 19-1485. New York: National League for Nursing, 1973.
9. Montag, M. Looking Back: Associate Degree Education Perspective. *Nurs. Outlook* 28(4):248, 1980.
10. National League for Nursing, Department of Baccalaureate and Higher Degree Programs. *Statement of Beliefs and Recommendations Regarding Baccalaureate Nursing Programs Admitting Registered Nurse Students.* New York: National League for Nursing, 1964.
11. National League for Nursing. *The Open Curriculum in Nursing Education.* New York: National League for Nursing, 1970.
12. Searight, M.W. *The Second Step Baccalaureate Education for Registered Nurses.* Philadelphia: F.A. Davis Company, 1976.
13. Stevens, B.J. Program Articulation: What It Is and What It Is Not. *Nurs. Outlook* 29(12):700, 1981.

Graduate Education

1. American Nurses' Association, Commission on Nursing Education. *Statement on Graduate Education.* New York: American Nurses' Association, 1969.
2. American Nurses' Association. *Statement on Graduate Education in Nursing.* Kansas City: American Nurses' Association, 1978.
3. Grossman, H. Diversity in Graduate Nursing Education. *Nurs. Outlook* 20:467, 1972.
4. Kelley, Jean A. Purposes of Graduate Education: An Evaluation. In Mary H. Smith (ed.), *Graduate Education in Nursing: Issues and Future Directions.* Atlanta: Southern Regional Education Board, 1981.
5. Lenz, Elizabeth. Position 1: The Master's Degree as Prerequisite. In Mary H. Smith (ed.), *Graduate Education in Nursing: Issues and Future Directions.* Atlanta: Southern Regional Education Board, 1981. Pp. 43-44.
6. McLane, A.M. Core Competencies of Master's Prepared Nurses. *Nurs. Res.* 27, 48-53, 1978.
7. National League for Nursing. *Master's Education in Nursing: Route to Opportunities in Contemporary Nursing,* 1979. P. 2.
8. Waltz, Carolyn. Position II: The Direct Route to the Doctorate. In Mary H. Smith (ed.), *Graduate Education in Nursing: Issues and Future Directions.* Atlanta: Southern Regional Education Board, 1981. P. 45-46.

Suggested Readings

Chaska, N.L. *The Nursing Profession: A Time to Speak.* New York: McGraw-Hill, 1983.

Clayton, G.M. Identification of Professional Competencies. In N. L. Chaska, *The Nursing Profession: A Time to Speak.* New York: McGraw-Hill, 1983.

Downs, F. Doctoral Education in Nursing: Future Directions *Nurs. Outlook* 26(1):56, 1978.

Ezell, A.S. Future Social Planning for Nursing Education and Nursing Practice Organizations. In N. L. Chaska, *The Nursing Profession: A Time to Speak.* New York: McGraw-Hill, 1983.

Grace, H.K. Doctoral Educational in Nursing. Dilemmas and Directions. In N.L. Chaska, *The Nursing Profession: A Time to Speak.* New York: McGraw-Hill, 1983.

MacPhail, J. Collaboration/Unification Models for Nursing Education and Nursing Service. In N. L. Chaska, *The Nursing Profession: A Time to Speak.* New York: McGraw-Hill, 1983.

Smith, G.R. Nursing Beyond the Crossroads. *Nurs. Outlook* 28:540, 1980.

Stokes, S.A., Werlin, E.L., Rauckhorst, L., and Gother, A.M. The Development of an Evaluation Process for Technical Level Competency. *Nurs. & Health Care* 2(4):192, 1981.

Wagner D.L. Nursing Administrators' Assessment of Nursing Education. *Nurs. Outlook* 28:557, 1980.

Werner, T. Joint Endeavors: The Way to Bring Service and Education Together. *Nurs. Outlook* 28:546, 1980.

Chapter 13

Continuing Education Issues

Arlene M. Putt, R.N., Ed.D.

Study Questions

1. What is the role of continuing education programs in nursing?
2. What role do continuing education programs have in changing the content of basic nursing programs?
3. Should continuing education be mandatory for relicensing? If so, how much, and what types of programs should be required?
4. Who should determine continuing education policies for nursing?
5. Why should continuing education courses not be accepted for degree credit?
6. How do four types of continuing education programs compare as to the needs addressed in the program?
7. What types of content should be included in continuing education offerings?
8. What resources can be utilized for continuing education programs?
9. How should continuing education programs be financed?
10. What is your personal philosophy regarding continuing education for nursing?

In the area of continuing education a number of issues confront faculty. These issues include the ongoing debate over the legislative mandates governing the practice, licensing, and relicensing of nursing, and related issues of allocation of resources, the role, and goals of continuing education, as well the amount, kind, and financing of continuing education courses. Finally, the faculty member must resolve the issue of personal philosophy, commitment, and obligation for self-development and the continuing education of others. To understand these issues, some background information is necessary.

The following aspects of continuing education in nursing will be discussed.

1. The role of continuing education in nursing
2. The goals of continuing education
3. The types of programs available
4. Content of the programs
5. Resources available
6. Financing options.

The Role of Continuing Education in the Nursing Profession

The role of continuing education in nursing can be viewed from three points of view: The roles in nursing programs, staff development, relicensing procedures will be discussed in this chapter.

In Nursing Programs

The role of continuing education in nursing programs is twofold. Continuing education can be viewed as an addendum to nursing programs. In the early years of the nursing profession, many nurses believed their education to be complete when they graduated from a nursing school. While they practiced their profession diligently, they did not view themselves as life-long learners. As the *American Journal of Nursing* developed, it did provide the rudiments of continuing education by publishing articles on aspects of nursing care which were of interest to those nurses interested in improving their knowledge and skills.

In an age of rapidly expanding knowledge and constantly changing technology, everyone in a professional capacity now recognizes the pressing need to keep individual knowledge and skills at a current level (7). Therefore, continuing education serves the ongoing purpose of bringing new content, ideas, and skills to former graduates, enabling them to stay abreast of the latest developments in their profession. Continuing education is aimed at satisfying the needs of adult learners.

Because of this need to keep older graduates abreast of new

knowledge and skills, continuing education programs may be a change agent for basic nursing programs by introducing new content and courses that then become incorporated into the basic nursing programs. Because continuing education programs are geared to respond quickly to expressed needs of the professional group they serve, continuing education programs may be among the first to offer certain new content in an organized program of study. Faculties of nursing programs frequently are slower to respond to rapid changes in societal needs and techniques as faculty-initiated changes in curricula usually require a slow, deliberate process of committee work and several levels of peer approval. Staffs of continuing education programs are in a more favored position to address the identified need promptly. Where faculties of the basic nursing program and the continuing education faculty share ideas and content freely, the likelihood of each segment reinforcing the offerings of the other group becomes stronger.

In Staff Development

In staff development the role of continuing education has become far greater in recent years. Every institution has a vested interest in keeping the personnel employed, intellectually challenged and technically competent. For this reason, all of the larger institutions have a staff position designated for nurse educator. This person has the functions of orienting new staff to basic procedures and policies, identifying problem areas for staff, planning and executing remedial programs, and upgrading staff skills by offering regularly scheduled short skills courses. Many times these offerings are made cooperatively with medical or speciality staff of an agency or an educational institution. Sometimes, these staff development programs are the stimulus needed by some nurses to encourage them to seek more formalized professional preparation. In these ways the personnel working in staff development are making a sizable contribution to continuing education in general.

In Relicensing Procedures

In recent years legislatures, in addition to defining the scope of practice, have required evidence of completion of continuing education programs as a necessary criterion for relicensing in some states (9). The arguments for such a requirement are strong. All professional personnel must continue to learn to remain competent in their fields. The public has a right to assume that a licensed professional person has the requisite knowledge and skills for the service offered (11). One way to mandate ongoing learning is to require proof of attendance at professional programs that have approved content, qualified faculty, and learner involvement. Numerous states have formalized this axiom into regulations requiring a stated number of continuing education units as a condition for relicensing. As agreed upon at a 1968 conference, one CE unit equals 10 contact hours of approved content given by qualified instructors under capable direction (5). Currently the states that have such a mandatory requirement are: California, Florida, Iowa, Kansas, Kentucky, Massachusetts, Michigan, Nebraska, Nevada, and New Mexico (14). In addition, states that require continuing education units for relicensing of nurse practitioners are: Alabama, Mississippi, New Hampshire, and Oregon. There are other states that strongly encourage continuing education participation but on a voluntary basis. Arizona is an example. Participation in continuing education may also be required in certification procedures (16).

Whether or not continuing education participation is mandatory, some employers are directing their employees to participate in continuing education offerings as proof of adequate professional performance (2, 9, 15). Sometimes the employer will offer compensatory time and pay the registration fees for such participation. With the growing emphasis on professional participation at several levels, continuing education has gone from relative obscurity to a substantial area of endeavor, worthy of time, attention, and funding.

Goals of Continuing Education

While continuing education is an extension of learning opportunities for the adult learner and is further professional development beyond a baseline, it generally does not lead to formal advanced professional standing. Exceptions to this are the nurse practitioner programs organized and offered under continuing education direction.

The goals of continuing education are stated in various ways but include:

1. Maintaining and improving nursing practice by keeping nursing practice skills current (9)
2. Staff development of employees
3. Career development of nurses desiring change of practice

area, certification, or refresher courses to return to active practice of nursing (2, 16)
4. Entry level for those with aspirations of higher degrees.

Currency of practice is the prime goal of continuing education programs. This goal is ongoing. As long as there is a profession of nursing, there is a large need to keep the practitioners of nursing at a current level of skill. Once a professional leaves the basic educational programs, there is need for that professional to articulate with some sort of intellectual challenge on a periodic basis. Continuing education courses serve that purpose. Most frequently, it is the learner who must approach the continuing education process and commit time and money in exchange for an update of knowledge and skill aimed at making professional practice more effective.

The goal of staff development is an important one, especially for continuing education departments within institutions. The employment procedure for each person employed is an expensive venture, representing an outlay of monies for position advertisement, application review, candidate interviews, paperwork processing, job orientation, and on-the-job training. It is to the employer's advantage to keep that employee functioning as effectively as possible. Functioning can be improved by well-designed and capably presented continuing education programs that offer needed information and assistance. Frequently, the gains from such investment of time and energy can be maximized by some sort of reward system to the employee who participates and utilizes the information gained. The variety of types of programs that can be utilized for staff development is almost endless. This reasoning also applies to continuing education for faculty (3, 4, 6, 12).

The goal of career development provides another focus for continuing education programs. Nurses frequently become disenchanted with the positions they hold. Some nurses aspire to management positions and seek continuing education courses to prepare them for entry-level administration positions. Other nurses want to be considered experts in a particular aspect of nursing care. They seek additional knowledge and skills in that area. A third group of nurses wish to switch practice areas and seek to learn about nursing care of another segment of the population. They need additional information in their chosen area.

A fourth group, those nurses who elect to be inactive in the profession for a segment of time and then decide to return to active practice, have need of refresher courses to prepare them to assume a current position with a competent level of knowledge and skills. Refresher courses may be organized and conducted by an educational institution or by a service agency which hopes to gain future employees from the enrollees in the course.

Finally, one goal continuing education courses serve is to introduce nurses to higher level preparation and to act as a stimulus to those nurses who are dubious about returning for more formal education. These nurses may try a continuing education course to test the academic waters and then decide they are challenged by the new content. They may then clarify their own goals and progress from continuing education offerings to degree programs.

Two problems develop when nurses try to go to degree programs from continuing education courses. Continuing education courses do not carry academic credit. Usually, the only requirement for registration in a continuing education course is licensure as a practical or a registered nurse. Academic credentials are not necessary. Because the course does not require academic standing as a prerequisite, academic credit is not given. This is true even though the course is offered by an educational institution. To the person unfamiliar with academic admission procedures, this fact is both confusing and frustrating. For this reason, brochures on continuing education offerings usually will state whether or not academic credit is offered. The second problem with offering credit for continuing education courses is the level at which the course is taught. If the course is open to all nurses, the level of the learners will vary widely. While the content of such courses may be equivalent to courses taught for academic credit, the course requirements for the learner are far less. Continuing education courses require far less projects, examinations, practice requirements, and effort on the part of the learner. For this reason also, academic credit is not offered. Continuing education courses and regular academic courses for degree credit are distinct from each other.

Types of Programs

The types of programs offered under continuing education are varied. One common offering is a single conference to address a specific need. For example, acquired immune deficiency disease,

AIDS, is a current health problem about which much hysteria exists. Therefore, a continuing education department may decide to sponsor a one-day conference on the topic of AIDS and its ramifications for other health workers. This is a timely way to meet a specific need in the shortest period of time.

Another type of offering by continuing education departments addresses the problems in a specific area of practice. For instance, in one urban area, the incidence of birth defects is higher than the national average. Therefore, the continuing education department may elect to offer some programs on birth defects. This offering can take the form of a single conference or a series of conferences or classes for the group of health workers most involved with birth defects—those nurses in maternal and child health. By this offering, the continuing education department contributes to a higher level of expertise in the maternal-child clinicians in that area.

A third type of offering presented by continuing education departments is a series of classes or conferences on one theme, such as Nursing Update or Nursing Autonomy. These offerings are more broadly based and usually include aspects of nursing theory, ethics, current issues, or dilemmas. This is one way continuing education departments respond to the broader issues confronting the profession and its future.

Finally, one large segment of continuing education offerings is those programs especially designed for students to acquire a higher level of skill. The various practitioner programs, certification procedures, and refresher courses are examples.

Thus, by these four types of program offerings, continuing education departments make a significant and ongoing contribution to the current skills of practicing nurses.

Content Trends of Continuing Education

While the content presented in continuing education programs runs the gamut of topics, there are some trends in common. Frequently, present social trends are points of focus. Along this line, the following topics are popular:

Cost containment
Foreign graduates
Governmental intervention
Health legislation

Interprofessional ventures
Licensing
Malpractice
Management problems
Opportunities for women
Paraprofessional interelationships
Personal fulfillment
Quality of care
Refresher courses
Shifting clinical content
Shifting population patterns and inherent problems
Specialist courses
Substance abuse

The aims of continuing education directors are to present diverse, comprehensive programs with a high degree of accessibility (1).

Resources

Since fully one-half of continuing education programs originate in institutions of higher learning (8), the total resources of that institution can be utilized to the advantage of continuing education. Most useful are the libraries, laboratories, classrooms, audiovisual departments, faculties of various disciplines, and news release department (13).

Service agencies and professional organizations contribute a large segment of continuing education offerings (10). The sponsorship may be shared among various organizations and agencies. Here again, the larger the agencies or organization, the greater the internal resources are likely to be. Usually these agencies have direct access to community publicity channels so that offerings can be publicized with ease. If a service agency sponsors a program, the costs are frequently reflected back to the consumer in increased cost of service.

A new provider upon the continuing education scene is the commercial provider who organizes and presents continuing education programs in various parts of the country for a fee. These companies contract with qualified instructors on a fee-for-service basis and offer well-designed, well-presented programs. As an added attraction, these programs may be presented at popular vacation spots so that vacation and professional education may be combined in a tax-deductible manner. These commercial ventures aim to make a profit from their services. When registration lags, they may open the offerings to persons with lesser preparation who are looking for advanced content for which they are not prepared. This practice can pose problems for the instructors who then have to teach to students with widely divergent backgrounds. Problems arise for the enrollees who do not feel the content is aimed at their level. Also, when professional programs are presented at resort settings, the full array of supporting equipment may not be at hand.

Another source of continuing education offerings is the independent authority who tours the country presenting short-term classes or conferences for a registration fee. These programs have more limitations in resources. Mainly, the success or failure of the programs tends to fall upon one or two people. So to be successful, the individual presenting a major part of a conference must be well prepared, have a large amount of content to share, and to be flexible enough to sense the desires of various audiences.

One of the basic resources for continuing education programs is adequate planning. Successful programs are more likely to occur if the planners have careful attention to the purpose, content financing, promotion and public relations aspects, and, finally, evaluation of the program. Usually, the aspects of financing come first. If special funding is being sought, then a proposal must be written outlining the project, objectives, content and method of presentation, equipment and facilities needed, fees to be assessed, and obligations to be met. Also to be included is a description of the way in which the project is to be evaluated. If the funding comes from current budget, then the plans must fit within the budget limitations. Further discussion of financing occurs in the next section.

Financing

Most continuing education is pay-as-you-go. Loring (8) cites data from the National Center of Educational Statistics which indicated 56 percent of enrollees in continuing education pay their own fees, while 27 percent have employer funding, and only 16 percent rely upon public funding in the form of federally funded short courses, state funding, foundation support, and corporate or individual underwriting.

The adult student is an expensive student, requiring more

individual counseling and administrative costs because of the high degree of variance in the backgrounds of the students. Adult students end up paying higher fees for services because such fringe services as counseling hours, parking, and child care are not available at night when most of the continuing education classes are offered.

For some courses, short-term grants from governmental or foundation funding are available. This support is usually given as stipends to be used for fees and lodging. As educational support shrinks, such funds tend to disappear. Some institutions do underwrite some continuing education offerings. It depends upon the educational mission of the institution. Most often this support is only meant to be supplementary and not the main support for programs. Occasionally, the state will contribute some funding for certain types of programs deemed to be of value to the state in general.

Finally, one source of funding in recent years has been the federal government. Cooper (5) mentions the Social Security Act of 1935 as having the first federal funds for continuing education in nursing, but assistance was sporadic until the Health Amendment Act of 1956, the Nurse Training Act of 1964, and the Health Manpower Act of 1968. In recent years the support has been less. While funding sources are changing, the method of requesting such funding remains proposal submission and peer review. The project proposal must address a specific need with a stated purpose, a description of the content and methods, a detailed budget, and a means to evaluate the program. There is no guarantee that every good program will be funded. Only a small number of proposals are financed.

Through all of this process, a continuing education specialist, who is developing skill and expertise in addressing the needs of adult learners seeking to extend themselves is emerging. This person must possess high levels of creativity and resourcefulness to meet increasing demands with meager funding and limited resources.

Continuing Education Issues Confronting Faculty

From the above discussion, it is evident that the issues in continuing education present ongoing challenges to faculty members. These issues cluster around three focal points: legisla-

221

tive mandates, allocation of resources, and philosophies of individuals and groups.

In the area of legislative mandates, questions arise. What is the scope of nursing practice in your state? Is continuing education a requirement for relicensing? If it is mandatory, how much, what kind, and how is the continuing education made available? Does the law fit the need? To what degree should the nursing profession determine its own destiny, rules, and regulations? What kind of lobbying activities are going on nationally and in your state? What role do you play in legislative matters? What role could you play, if you so chose? In short, what is your individual and your faculty obligation and commitment to legislative matters affecting nursing?

In the allocation of resources to continuing education, what roles do the federal, state, and local governments play? What activities are carried on by national and state nursing organizations? What roles do the educational institutions and the health care agencies have in providing continuing education? What are the sources of financial support? Are the sources adequate to the need? Are the sources of support stable? If the financial support needs to be increased, how much and from what sources? As a faculty member, what is your obligation to be a resource for others seeking continuing education?

In the area of philosophy, what is the commitment of your institution to continuing education? Do you agree with that philosophy? What is your personal philosophy regarding the goals of continuing education? What is your stand on the legislative mandates? What is you personal commitment to continuing education for yourself? How much time and effort are you willing to spend on your own development and the development of others? As a professional health care giver, what has been your commitment to continuing education activities in the past, and what will it be in the future?

These questions require a series of ongoing answers. Solutions to the issues of continuing education confronting faculty evolve from the composite actions of legislatures, public, and private institutions, and individuals in the various settings.

References

1. Boissoneau, R. *Continuing Education in the Health Professions.* Rockville: Aspens Systems, 1980.

Suggested Readings

2. Brown, S., Continuing Education Must Impact on Practice. *J. Cont. Educ. Nurs.* 11:8, 1980.
3. Buckner, K. Continuing Education for Nurse Faculty Members. *Nurs. Forum* 13:393, 1974.
4. Chaska, N.L., *The Nursing Profession: A Time to Speak.* New York: McGraw-Hill, 1983.
5. Cooper, S.S. and Hornback, M.S. *Continuing Nursing Education.* New York: McGraw-Hill, 1973.
6. Edgil, A.E. CE For the Educator Role of Nursing Faculty. *Nurs. and Health Care* 11:12, 1981.
7. Houle, C.D. *Continuing Learning in the Professions.* San Francisco: Jossey-Bass, 1980.
8. Loring, R.K., Finance. In P.F. Franson (consulting ed.), *Power and Conflict in Continuing Education: Survival and Prosperity for All?* Belmont: Wadsworth Publishing and National University Extension, 1980.
9. Lorni, P. Continuing Education Versus Continuing Competence. *J. Nurs. Admin.* 5(9):34, 1975.
10. Maxwell, J.F. Who Will Provide Continuing Education for Professionals? *AAHE Bulletin* 33(4):1, 1980.
11. McGriff, E.P. and Cooper, S.S. *Accountability to the Consumer Through Continuing Education in Nursing.* NLN Publ. No. 14–1507. New York: National League for Nursing, 1974.
12. O'Conner, A. Educating Nursing's Leadership: Agenda for Action. *Nurs. Leadership* 5:44, 1982.
13. Presler, E.P. and Bolte, I.M. Discovering Resources for Continuing Education. *Nurs. Outlook* 30:454, 1982.
14. Putney, J.C. Continuing Education Requirements: Not as Complicated as They Seem. *Nurs. Life* 1:17, 1981.
15. Strauss, M.B. The Impact of Continuing Education on the Nursing Profession. *J. Cont. Educ. Nurs.* 13:4, 1982.
16. Warmuth, J.F. Certification and Continuing Education. *J. Cont. Educ. Nurs.* 13:35, 1982.

Suggested Readings

Arney, W.R. Evaluation of a Continuing Nursing Education Program and Its Implications. *J. Cont. Educ. Nurs.* 9:45, 1978.

Bell, D.F. Assessing Educational Needs: Advantages and Disadvantages of Eighteen Techniques. *Nurse Educator* 3:(5)15, 1978.

Belle, D.A. Successful Educational Programming: Increasing Learner Maturation Through Involvement. *J. Nurs. Admin.* 9:(5) 36, 1979.

Binger, J.L. and Huntsman, A.J. Keeping Up: The Staff Development Educator and the Professional Literature. *Nurse Educator* 4:(3)19, 1979.

Chaska, N.L. *The Nursing Profession: A Time to Speak.* New York: McGraw-Hill, 1983.

Cooper, S.S. *The Practice of Continuing Education in Nursing.* Gaithersburg: Aspen Systems, 1982.

Cooper, S.S. *Self-Directed Learning in Nursing.* Gaithersburg: Aspens Systems, 1980.

Dinsmore, V.K. and Pollow, R.L. Credit-for-Faculty Practice Model: A Proposal. *Nurs. & Health Care* 2:17, 1981.

Houle, C.D. *Continuing Learning in the Professions.* San Francisco: Jossey-Bass, 1980.

Maxwell, J.F. Who Will Provide Continuing Education for the Professionals? *AAHE Bulletin* 33(4):1, 1980.

McGriff, E.P. and Cooper, S.S. *Accountability to the Consumer Through Continuing Education in Nursing.* NLN Publ. No. 14–1507. New York: National League for Nursing, 1974.

O'Connor, A. Educating Nursing's Leaders: Agenda for Action. *Nurs. Leadership* 5:4, 1982.

Palmer, I.S. Continuing Education: Professional Responsibility or Societal Mandate? *Nurs. Forum* 13:402, 1974.

Presler, E.P. and Bolte, I.M. Discovering Resources for Continuing Education. *Nurs. Outlook* 30:454, 1982.

Puetz, B.E. and Peters, F.L. *Continuing Education for Nurses: Complete Guide to Effective Programs.* Gaithersburg: Aspen Systems, 1981.

Shockley, J.A. Multi-Faceted Program for Continuing Education in Nursing. *JNE* (3):20, 1981.

Strauss, M.B. The Impact of Continuing Education on the Nursing Profession. *J. Cont. Educ. Nurs.* 13:4, 1982.

Tarnow, K.G. Working with Adult Learners. *Nurse Educator* 4:(5)34, 1979.

Chapter 14

Faculty Role Issues

Suzanne Van Ort, R.N., Ph.D.

Study Questions

1. What is included in the issue of faculty clinical practice? What are some of the models that have been developed to provide for faculty practice?
2. What is the concept of academic freedom? How does this affect teaching in collegiate schools of nursing?
3. What is involved in collective bargaining? What effects does collective bargaining have on shared governance in colleges and universities? What are the primary effects on the faculty role?

Faculty Clinical Practice

The issue of faculty clinical practice came to the forefront in the 1970s and is based on the premise that in order to effectively teach nursing, one must be a competent clinician. While few would argue philosophically with this premise, the logistics involved in incorporating faculty clinical practice into the faculty role create a dilemma for nurse educators.

Historically, clinical nursing practice for faculty was inherent in the faculty role until the 1950s. With the growing emphasis on teaching in evolving baccalaureate programs in the 1950s and 1960s, less emphasis was placed upon the clinical competence of faculty (2). By the 1960s, leaders in nursing became increasingly concerned with the separation of nursing service and nursing education.

In the early 1970s, organizational structures in several institutions were changed to implement the unification model for nursing education and nursing service (5). These models incorporated

225

faculty clinical practice as an expectation within the organizational structure. In the unification models, faculty practice in the nursing service setting and nursing service personnel participate in nursing education. Thus, collaboration between nursing service and nursing education is facilitated by the organizational structure.

In 1979, thirteen nursing leaders published a *Statement of Belief Regarding Faculty Practice* (7). This statement advocated unification and development of collaborative mechanisms to provide for faculty practice as an integral part of the faculty role. During the last few years, national and regional meetings have been held to discuss mechanisms for promoting the concept of faculty practice.

Although unification models are one way to incorporate clinical practice into the faculty role, other mechanisms have also been implemented (3). Joint appointments in which faculty are employed part-time by both nursing education and nursing service institutions are one mechanism. One nursing education setting sets aside one day each week for faculty clinical practice and compenstates faculty for their practice (6). Faculty in settings in which nine-month appointments are used may engage in practice during the summer months or on breaks when classes are not in session. Also, some faculty develop a private practice or a collaborative practice. In addition, sabbatical leaves may be utilized to improve faculty competence in a given clinical area.

Those who question the feasibility of faculty clinical practice as a role expectation usually cite time commitment and logistics as the major concerns (1). Faculty who are expected to be experts in teaching, research, and community service may feel too overburdened to be practitioners too.

In addition, in institutions that reward research and teaching—often in that order—faculty who desire tenure and/or promotion elect to allocate their time to research at the expense of practice.

Three questions are crucial in considering faculty clinical practice (4):

1. How do you find time for faculty clinical practice?
2. How do you work out appropriate reimbursement?
3. How do you manage to have the faculty practice not interfere with academic career advancement, which is usually based on research and writing activities?

Responses to these questions by colleagues in nursing education and nursing service will determine the future of faculty clinical practice as an integral part of the faculty role in collegiate nursing education. Creative strategies are needed to demonstrate the feasibility of the faculty practice concept.

Academic Freedom and Tenure

The concept of *academic freedom* in American education has been a concern of educators since the early 1900s. Academic freedom is defined as the "freedom of a teacher or student to hold and express views without fear of arbitrary interference by officials" (5). Academic freedom allowed colleges to be centers of dialogue among scholars in which controversial topics could be examined without fear of reprisal. The concept of tenure was introduced in 1915 by the American Association of University Professors (AAUP) as a mechanism to protect the academic freedom of faculty (3). Faculty believed that *tenure*, as a protector of academic freedom, was essential if the free exploration of ideas and the search for truth were to be unimpeded by political, social, or economic forces.

Tenure is defined as

> an arrangement under which faculty appointments in an institution of higher education are continued until retirement for age or physical disability, subject to dismissal for adequate cause or unavoidable termination on account of financial exigency or change of institutional program (4).

Implementation of this definition means that tenured faculty essentially have job security in an institution until retirement. Thus, although originated to protect academic freedom, tenure has come to connote job security. It is the job security aspect of tenure which is at issue today.

The advantages of tenure include protection of academic freedom, job security for faculty, stability of faculty, and ability to recruit high-quality faculty. Disadvantages include decreased flexibility and diminished self-renewal of the institution, protection of mediocre faculty, and inability to recruit and retain young, dynamic faculty. In fact, the allegation is often made that tenure is a refuge of mediocrity because tenured faculty may resist change and professional growth.

An additional concern in nursing is the requirement of the doctoral degree for achieving tenure in many institutions. Since only a minority of nursing faculty are prepared at the doctoral level, the potential for losing creative, capable master's-prepared faculty is great. However, as the supply of doctorally prepared nurse educators increases, this concern will be self-mitigated.

Another issue in nursing education is the reward system for faculty clinical practice. Traditionally, tenure criteria focus on teaching, research, and community service. If nursing as a practice profession is to value faculty clinical practice, this needs to be reflected in tenure criteria (6). This value will also need to be communicated to nonnursing academic colleagues since they often participate in decisionmaking regarding tenure.

The American Association of University Professors has published guidelines for tenure that are adopted by most higher education institutions (1, 2). In most institutions the process for granting tenure encompasses a six-year period of time during which the faculty member participates in activities to meet tenure criteria. If tenure is denied, the faculty member is usually granted a seventh, terminal year at the institution.

Tenure criteria are developed by the institution and the school of nursing. Typically, the criteria reflect the institutional missions of teaching, research, and community service. For example, research productivity is more heavily emphasized in research universities. Teaching receives primary emphasis in comprehensive colleges and universities.

A committee process is utilized for tenure decisionmaking. Usually the review process begins at the department level in the school of nursing and proceeds through the administrative levels to the campus-wide committee and then to the university administration. Since each tenure decision involves a lifetime commitment of resources, the potential contributions of the candidate as well as his/her past performance are carefully scrutinized.

Tenure and the protection of academic freedom are controversial issues in higher education at present. Whether the tenure system will be continued or abolished will depend in part on the ability of faculty to convince legislative decisionmakers that tenure is protective of academic freedom rather than a self-serving job security mechanism.

Collective Bargaining

Over the past two decades, faculty members in public and private institutions of higher education have considered the issue of *collective bargaining*. Collective bargaining may be prohibited by law in some state institutions. Faculty in two-year colleges have been more likely to adopt collective bargaining than those in four-year institutions. However, in the current economic atmosphere, collective bargaining appears to be an increasingly attractive alternative for many faculty in higher education.

Collective bargaining is a process of negotiation in which faculty, as members of a bargaining unit, are represented as a group in seeking accommodations on salaries, benefits, and working conditions (1). Collective bargaining in higher education became more popular in the 1960s and 1970s in response to changes in institutional size, structure and function, controversies over the concept of tenure, and a new legal environment that sanctioned collective bargaining in colleges and universities (2). During the 1960s many institutions grew in size and complexity as multicampus systems and consortia were organized. Institutional missions were expanded to serve diverse clientele. Concomitantly, many faculty felt removed from policymaking and believed their ability to influence institutional policy and programs had diminished. In this climate collective bargaining became an alternative to shared governance.

According to Thomson (3), the traditional concept of university organization is that of a self-governing community of scholars, an ideal which stretches back to medieval times and sharply differentiates university structure from the hierarchical structure of industrial organizations. Traditionally, higher education has adopted this concept of shared governance in which faculty and administration participate together in the community of scholars. Students are also included in a shared governance model. Shared governance involves faculty in policymaking and programmatic decisions. The Faculty Senate is usually the arena through which faculty have a voice in academic decisionmaking. On an individual level, faculty have traditionally "bargained" individually with administrators in terms of salary, benefits, and working conditions.

In a collective bargaining model, faculty are members of a bargaining unit and are represented at the bargaining table by an elected or appointed negotiator. Three national organizations represent the majority of faculty in higher education who engage in collective bargaining (1). The National Education Association (NEA), founded as a professional organization for elementary and secondary school teachers, has expanded its scope to include faculty in higher education. The NEA is particularly popular among faculty in two-year colleges.

The American Federation of Teachers (AFT), an AFL-CIO affiliate, utilizes the trade union model for collective bargaining on behalf of teachers. This model assumes an adversary relationship between faculty and administrators. The American Federation of Teachers is accepted in many two-year and four-year public universities because it has extensive experience and sound financial backing for bargaining activities.

The American Association of University Professors (AAUP) has spoken for faculty in colleges and universities since the early 1900s. The American Association of University Professors has the protection of academic freedom as its primary concern. Its scope was expanded to include collective bargaining in the early 1970s. The American Association of University Professors has appeal for many faculty in four-year colleges and universities because it is more familiar with the academic model and the notion of the university as a community of scholars.

The primary effects of collective bargaining are the formalization of governance procedures, the leveling effect of salaries and benefits, and the utilization of formal evaluation processes for job security (2). Under collective bargaining, governance procedures are explicit and contractual. The Faculty Senate model may be replaced by a professional association model such as the National Education Association or the American Association of University Professors or a trade union model such as the American Federation of Teachers. An effective grievance procedure is an integral part of all collective bargaining agreements.

The effect of collective bargaining on job security involves the development and utilization of formal evaluative criteria. Faculty members' input into evaluation is increased, and the tenure process is opened up. Detailed evaluative and appeal procedures are utilized.

In the areas of salaries and fringe benefits, there is a leveling effect. Typically, because of the egalitarian emphasis in collective bargaining, faculty with lower salaries gain at the expense of those with higher salaries. The concept of merit increases is antithetical to the purist idea of collective bargaining. Egalitarianism is seen by opponents of collective bargaining as having an adverse effect on academic values of research and creativity (4). Since working conditions are a negotiable item, faculty workloads, research time, community service expectations, and teaching expectations may all be explicitly contracted. The individual teacher's opportunity for enhancing his/her productivity is diminished as the leveling process fosters egalitarian productivity.

The issue of collective bargaining deserves careful consideration by all faculty in nursing education. Advantages of collective bargaining in one institution may be detractors in another institution. As nursing strives to enhance its professional autonomy, efforts to collectivize the academic community may have a lasting impact upon our emerging profession.

References

Faculty Clinical Practice

1. Bevis, Mary. Can Faculty Meet Role Expectations? In J.C. McCloskey, and H.K. Grace, *Current Issues in Nursing.* Boston: Blackwell, 1981. Pp. 654–660.
2. Christy, T.E. Clinical Practice as a Function of Nursing Education: An Historical Analysis. *Nurs. Outlook* 28:493, 1980.
3. Collison, C.R., Parson, M.A. Is Practice a Viable Faculty Role? *Nurs. Outlook* 28:677, 1980.
4. Mauksch, I.G. Faculty Practice: A Professional Imperative. *Nurse Educator* 5(3):21, 1980.
5. Nayer, D.D. Unification: Bringing Nursing Service and Nursing Education Together. *Am. J. Nurs.* 80:1110, 1980.
6. Smith, G.R. Compensating Faculty for Their Clinical Practice. *Nurs. Outlook* 28:673, 1980.
7. Smith, G.R. Statement of Belief Regarding Faculty Clinical Practice. *Nurse Educator* 4(3):5, 1979.

Academic Freedom and Tenure

1. American Association of University Professors. Academic Freedom and Tenure. 1940 Statement of Principles and 1970 Interpretive Comments. *AAUP Policy Documents and Reports.* Washington D.C.: American Association of University Professors, 1977.
2. American Association of University Professors. 1976 Recommended Institution Regulations on Academic Freedom and Tenure. *AAUP Policy Documents and Reports.* Washington D.C.: American Association of University Professors, 1977.
3. Bueche, M.N. Academic Tenure: A Reexamination for the Eighties. *Nurse Educator* 8(1):3, 1983.
4. Commission on Academic Tenure in Higher Education. *Faculty Tenure.* San Francisco: Jossey-Bass, 1973. P. 256.
5. Guralnik, D.B. (ed.). *Webster's New World Dictionary of the American Language.* New York: The World Publishing Co., 1972. P. 7.
6. Henry, J.K. Nursing and Tenure. *Nurs. Outlook* 29:244, 1981.

Collective Bargaining

1. Clements, I.W. and P.L. Hayes. Collective Bargaining: Dilemma for Nurse Educators. *Nurse Educator* 6(7):13, December 1981.
2. Garbarino, J.W. *Faculty Bargaining: Change and Conflict.* New York: McGraw-Hill, 1975. P. 20.
3. Thomson, A.W.J. *An Introduction to Collective Bargaining in Higher Education.* Ithaca: Cornell University, 1974. P. 3.
4. Weisberger, June. *Faculty Grievance Arbitration in Higher Education: Living with Collective Bargaining.* Ithaca: Cornell University, 1976. P. 1.

Suggested Readings

Baker, C.M. Faculty Unionism: Issues and Impact. In N.L. Chaska, *The Nursing Profession: A Time to Speak.* New York: McGraw-Hill, 1983.

Chaska, N.L. *The Nursing Profession: A Time to Speak.* New York: McGraw-Hill, 1983.

Cleland, V.S. Reimbursement for Nursing Practice. In N. L. Chaska, *The Nursing Profession: A Time to Speak.* New York: McGraw-Hill, 1983.

Dinsmore, V.K. and Pollow, R.L. Credit-For-Faculty Practice Model: A Proposal. *Nurs. & Health Care* 11:17, 1981.

Gorney-Fadiman, M.J. A Student's Perspective on the Doctoral Dilemma. *Nurs. Outlook* 29:650, 1981.

Holm, K. Faculty Practice—Noble Intentions Gone Awry? *Nurs. Outlook* 29:655, 1981.

Kuhn, J.K. An Experience with a Joint Appointment. *Am. J. Nurs.* 2:1570, 1982.

Murphy, J.F. Doctoral Education in, of, and for Nursing: An Historical Analysis. *Nurs. Outlook* 29:645, 1981.

Perry, S.E. A Doctorate—Necessary but Not Sufficient. *Nurs. Outlook* 30:95, 1982.

Smith, M.M. Career Development in Nursing: An Individual and Professional Responsibility. *Nurs. Outlook* 30:127, 1982.

Wakefield-Fisher, M. The Issue: Faculty Practice. *JNE* 22:207, 1982.

Chapter 15

Professional Autonomy Issues

Suzanne Van Ort, R.N., Ph.D.

Study Questions

1. What is involved in the issue of professional autonomy? How does this issue affect teaching in collegiate schools of nursing?
2. What is the impact of economics on teaching in collegiate schools of nursing?
3. What is the credentialing issue? Describe the Credentialing Study and its recommendations. What are the implications of credentialing for teaching in schools of nursing?
4. What are possible future directions for nursing as a profession? What impact will teachers in collegiate schools of nursing have on determining the future of the profession?

Autonomy of the Profession

The issue of professional autonomy for nursing is broad, complex, and touches every aspect of the nursing profession. This section will focus upon professional autonomy as it relates to collegiate nursing education.

Education is often assumed to be directly related to professional autonomy. That is, some nursing leaders assume that increased education will lead to better, more well-recognized nursing services and, thus, greater autonomy for the profession. However, as Smith so aptly asserts

> There is no evidence to support the notion that education alone can overcome such obstacles to professional recognition as the lack of autonomy or significant organizational influence, the lack of a clear mandate or public legitimation and of knowledge of nursing's scope, the unavailability of direct third-party reimbursement,

233

and the absence of a clear-cut definition of nursing's relationship to other disciplines (5, p.545).

The critical issue for nursing and nursing education is the lack of economic or political power that can be used to influence the public, other health professionals, colleagues in higher education, and the legislators that support both education and health care. At present, nursing is physician-dependent, lacks client ownership, lacks independent sources of funding for nursing care, and lacks a clear definition of its unique contribution (actual and potential) to health care (5).

Lewis Thomas (7) in his treatise on medicine, describes nursing's drive for professional autonomy as complicated by the changing role of women and the increasing routine tasks nurses are obligated to assume. Thomas asserts that

> Eventually the arguments will work themselves out, and some sort of agreement will be reached, but if it is to be settled intelligently, some way will have to be found to preserve and strengthen the traditional and highly personal nurse-patient relationship (7, pp. 65–66).

He sees this relationship as nursing's unique contribution.

Sovie suggests that, as an emergent profession, nursing is clarifying its unique, essential knowledge base, identifying its specialty areas, and increasing its bureaucratization (6, p. 373). This being the case, nursing is maturing toward professional autonomy. Within the last twenty years, nursing has indeed identified the disciplines upon which it is based, divided the profession into specialty and subspecialty areas, and become increasingly bureaucratic in its organizational and professional practice activities. The Code of Nursing Ethics, Standards for Nursing Education, and the various Standards for Nursing Practice developed through the American Nurses' Association provide evidence of increasing bureaucratization (6).

Numerous authors suggest models for the future that may enhance nursing's autonomy. Two examples are presented as illustrations. Cleland advocates a nursing practice model that combines shared governance and collective bargaining in order to facilitate greater autonomy by nurses in practice (1). She proposes that this combination will respond to professional values and institutional changes in the practice setting. In contrast, Schlotfeldt envisions a future in which nurses will provide comprehensive health care through primary patient contact in community health centers (3). Nurses would be involved in patient assessment, community assessment, and broad health-related activities. In this model, nursing's professional autonomy would be recognized by the public since nurses would provide essential health care services in the community as visible community leaders.

Each of the diverse possibilities described by the authors in previous paragraphs could have a potential impact on the teaching of nursing in collegiate institutions. For example, curricula could be designed to prepare nurses to strengthen the bureaucratic-leader relationship in order to function in a practice setting that incorporated a combination of shared governance and collective bargaining. Such a curriculum would need coursework and experiences in collaborative and independent interactions, nurse leadership and management skills, and assertiveness and group dynamics experiences. While each of these topics is provided in most nursing curricula today, the interweaving of these concepts might necessitate reconceptualizations. If Schlotfeldt's vision of community health centers were adopted, additional curricular reconceptualizations and new learning opportunities would be needed to prepare the autonomous professional to function in this community model. Clarification of these models could help to define nursing's uniqueness and in so doing, address Smith's concern for nursing's lack of power (5).

Another area of concern for nursing's autonomy is in the academic milieu itself. According to Sleicher (4, p. 189), "the variety of (nursing) degrees and educational institutions results in the low academic prestige of nursing within the university and the historical affiliation with professional schools of education." As a relatively new member of the academic community, nursing is striving to participate fully in governance, be accorded full partnership in academic circles, have more qualified faculty promoted to the upper ranks, and have graduate programs recognized for their quality and uniqueness. Thus, in addition to concerns for professional autonomy in nursing per se, nurse educators in collegiate programs are working to be recognized as full-fledged academicians and contributing members of the academic community.

Since nursing education has a primary role in preparing nurses for the future as well as the present, nurse educators need to explore the dilemmas of professional autonomy, participate in the development of clear, well-defined roles for nursing, and

235

assume a proactive leadership role in promoting nursing's professional autonomy (2). Nurse educators have an opportunity to creatively design nursing education that will prepare nurses to collaborate in health care as autonomous professionals.

Economics

The economics of higher education, and, in particular, nursing education is changing rapidly as the educational goals of American society change and are refined. Historically, funding for education was a state prerogative. Federal funding became more important after World War II when the GI Bill for students initiated an era of federal student loans and grants. Also, especially since the 1960s, the federal government has played a significant role in funding higher education programs and institutions.

The federal government's role in support of nursing education has been growth producing. The Nurse Training Act funds have supported nursing education program development, nursing research development, and student aid for graduate and undergraduate students. This support is expected to decrease or be eliminated in the future as federal funding priorities are revised in response to the marketplace in health care. Alternatives will need to be actively explored by nurse educators and nurse researchers so that the progress made in the past two decades is not eroded.

In spite of the emphasis on federal funding for nursing education, state and local governments remain the largest source of current operating income for higher education institutions (1). Tax revenues are the primary source of funds for higher education and, therefore, nursing education in public collegiate settings.

State support for higher education provides student aid as well as institutional operating income. Since tuition typically covers less than 30 per cent of the cost of each student's education, the state support of institutions is essential. In times of economic recession or depression, education is often viewed as a luxury item rather than an investment in the future. Thus, educators need to continually validate the essentiality of education for society's well-being.

Private funding is a third source of income for higher education. However, private funding for public collegiate nursing education is minimal and remains an untapped resource. Foundation sources and alumni support are two areas of private funding that nursing needs to capitalize on in the future.

One unique dilemma for nursing concerns the profession's goal to prepare more nurses with baccalaureate and higher degrees. According to Ginsberg

> the education of a larger number of baccalaureate nurses would involve: (1) additional outlays by state governments—the primary source of funding; (2) expanded support from the federal government for the training of additional faculty, scholarship funds, and other infrastructure assistance; and (3) most importantly, the willingness of more potential nursing students (and their families) to assume the substantial short-run connected with a four-year program of undergraduate studies (2, p. 30).

Until the employment settings encourage or reward baccalaureate preparation for nursing practice, additional support to collegiate nursing education is difficult to justify. Nursing service and nursing education need to collaborate in using cost-analysis techniques to document the cost-effectiveness of collegiate education (3).

Since faculty salaries, benefits, and working conditions as well as student enrollment, retention, and progression are inextricably linked to financing of higher education, nursing education needs to document its educational strategies and outcomes in terms of cost-effectiveness. As preparation for a practice profession, nursing education is usually one of the most expensive undergraduate programs on any campus. Many of our teaching-learning strategies need to be examined in terms of cost-effectiveness in the future. For example, is a 1:10 (or less) faculty-student ratio essential in the clinical area? Could more use be made of audiovisual or simulation methods? Is clinical laboratory time used to its utmost effectiveness?

Faculty in collegiate nursing education need to reaffirm their goals, develop cost-effective mechanisms to deliver high-quality nursing education, and collaborate with nursing service to justify the contributions of nurses educated in collegiate settings. Also, faculty need to become aware of external sources of funding and seek supplemental support for research and special educational projects. Only when nursing education actively and successfully competes in the economic marketplace of higher education will its goals be realized.

Credentialing

Credentialing is defined as the process by which individuals or institutions, or one or more of their programs, are designated by a qualified agent as having met minimum standards at a specified time (3, p. 316). Credentialing mechanisms include licensure, certification, academic degrees, accreditation, and approval or recognition by certain voluntary or governmental agencies. Essentially, credentialing has four components: "(1) it seeks to produce quality, (2) it confers unique identity on a person or institution, (3) it is protective, and (4) it is an instrument of control" (3, p. 317). In nursing, the issue of credentialing focuses upon two questions (3, p. 325) "Who should control the process of credentialing? and Who should set the standards for use in credentialing?"

The credentialing issue involves society in general, and its impact is not restricted to the nursing profession. Within the last two decades, America has become a credentialed, regulated society. When utilized for the benefit and protection of the public—its intended purpose—credentialing is an effective force in promoting high-quality human services. However, the process itself is questioned because, in its attempts to serve the public, credentialing also benefits those who are credentialed. For example, the licensure of nurses, designed to ensure safe nursing practice, also restricts membership in nursing practice to those who meet the standards for licensure. Thus, an allegation can be made that an elite group is created by the licensure process. Similarly, accreditation proffers certain status on those schools that meet accreditation standards. For example, schools of nursing that are accredited by the National League for Nursing are more apt to be approved for federal funding by the U.S. Office of Education. Although accreditation is touted as a voluntary process, the use of accreditation as a mechanism for governmental approval detracts from the voluntary nature of the process.

Historically, the National League for Nursing has been the organization that controls accreditation of nursing education. However, in 1974 the American Nurses' Association House of Delegates adopted a resolution calling for a feasibility study to determine the potential for American Nurses' Association accreditation of basic and graduate nursing education (2). Thus, an intraprofessional conflict that had been evolving for some time was brought to the surface.

The National League for Nursing, through its educational councils, has conducted accreditation of diploma, associate, baccalaureate and higher degree nursing programs. Procedures for accreditation were adopted by the membership of the various councils and supported by the National League for Nursing Board of Directors. One of National League for Nursing's strongest rationales for its continuing as the accrediting body was the participation of public members in the National League for Nursing. In the present era of consumerism, this participation was seen as advantageous to nursing. Also, the National League for Nursing already had well-defined processes and procedures for accreditation.

The American Nurses' Association's view of the need for a review of credentialing focused primarily upon control of credentialing by the professional society. The American Nurses' Association believed that control of credentialing and standard-setting for nursing should rest with the American Nurses' Association as the professional organization for nurses. Also, the American Nurses' Association already had mechanisms for accreditation of continuing education and for certification of expert practitioners.

In response to the 1974 resolution by the House of Delegates, the American Nurses' Association proposed that a national study of credentialing be conducted to determine the best mechanisms for nursing in the future. The National League for Nursing and numerous other groups were invited to participate in the study. The National League for Nursing declined to co-sponsor the study, but did participate as a cooperating group (4, p. 2). A Committee for the Study of Credentialing in Nursing was appointed by American Nurses' Association to conduct a comprehensive study of credentialing in nursing. The Committee's report, published in 1979 and entitled *The Study of Credentialing in Nursing: A New Approach*, recommended a freestanding credentialing center that would control accreditation and certification (2). Licensure as a state statutory responsibility would be left to the states. Subsequent to the Committee's report, a Task Force on Credentialing was appointed to refine the concept of a national credentialing center and make specific recommendations for the future. The 1982 American Nurses' Association House of Delegates voted to support the establishment of a national credentialing center under the auspices of the American Nurses' Association (1).

Concurrently with the American Nurses' Association study of credentialing, various other nursing groups conducted their own studies of credentialing mechanisms. The National League for Nursing conducted an ongoing study of its accreditation process. The American Association of Colleges of Nursing, the organization of deans of accredited baccalaureate and higher degree programs, studied its potential role in accreditation. Various specialty organizations are examining certification mechanisms. Also, the entry-into-practice issue has raised questions at the national and state levels regarding state approval of educational programs and licensure for the various types of nurses.

Thus, although the American Nurses' Association position has been defined, the attitude of the profession as a whole has yet to be clarified. Until the entry-into-practice issue of licensure, the question of control of credentialing, and the issues of professional standard-setting are resolved, nursing credentialing will be in limbo.

Since credentialing mechanisms such as licensure, certification, and accreditation have a direct impact upon nursing education, faculty need to be well-informed and participate in defining an appropriate mechanism for credentialing in nursing. This issue challenges the leadership in nursing and will have a profound impact on nursing in the future.

Future Directions

Nursing as a profession has evolved in response to societal need for well-prepared, caring practitioners who function in episodes of illness and promote health among all age groups. In response to society's need for health care, nursing education has evolved from the apprenticeship model into the educational model typified by two-year and four-year collegiate schools of nursing. At the present time the evolutionary process is continuing as increasing numbers of nurses are educated in postsecondary education institutions.

McCloskey and Grace (2) enumerate six professional issues that are dilemmas for nursing: "unity versus diversity, standards versus access, quality versus cost, independence versus dependence, inside control versus outside control, and safety versus risk." Each of these issues affects nursing education as an integral part of the nursing profession. Nurse educators have a responsibility to prepare competent practitioners and nursing leaders for the future to ensure nursing's survival by demonstrating nursing's ability to respond to societal needs. It is incumbent upon nurse educators to: (1) strengthen their ability to teach, (2) promote research-based nursing practice, (3) participate in community service, (4) participate in the academic milieu as a scholarly colleagues, and (5) strengthen the profession of nursing by promoting collaboration between nursing service and nursing education.

Leininger (1) proposes that specific preparation is essential for nurses to face the future. She advocates five essential requirements of a nurse-futurist: "the ability to take risks, to analyze the past and present astutely, to predict goals, to fend off intimidation, and to evaluate predictions (1, p. 379)." Although these are characteristics of effective leaders in any situation, Leininger's predictions for the future of nursing call for using these requirements in an age of "escalating technology"; enhanced "modes of communication," greater "transcultural nursing practices"; "advances in space and oceanic nursing"; greater "marketing of nursing services," "new modes of health care delivery"; and "control of common conditions such as colds, cancers and stress" (1, p. 379). In order to achieve her vision of the future, Leininger suggests that nursing education will require the master's degree for professional practice and the doctoral degree for leadership roles in education or service (1). Baccalaureate and graduate programs will be more flexible and oriented toward self-paced learning with instructional technology available to facilitate learning. Major reconceptualizations will be necessitated by Leininger's model but nursing's autonomy and professional future would be enhanced by the preparation of nurses who would lead health care delivery into the future. This is our challenge—and our opportunity as nurse educators.

References

Autonomy of the Profession

1. Cleland, V. Nurses' Economics and the Control of Nursing Practice. In L.H. Aiken (ed.), *Nursing in the 1980s: Crises, Opportunities, Challenges.* Philadelphia: Lippincott, 1982.
2. Leininger, M. Futurology of Nursing: Goals and Challenges for Tomorrow. In N.L. Chaska (ed.), *The Nursing Profession: Views Through the Mist.* New York: McGraw-Hill, 1978.
3. Schlotfeldt, R.M. The Nursing Profession: Vision of the Future. In N.L.

Chaska (ed.), *The Nursing Profession: Views Through the Mist*. New York: McGraw-Hill, 1978.
4. Sleicher, M.N. Nursing IS NOT A Profession. *Nurs. and Health Care* 2:189, 1981.
5. Smith, G.R. Nursing Beyond the Crossroads. *Nurs. Outlook* 28:543, 1980.
6. Sovie, M.D. Nursing: A Future to Shape. In N.L. Chaska (ed.), *The Nursing Profession: Views Through the Mist*. New York: McGraw-Hill, 1978.
7. Thomas, Lewis. *The Youngest Science*. New York: Viking, 1983. P. 65.

Economics

1. Derby, V.L. Financing Nursing Education. *Nurs. Educator* 5(2):21, 1980.
2. Ginsberg, Eli. The Economics of Health Care and the Future of Nursing. *Nurs. Educator* 6(3):29, 1981.
3. Knopf, Lucille. Applying Cost-Analysis Techniques to Nursing. *Nurs. and Health Care* 3:427, 1982.

Credentialing

1. Dolan, J.A., Fitzpatrick, M.L., and Herrmann, E.K. *Nursing in Society: a Historical Perspective*. Philadelphia: Saunders, 1983. P. 337.
2. Committee for the Study of Credentialing in Nursing. *The Study of Credentialing in Nursing: A New Approach, Vol. 1*. Kansas City: American Nurses' Association, 1979.
3. Hinsvark, I.G. Credentialing in Nursing. In J.C. McCloskey and Grace, H.K. *Current Issues In Nursing*. Boston: Blackwell, 1981.
4. National League for Nursing. *Historical Perspective of NLN's Participation in the ANA Credentialing Study*. New York: National League for Nursing, 1979.

Future Directions

1. Leninger, M. Futurology of Nursing: Goals and Challenges for Tomorrow. In N.L. Chaska (ed.), *The Nursing Profession: Views Through the Mist*. New York: McGraw-Hill, 1978.
2. McCloskey, J.C. and Grace, H.K. *Current Issues in Nursing*. Boston: Blackwell, 1981. P. 765.

Suggested Readings

Aiken, L.H. (ed.). *Nursing in the 1980s: Crises, Opportunities, Challenges*. Philadelphia: Lippincott, 1982.

Chaska, N.L. (ed.). *The Nursing Profession: Views Through the Mist*. New York: McGraw-Hill, 1978.

Chaska, N.L. *The Nursing Profession: A Time to Speak*. New York: McGraw-Hill, 1983.

Chinn, P.L. Nursing Theory Development: Where We Have Been and Where We Are Going. In N.L. Chaska (ed.), *The Nursing Profession: A Time to Speak*. New York: McGraw-Hill, 1983.

Suggested Readings

Cleland, V. Nurses' Economics and the Control of Nursing Practice. In L.H. Aiken (ed.), *Nursing in the 1980s: Crises, Opportunities, Challenges*. Philadelphia: Lippincott, 1982.

Donley, R. Nursing and the Politics of Health. In N.L. Chaska (ed.), *The Nursing Profession: A Time to Speak*. New York: McGraw-Hill, 1983.

Elliott, J.E. and Osgood, G.A. Federal Nursing Priorities for the 1980s. In L.H. Aiken (ed.), *Nursing in the 1980s: Crises, Opportunities, Challenges*. Philadelphia: Lippincott, 1982.

Ezell, A.S. Future Social Planning for Nursing Education and Nursing Practice Organization. In N.L. Chaska (ed.), *The Nursing Profession: A Time to Speak*. New York: McGraw-Hill, 1983.

Fagin, C.M. Nursing's Pivotal Role in American Health Care. In L. H. Aiken (ed.), *Nursing in the 1980s: Crises, Opportunities, Challenges*. Philadelphia: Lippincott, 1982.

Fleming, J.W. Consumerism and the Nursing Profession. In N. L. Chaska (ed.), *The Nursing Profession: A Time to Speak*. New York: McGraw-Hill, 1983.

Froebe, D. Marketing Strategies Applied to Nursing. In N. L. Chaska (ed.), *The Nursing Profession: A Time to Speak*. New York: McGraw-Hill, 1983.

La Monica, E.L. The Nurse as Helper: Today and Tomorrow. In N. L. Chaska (ed.), *The Nursing Profession: A Time to Speak*. New York: McGraw-Hill, 1983.

Leininger, M. Futurology of Nursing: Goals and Challenges for Tomorrow. In N.L. Chaska (ed.), *The Nursing Profession: Views Through the Mist*. New York: McGraw-Hill, 1978.

McCloskey, J.C. and Grace, H.K. *Current Issues in Nursing*. Boston: Blackwell, 1981.

Peterson, C.W. Overview of Issues in Nursing Education. In N.L. Chaska (ed.), *The Nursing Profession: A Time to Speak*. New York: McGraw-Hill, 1983.

Rogers, M.E. Beyond the Horizon. In N.L. Chaska (ed.), *The Nursing Profession: A Time to Speak*. New York: McGraw-Hill, 1983.

Schlotfeldt, R.M. The Nursing Profession: Vision of the Future. In N.L. Chaska (ed.), *The Nursing Profession: A Time to Speak*. New York: McGraw-Hill, 1983.

Sovie, M.D. Nursing: A Future to Shape. In N.L. Chaska (ed.), *The Nursing Profession: Views Through the Mist*. New York: McGraw-Hill, 1978.

Thomas, Lewis. *The Youngest Science*. New York: Viking, 1983.

Index

Abdellah, F.G., 82
An Abstract for Action (Lysaught Report), 16
Academic freedom, 33, 227–228
Accountability, 8, 16, 105, 169
Accreditation, 13, 191–194, 238–240
Adaptation model, 82–83
Administration:
  and accreditation, 192
  evaluation of, 185
  faculty responsibilities for, 36–37
  and personnel decision making, 29–30, 33, 174, 228
  and program development, 72–73
  and program evaluation, 105
  role in clinical instruction of, 135, 137
  role in organizational structure of, 20–21
Advising of students, 21, 24
Affective domain, 49, 60–61, 153–154
Agassiz Region Nursing Education Consortium, 202
Agranoff, B.W., 52
Alverno College, 203–204
American Association of Colleges of Nursing, 240
American Association of University Professors (AAUP), 227–228, 230
American Cancer Society, 22, 185
American Federation of Teachers (AFT), 230
American Heart Association, 22, 185
American Journal of Nursing, 213

American Lung Association, 185
American Nurses' Association, 14, 15, 27, 185, 200–201, 203, 208, 234, 238–240
Applegate, M., 171
Appointment of faculty, 29–30
Apprenticeship, 10, 240
Area chairpersons, 20, 105, 120, 164–165, 174
Aristotle, 57
Army Nurse Corps, 10
Army School of Nursing, 10
Articulation program, 203–204
Associate degree nursing education:
  accreditation of, 238–239
  clinical instruction for, 134, 138
  described, 75–76
  evolution of, 12, 13, 14, 15, 16, 75
  faculty workload in, 36
  issues in, 200–203, 206
Audiovisual instruction:
  and classroom strategies, 119
  and course development, 97–98, 100
  as evaluation criterion, 188
  evolution of, 7
  materials for, 109–114
Autonomy of nursing, 9, 21, 233–236, 241

Baccalaureate programs:
  accreditation of, 238–240
  clinical instruction for, 134, 138
  described, 76–77
  evolution of, 10–16, 72, 75
  faculty characteristics for, 74
  faculty workload in, 36

Index

future of, 237, 241
issues in, 200–206
Behavioral objectives, 95–96, 112, 136, 182 (*see also* Course objectives; Program objectives)
Behavioral systems model, 82
Behaviorism, 58–59, 61
Bellevue Hospital School of Nursing, 9
Bertalanffy, L., 82
Bevil, C.W., 187
Bevis, E.O., 69, 182, 191
Bloom, B., 49, 60, 153–154
Bolton Act of 1942, 12
Bosk, C.L., 142
Boston University, 14
Bower, D., 37
Brown, Dr. Esther Lucile, 12
Brown, J.W., 113
Brown Report, 12, 200
Bruner, J., 58, 59

Career development, 215–216
Career mobility, 15, 78, 201–204
Carlson, J.H., 136
Carnegie Commission on Higher Education, 7
Carnegie Council on Policy Studies in Higher Education, 8
Case Western Reserve University, 78
Cazalas, M., 136
Centra, J.A., 174
Certificate programs, 16, 238–240
Changeux, J.P., 62
Chase, B.M., 139
Chomsky, N., 62
Civil War, 5
Classics in education, 3–6
A Classification of Institutions of Higher Education, 7
Classroom strategies, 118–125
Cleland, V., 234
Clinical practice of faculty, 225–228

Clinical specializations of nurses, 78–79, 208
Clinical teaching:
agency administration perspective on, 143–151
evaluation of, 169–170
factors in planning, 131–142, 144–151
faculty perspective on, 129–142
as faculty role, 21, 24, 36, 118
objectives of, 131
as practice teaching, 117–118
staff role in, 138, 150–151
time constraints of, 132–135, 138
value of, 129–131, 143–144
Cognitive domain, 49, 59–61, 153–154
Collective bargaining, 228–230, 234–235
Colonial education, 3–5, 8–9
Columbia University Teacher's College, 13
Committee on Grading of Nursing Schools, 11
Committee work of faculty, 25, 36–37
Community colleges, 6, 13, 75
Community health nursing, 206, 234–235
Community service:
in clinical instruction, 138
as educational mission, 19–21, 27–28, 30, 33, 35, 185, 188, 228
as faculty role, 21–22, 26, 36–37, 169, 226, 230, 241
Competency-based education, 201–204, 206
Computer-assisted instruction, 7, 123–125, 130–131, 144
Computers, 109, 124–125
Concepts model of instruction, 82
Conceptual framework for curriculum development, 84–85, 91, 188–190
Conley, V., 69

246

Index

Connecticut Training School for Nurses, 9
Conrad, C.E., 184
Consulting by faculty, 22, 28, 38
Consumers, 72, 171–172, 239
Continuing education:
  content trends in, 218–219
  financing of, 220–221
  goals of, 15, 215–217
  issues in, 212–222
  resources for, 219–220
  role in nursing, 213–215
  types of, 217–218
Cooper, S.S., 221
Costs of clinical instruction, 133–134
Coudret, N.A., 36
Counseling, 6, 21, 24, 138
Course content, 96–97 (*see also* Curriculum)
Course development:
  and allocation of credit, 93
  and content, 96–97
  and course description, 91, 93
  as faculty role, 21
  and prerequisites, 93–94
  process of, 90–105
  and teaching method selection, 97–98
Course evaluation, 102–105
Course objectives:
  and audiovisual materials, 109, 112
  and clinical instruction, 132, 136–138, 146
  and curriculum development, 87, 95–96, 100
  and evaluation, 101–102, 141–142, 154, 164, 173, 175, 190
Course placement, 94–95
Coronary care nursing, 15
Credentialing, 238–240
Credit allocation for courses, 93
Credit for life experiences, 204
Creighton, M., 136
Crisis intervention, 138

Curriculum:
  defined, 69–70
  development of, 69–74
  in early U.S. colleges, 3–6
  experimentation with, 13
  and institutional mission, 70–72
  issues in, 200, 205–206, 235
  models of, 10, 13, 75–78, 80
  patterns for, 74–80, 105
  process of, 80–87
Curriculum threads, 84–87, 138, 189

Deans of schools of nursing:
  and grade appeals, 164–165
  role in organizational structure, 20
  and personal decisionmaking, 29–30, 33, 174
Deloughery, G.L., 11
Diploma schools of nursing:
  accreditation of, 238–239
  affiliations of, 13, 75
  autonomy of, 9
  described, 75
  evolution of, 9, 10, 14–16, 74
  issues in, 200–202
Dressel, P., 174
Department chairmen, 20, 105, 120, 164–165, 174
Descartes, R., 57
deTornyay, R., 61, 97, 115
Dewey, J., 57–58
DiCara, L.V., 47
Dickoff, J., 82

Economics and nursing, 234–237
Educational Testing Service, 158
Electives, 5
Entry-into-practice issues, 199–200, 240
Essay examinations, 101, 155–156
Europe, 3–5
Evaluation (*see also* Tests):
  of courses, 102–105
  of faculty, 8, 168–178, 230
  as faculty role, 21, 24

247

Index

of instructional materials, 113–114
of learning, 101, 120, 141–142, 153–166
measures for, 174–176
models of, 171, 175, 177–178
of programs, 85, 87, 181–194
research on, 172–173
reliability/validity of, 172–174
of students, 85, 101–102, 190–191
subjectivity in, 142, 156, 164, 174
techniques for, 101, 141, 190

Facilities for instruction, 134–135, 187, 200
Faculty:
attitude of, 138–140, 149, 170
clinical associations of, 135–136
clinical practice of, 225–228
competency of, 139–140, 148, 150, 169–170, 184–185, 200, 225
continuing education concerns of, 221–222
development activities for, 22–23
evaluation of, 8, 168–178, 230
growth of, 169, 171, 175, 177–178
part-time, 37–38
personnel decisions on, 28–35, 102, 171, 175, 177–178
professional involvement of, 27–28, 185
and program development, 72, 74
position description of, 23–28
ranks and responsibilities of, 27–28, 30, 33, 172–173
salary for, 102, 169, 171, 178, 230
workload of, 36–37, 230
Faculty role:
in accreditation, 192
in clinical instruction, 138–40, 148–151
in collegiate setting, 19–38
community service as, 21–22, 26, 36–37, 169, 226, 230, 241
and institutional governance, 19–21, 23, 25, 27–28
and institutional mission, 19–21, 27–28
issues in, 225–231
in nursing education, 1–40
preparation for, 22–23
research as, 21, 25–26, 36–38, 169, 226, 230, 241
teaching as, 21, 23–24, 36, 169, 226, 230, 241
Federal government, 6, 221–222, 236–238
Fine arts, 4, 6
Flexible scheduling, 37, 38
Flexner Report, 11
Forgive and Remember, 142
Formative evaluation, 178, 183–184
Four-year colleges/universities:
affiliated with nursing schools, 75
faculty role in, 21, 229–230
nursing degrees in, 72, 76, 79, 240
Fox, J., 62
Fuhrmann, B.C., 105
Funding:
for audiovisual materials, 109, 111, 112
for continuing education programs, 220–222
by the federal government, 6, 221, 236–238
by foundations, 221, 237

Gaming, 7, 123, 130
Gentile, J.R., 162, 164
Germany, 5, 61
Gestalt, 61
GI Bill, 6, 236
Ginsberg, E., 237
Gleit, C.J., 134

Index

Goldmark, Josephine, 11
Goldmark Report, 11, 200
Grace, H.K., 240
Grading, 101–102, 162–166
Graduate nursing education:
   accreditation of, 239–240
   curriculum patterns for, 78–80
   doctoral programs, 13–14,
     15–16, 72, 78–80, 207–209,
     241
   evolution of, 12, 13–14
   issues in, 207–209
   masters programs, 13, 16, 72,
     78–79, 117–118, 193, 201,
     207–209, 241
   and mission, 70–71, 208–209
   trends in, 16–17, 237, 241
Graham, B.A., 134
Grasha, A.F., 105
Great Britain, 3–5
Great Depression, 12
Grievance procedures, 35–36, 230
Gross, L.C., 187
Guinee, K.K., 70
Guthrie, E.R., 57

Habituation, 48, 61
Halstead, W.C., 52
Hanson, K.H., 121
Harcleroad, F.F., 113
Harvard College, 3–5, 9
Health Amendment Act of 1956,
   221
Health care agencies:
   clinical instruction in, 129–151
   evaluation of, 187
   mission of, 144–145
Health Manpower Act of 1968, 221
Health science centers, 21, 72
Hebb, D.O., 52
Herbert, W., 52
Higher education (*see also* Graduate nursing education):
   access to, 6, 8
   development of in America, 3–8
   economics of, 236–237

evolution of nursing in, 3–17
missions of, 19–21
Hospital schools of nursing, 8–10,
   74–75
Hull, C.L., 57
Hume, D., 57

Independent study, 111, 121
Input measures, 174–175, 182–184
Institutional governance:
   faculty role in, 23, 25, 27–28,
     229–230, 234–235
   structure for, 19–21
Institutional governing boards, 30,
   33, 135
Institutional mission:
   and clinical instruction,
     144–145
   and curriculum, 70–72, 81, 83
   and evaluation, 169, 185, 188
   and faculty role, 19–21, 27–28,
     228
   and graduate programs,
     208–209
   and personnel decisions, 30
Instructional materials, 24,
   109–112, 175, 187–188
Integrated curriculum model,
   13, 96, 120
Irby, D.M., 169

James, P., 82
Job security, 33, 38, 227
Job sharing, 37–38
Johns Hopkins University, 5
Johnson, D.E., 82
Joint appointments, 37–38, 226

Kaiserworth Hospital, 129
Kancel, E.R., 62
Kansas State University, 172
Kant, E., 57
W.K. Kellogg Foundation, 203
Kemp, J.E., 111
Kennedy administration, 14
Kim, M.J., 136

249

Index

King, I., 82
King's College, 4, 9
Kuhn, T.K., 38

Lazarus, R., 58
Learning:
  and brain structure, 49–51
  domains of, 49, 59–61, 152–154
  evaluation of, 101, 120, 141–142, 153–166
  levels of, 158
  nature of, 43–53
  neurological basis of, 43–48
  patterns of, 62–64, 170
  techniques for, 100, 108–125
  theories of, 56–64
  types of, 48–49, 60–61
Learning experiences, 87, 100, 105, 136–141
Learning resource centers, 7
Leininger, M., 241
Lenz, E., 209
Lesson plans, 98–100
Level objectives, 84–87
Lewin, K., 61
Lewis, R.R., 113
Liberal arts, 4–5, 13, 75–76, 80–81
Licensure, 238–240
Likert, R., 62
Locke, J., 57
Loring, R.K., 220
Lysaught, Dr. Jerome, 16
Lysaught Report, 16

McCloskey, J.C., 240
McLane, A.M., 208
MacQueen, J., 37–38
Mager, B.F., 95
Mann, R., 170
Maslow, A., 61
Mastery learning, 102, 121–123, 131, 162–164
Medical education, 4–5, 11, 137
Medical model, 21
Medical schools, 9
Memory, 50–53

Mentorship, 22
Meyer, M., 38
Microteaching, 115–117
Milgram, S., 44
Miller, N., 43, 47, 58
Miskin, 53
Modules, 7, 121–122
Montag, Dr. Mildred, 13, 75, 206
The Morrill Act of 1862, 4
Multiple-choice tests, 101, 156–158

National Center of Educational Statistics, 220
National Commission for the Study of Nursing Education in the United States, 16
National Council of State Boards of Nursing, 158
National Education Association (NEA), 229–230
National League for Nursing, 27, 73, 75–78, 81, 101, 158, 171, 191–194, 200, 203, 205, 206, 208, 238–240
Navy Nurse Corps, 10
Neuman, B., 82
Neurological basis for learning, 43–48, 62
New England Hospital School of Nursing, 9
Nightingale Endowment Fund, 9
Nightingale, Florence, 9, 10, 129, 199
Nightingale School, 9
Nordmark, M.T., 82
Nurse educators, 214–216
Nurse practitioners, 15, 16, 72, 215–216
Nurses:
  competency standards for, 201–204, 206
  as instructors, 10, 150–151
Nurse Training Act of 1964, 14, 221, 236
Nursing:
  categories of, 200–202

250

Index

and economic and political power, 234–235
evolution of in higher education, 3–17
and the faculty role, 1–40
future directions of, 240–241
professional autonomy of, 9, 21, 233–236, 241
and the role of women, 234
specialties in, 15
Nursing assistant, 202
Nursing education:
  autonomy of, 9, 21, 233–236, 241
  costs of, 204, 205
  curriculum patterns for, 74–78
  evolution of in America, 8–17
  issues in, 199–209
  and nursing service, 225–226, 241
  for registered nurses, 16, 75, 94–95, 132, 205–206
  standards for, 14
  for technical nurses, 14–16, 75, 206
Nursing for the Future (Brown Report), 12
Nursing model, 82–83
Nursing and Nursing Education in the United States, 11 (*see also* Goldmark Report)
Nursing specialist programs, 78–79, 208
Nursing specialty organizations, 27
Nursing staff development, 38, 214 (*see also* Continuing education)
Nursing theory:
  and course development, 102
  instruction in, 76, 79, 80, 208–209
  and nursing practice, 129, 208

Objectives (*see* Course objectives; Program objectives)
Objective tests, 101, 156–158
O'Kane, P.K., 38

Oncology nursing, 79
One-track programs, 205–206
Open curriculum, 205
Orange County Community College, 13
Orem, D.E., 82
Organizational structure of educational institutions, 20–21, 25, 226
O'Shea, H.S., 38, 141
Output measures, 174–175, 182–185

Parsons, M.K., 141
Part-time study, 8
Patient advocacy, 138
Patient care:
  as criterion for evaluation, 141
  faculty role in, 38
  versus student needs, 137, 145–147, 150
Pavlov, I.P., 57, 62
Pennsylvania Hospital, 8
Peplau, H.E., 82
Perioperative care, 138
Personnel decisionmaking, 28–35, 174, 175, 177–178
Phillips, M.K., 141
Philosophy:
  and clinical instruction, 132, 144–145
  and continuing education, 222
  and course development, 91
  and curriculum development, 83–84
  as evaluation criterion, 188–189
Piaget, J., 59
Plato, 57
PLATO, 124
Politics and nursing, 234, 235
Position Paper on Education (1965), 14, 15, 200
Practical nurses, 147, 202
Practice teaching, 117–118
Prerequisites and course development, 93–94

251

Index

Pribram, K., 52
Primary care nursing, 79
Princeton University, 4
Process measures, 174–175, 182–183
Professional autonomy issues, 233–241
Professional judgment, 102, 131, 141–142
Professional organizations, 219, 222, 227–230
Program administrators, 29–30, 33
Program development, 72–74, 90–91 (see also Course development)
Program evaluation, 85, 87, 181–194
Programmed instruction, 122–123
Program mission, 19, 169 (see also Institutional mission)
Program objectives:
  and clinical instruction, 135, 138
  and course development, 91
  and curriculum development, 84–85
  and program evaluation, 182, 188–191
Promotion of faculty, 30, 32, 37, 102, 171, 178, 226
Psychomotor domain, 49, 60–61, 153–154
Psychiatric-mental health nursing, 12, 14
Psychology, 58–59, 61
Public health nursing, 12
Pulmonary nursing, 79
Purdue University, 172
Putt, A.M., 82

Rambo, B.J., 136
Reappointment of faculty, 30–31, 171, 178
Red Cross, 10
Regents of the University of the State of New York, 78

Registered nurses, 16, 75, 94–95, 132, 147, 205–206
Relicensing procedures, 214–215, 222
Religion, 3–5, 8, 70
Research:
  in clinical setting, 138–139
  and curriculum, 70–72, 79
  as educational mission, 19–21, 27–28, 30, 32, 33, 35, 185, 188, 228
  as faculty role, 21, 25–26, 36–37, 38, 169, 226, 230, 241
  in graduate programs, 208–209
Resources for education, 109–110, 187–188, 219–220, 222
Riehl, J.P., 82
Rockefeller Foundation, 11
Rogers, C., 61
Rogers, M., 82–83
Rohweder, A.W., 82
Roy, C., 82–83
Rucker, W.B., 52
Rural institutions, 72, 74, 134–135
Russel Sage Foundation, 12

St. Thomas Hospital, 9
Salary for faculty, 102, 169, 171, 178, 230
Schlotfeldt, R.M., 234, 235
Scholarship (see Research)
Science in curriculum, 4–6, 13, 75–76, 80–81
Seaman, Dr. Valentine, 9
Second step model, 77–78, 203
Seldin, P., 169–170
Self-pacing, 121–122
Sensitization, 48, 60
Shared governance, 229–230, 234–235
Simulation, 7, 100, 123–124, 130–131, 143–144, 158
Singer, 62
Skinner, B.F., 57–59
Sleicher, M.N., 235
Smith, G.R., 233, 235

252

Index

Social Security Act of 1935, 220
Sonoma State University (California), 77, 203
Sorensen, G.E., 35
Southern Regional Education Board, 22
Sovie, M.D., 234
Staff development, 38, 214 (*see also* Continuing education)
Standard Curriculum for Schools of Nursing, 10
Standardized tests, 158, 204
State boards of nursing, 73, 75, 184, 193–194
Stevens, B.J., 204
Stevens-Haslinger, C.A., 162, 164
Stimulus-response theory, 57–58
Students:
　ability levels of, 109
　and accreditation, 192
　course evaluation by, 102
　evaluation of, 85, 101–102, 190–191
　faculty evaluation by, 172–173
　and patient care, 137, 145–147, 150
　and program development, 72, 74
Student teaching, 117–118
The Study of Credentialing in Nursing: A New Approach, 239
Summative evaluation, 178, 183–184
Surgeon General's Consultant Group on Nursing, 14, 16
System for Nursing Articulation Program (SNAP), 203

Tanzi, R.E., 53
Tarnow, K.G., 136
Teacher training, 5–6
Teaching (*see also* Clinical teaching; Student teaching):
　as educational mission, 19–21, 27–28, 30, 32, 33, 35, 185, 188, 228

　evaluation of, 168–178
　as faculty role, 21, 23–24, 36, 169, 226, 230, 241
　issues in, 197–243
　for large groups, 111, 119
　and the learning process, 53, 64
　for small groups, 111, 119
　strategies for, 67–196
　styles of, 170, 175
Teaching methods:
　described, 108–125
　evaluation of skill in, 186–187
　selection of, 97–98
Team teaching, 120–121
Technical institutes, 14, 75
Technical nursing, 14–16, 75, 206
Technology, 6, 7, 149, 213, 241
Television, 7
Tenure, 33–35, 37, 102, 171, 178, 226–230
Terminal objectives, 85–87, 138
Tests:
　cheating on, 155, 157, 165
　construction of, 159–161
　design of, 154–158
　development of, 154–161
　grading of, 162–166
　reliability and validity of, 161–162, 204
　types of, 101, 155–158
Thomas, L., 234
Thompson, M.A., 61, 97, 115
Thompson, A.W.J., 229
Thorndike, E.L., 57–58
Time constraints:
　and clinical instruction, 132–133, 138
　and computers, 124–125
　and materials development, 109, 111–113
　and testing, 156–157
Toward Quality in Nursing, 14
True-false questions, 156
Two-track programs, 205–206
Two-year colleges, 229–230, 240

253

Index

Unification model, 225–226
Unions, 228–231
United States Cadet Nurse Corps, 12
United States Department of Education, 12, 192, 238
United States Public Health Service, 12
University of Arizona, 32, 71, 172
University of California, 14
University of Colorado, 15
University of Iowa, 21
University of Minnesota, 10
University of Pennsylvania, 9
University of Pittsburgh, 13–14
University of Texas, Austin, 37
University of Wisconsin–Eau Claire, 31, 32, 85, 86
Urban institutions, 72, 74, 134–135

Van Ort, S.R., 35
Vassar Training Camp Program, 10
Vietnam War, 15
Vocational training, 6, 14

Waltz, C., 209
Watson, J., 57
Welch, L.B., 182
West Virginia University School of Nursing, 203
William and Mary College of, 4
Women's roles and nursing, 234
Wood, L.A., 136
Work-study programs, 8
World War I, 10
World War II, 6, 7, 10, 12, 13, 236

Yale School of Nursing, 11, 13
Yale University, 4, 5
Yura, H., 80